The Politics of
Policy Making in America

The Politics of Policy Making in America

Five Case Studies

EDITED BY

David A. Caputo
PURDUE UNIVERSITY

W. H. FREEMAN AND COMPANY
San Francisco

Library of Congress Cataloging in Publication Data
Main entry under title:

The Politics of policymaking in America.

  Includes bibliographical references and index.
  1. Policy sciences—Case studies. 2. United States
—Politics and government—1945–   Case studies.
I. Caputo, David A., 1943–
JK271.P56   320.9′73′092   77–24516
ISBN 0–7167–0194–4
ISBN 0–7167–0193–6 pbk.

320.973
P769-P

Printed in the United States of America

9 8 7 6 5 4 3 2 1

For our families

Contents

Preface

The purpose of this volume is to describe and analyze the dynamics and implications of American politics and public policy making. The dual emphasis on politics and policy should provide a realistic assessment of the relationship between the two. The book is intended for use in introductory undergraduate courses in American politics and policy analysis.

As the ensuing chapters indicate, policy making in America is complicated and often confusing, but seldom dull. By combining the theoretical overviews of the opening and concluding chapters with the specifics of the case chapters, the reader should acquire a much keener perception of both policy making and American politics.

The idea and need for the volume emerged from my experiences in undergraduate teaching at Purdue. I am grateful to Richard Lamb of W. H. Freeman and Company for encouraging the development of my ideas and providing assistance when needed. As a review of the chapters indicates, the four contributors are all experts in the areas they cover. Their willingness to keep deadlines and to consider suggested changes is appreciated. Their work was difficult but was completed in excellent fashion, with humor still remaining. I would especially like to thank each of them. As the dedication indicates, their families are also to be thanked. My wife, Alice, and children, Christopher, Elizabeth, and Jeffrey, are now free from my preoccupation with word counts and postal deliveries, but their patience and encouragement must be acknowledged with great appreciation.

Numerous others assisted me. Betsey McCormack skillfully typed the final manuscript, and the chapters and entire volume received helpful comments and suggestions from numerous developmental reviewers and friends.

Despite the shared responsibilities involved in an edited volume such as this one, I alone am responsible for its overall concept and content. I hope it will be a useful contribution to the increased understanding of policy making in the United States. Finally, to those policy makers who make the study of policy making both interesting and perplexing go my thanks, admiration, and fond wish that this volume captures the true nature of their enterprise.

David A. Caputo
April 1977

The Contributors

WILLIAM I. BACCHUS has most recently been a consultant on personnel system reform to the Director General of the Foreign Service, U.S. Department of State. He received his Ph.D. from Yale University in 1970. From 1973 to 1975 he served as a staff member and Associate Research Director of the Commission on the Organization of the Government for the Conduct of Foreign Policy. He has taught at the University of Virginia and has served as an American Political Science Association Congressional Fellow. His publications include *Foreign Policy and the Bureaucratic Process: The State Department's Country Director System* and articles in *American Political Science Review, Orbis,* and *Policy Sciences.* He is currently preparing a book on alternative foreign affairs personnel systems for the future and is carrying out research on comparative foreign policy processes.

DAVID A. CAPUTO is presently Professor of Political Science at Purdue University, where he teaches courses in American politics, urban politics, and intergovernmental relations. He received his Ph.D. from Yale University. He has published four books: *Urban America: The Policy Alternatives, Urban Politics and Decentralization, Revenue Sharing: Methodological Approaches and Problems,* and *American Politics and Public Policy: An Introduction.* He has edited several major symposium issues dealing with general revenue sharing, has served as a consultant to the Treasury Department's Office of Revenue Sharing, and has published articles in *Public Administration Review, Midwest Journal of Political Science, Political Methodology, Municipal Year Book, Publius, Urban Affairs Quarterly,* and *Annals of the American Academy of Political and Social Science.* He is currently conducting research on the relationship between population growth and political decision making.

RICHARD L. COLE is currently Assistant Professor of Political Science and Public Affairs at George Washington University. He received his Ph.D. from Purdue University in 1973 and has done teaching and research in the areas of urban policy analysis, decentralization politics, and political methodology. He has published three books: *Citizen Participation and the Urban Policy Process, Urban Politics and Decentralization,* and *Revenue Sharing: Methodological Approaches and Problems.* He has published articles in *American Journal of Political Science, Tax Review, Municipal Year Book, Social Science Quarterly, Publius, Urban Affairs Quarterly,* and *Annals of the American Academy of Political and Social Sciences.*

DAVID HOWARD DAVIS is Associate Professor of Government at Cornell University. He received his Ph.D. from Johns Hopkins University, where he held a Woodrow Wilson Foundation Dissertation Fellowship. Professor Davis was on leave from Rutgers in 1973-1974 as an NASPAA Public Administration Fellow assigned to the U.S. Environmental Protection Agency headquarters in Washington, D.C., where he worked in the Office of Planning and Evaluation and the Office of Legislation. In 1976 he served as a consultant to the National Academy of Sciences Committee on Nuclear and Alternative Energy Systems. He has written two books: *How the Bureaucracy Makes Foreign Policy* and *Energy Politics.*

MARCIA M. LEE is Assistant Professor of Political Science at Rutgers University, where she teaches courses in American politics. She received her Ph.D. from Tufts University in 1973 and has spent considerable research effort in examining the influence of sex roles on individual political behavior. She has had extensive experience in developing undergraduate programs at Rutgers and is currently working on a book on constitutional amendments and public policy making.

The Politics of
Policy Making in America

1

Public Policy Making in America: An Introduction

David A. Caputo

Public policy has been a major concern of social scientists and the general public for a long time. Extensive research has been done in the attempt to isolate and explain the specific sequences of events and the roles played by individuals and institutions in the formulation and implementation of public policy. Yet there is considerable disagreement over the "best" way to study public policy, and disagreement, even, over what public policy is (and is not). This volume will not attempt to resolve this debate, but it will provide the beginning student with a variety of case studies illustrating various analytical approaches to the study of public policy.

To the general public, public policy usually means a goal—that is, something to be gained by a governmental decision or set of decisions. Social scientists studying public policy as a goal attempt to determine whether the policy enacted is in fact achieving its stated goal. In order to conduct this type of research, it is necessary to assume, first, that definite goals can be set, and second, that their attainment or lack of it can be clearly attributed to policy decisions. This is a difficult and often impossible task to accomplish.

There are two other standard definitions of public policy—one broader and one narrower than the first. The narrower definition of public policy focuses on the direct impact of specific governmental decisions. Policy results are studied by a method called *policy analysis,* which employs scientific techniques for evaluating and measuring the impact of a particular policy and determining the effectiveness and efficiency of that policy or its implementation. This definition of public policy in terms of its measurable impact is limited largely to technical use by policy analysts in government and the social sciences.

The third definition of public policy assumes a more comprehensive view. This definition includes not only the specific governmental decisions (public policies) reached, and the impact of those decisions, but also the governmental and nongovernmental factors influencing those decisions. Researchers using this definition attempt to explain not only the specific public policy under consideration, but also the reasons for its adoption and its probable impact.

There is no need for the reader to choose one of the above three definitions of public policy. Students of public policy have long utilized all three. In fact elements of all three are found in the case studies which follow. Each of the case studies has its unique approach to the study of public policy, but all demonstrate aspects of the third definition in their approaches.

Just as there is no one accepted definition of public policy, there is no one accepted method for the study of public policy. It should be kept in mind that numerous approaches are available, each with its own advantages and disadvantages. For example, policy analysis, which we have already observed to be concerned with gauging the impact of a particular policy, emphasizes the development of precise quantitative measures for interpreting causal connections—establishing, say, that C happened because of B and not because of another policy or random effect. Since effective policy analysis requires that the methodology be adapted to a particular set of circumstances, the results are ordinarily difficult to generalize about. Similarly, other approaches have other advantages and disadvantages.

For this volume, the illustrative case study approach was chosen. Because of the various complexities and subtleties of policy making in the United States, it is often difficult to develop generalizations from specific cases which are applicable to other events and developments. Despite this difficulty, it is possible to place specific cases and the conclusions gained from them into a broader perspective *if* certain basic information about them and the American political system in general is clearly understood and if the limitations of the case studies are appreciated. The five case studies presented here—the drive for ratification of the Equal Rights Amendment, the energy policy of the Ford administration from August, 1974, to August, 1975, the campaign finance reform legislation of 1974, the Housing and Community Development Act of 1974, and the European Conference on Security and Cooperation, concluded in 1974—all are recent (since 1974) and illustrative of public policy making in the United States. They not only offer insights into the "who, what, and why" of the particular cases under examination, they also permit the development of certain conclusions about American politics and policy making in general. For these reasons they deserve careful reading and consideration.

The case studies in this volume can be analyzed and compared more easily if they are given a common frame of reference. One such frame of reference, which is widely used in the study of public policy making, and which seems particularly well suited to our study, is the *systems model*.

THE SYSTEMS MODEL

The systems model can take a variety of different forms, but a common example of it is depicted in Figure 1.1. As indicated there, a very complicated decision-making process resulting in public policy can be analyzed by looking at each of the components of the process. Each of these components is important and will be briefly described here since a clear understanding of the systems model will be useful in studying the case material that follows.

Inputs include a variety of factors which go into any specific policy-making process. Most common are demands and supports. *Demands* are the specific policy requests made by various groups or individuals of the political system. For instance, if a labor union desires legislation to permit its representation in the labor-manage-

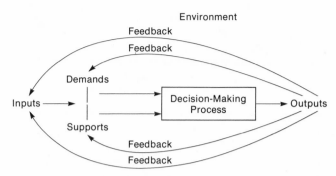

FIGURE 1.1. The Systems Model of Public Policy Making.

ment bargaining process, this would be considered a demand. Or if citizens request, through the city council, that the sanitation department improve its garbage service in their neighborhood, this would also be a demand. Demands for governmental action can be either requests for positive action to improve a situation or requests for corrective action to reverse the negative results of another policy. Political scientists have usually concentrated their attention on demands to improve a particular situation rather than on those demands which might take the form of protest. (Violence is one form of protest which, until recent years, has been widely overlooked as a political demand.)

Supports, which constitute the second type of input, are more difficult to explain. In essence, they represent the backing that policy makers receive—for particular policies and, ultimately, for their own tenure in office—from the general populace or specific segments of the populace. For instance, a President may have the support of certain segments of the population but not others on a controversial issue such as public housing. In this case, the social composition as well as the extent of the support may be important in determining the impact it will have on policy making. Remember that Lyndon B. Johnson and Richard M. Nixon both had unrivaled public popularity and support in 1964 and 1972 respectively, but that their popular bases of support quickly eroded when decisions were reached and policies implemented which were unpopular with many Americans.

Supports also involve specific consensus on the right of a governmental system to exist. It is possible to have the government become so unpopular that the support level for it drops to such an extent that there are widespread demands that the government be replaced or the form of government be altered. Certainly the revolutionary fever of 1776 and the dissatisfaction of many Southern leaders just prior to the Civil War are excellent examples of support for a political system being at a low ebb. It will be interesting to observe how historians treat the impact of the Watergate experience and President Nixon's resignation on the basic legitimacy of the American governmental system. Certainly the legitimacy of the American system, as represented by its underlying basic support, may be weakened if any more events as damaging as Watergate occur.

Demands and supports, in their various forms, are introduced into the *decision-making process,* which generates outputs. The decision-making process (often referred to as the "black box" because it is virtually impossible to describe all its mechanisms) is most often identified with specific governmental institutions such as the legislature, the judiciary, and the executive. Each of these institutions is responsible for reaching numerous decisions via a variety of complex and often confusing rules and procedures, which may sometimes be applicable only to that particular institution at that particular time. Consequently, it is often difficult for the casual observer to recognize the subtleties of policy making in differing arenas. The existence of these subtleties requires that an individual desiring a particular policy outcome spend considerable time and energy attempting to influence the course of the decision-making process. The decision-making process thus becomes the main focus of attention in descriptive analyses of public policy making.

In the United States, as the subsequent case studies will indicate, the decision-making process often involves more than one political institution and usually includes a variety of participants. For instance, a new law must be passed by Congress, acted upon by the President, and subsequently implemented by the appropriate government agencies. Local ordinances or state laws also face a variety of decisions before they can be adopted. Because of the large number of different participants, the decision-making process in the United States often appears to be indecisive and cumbersome, yet decisions do get made and policies get adopted and implemented. The policy-making process refers to all the specific decisions and events which are required for a policy to be proposed, considered, and finally either enacted and implemented or set aside. Thus descriptive emphasis on a particular institution will be helpful only to the extent that that institution alone is involved in a particular policy decision. The five cases which follow offer excellent examples of the complex interactions of institutions and individual participants throughout the policy-making process. The emphasis in these cases is not on a particular institution, but rather on specific policy decisions.

Eventually, the decision-making process results in *outputs*. For our purposes, there are two types of outputs. One, obviously, is the specific policies or decisions which are reached during the decision-making process. These policies, or particular sets of rules or decisions which have been sent down to be implemented by the appropriate authority, include such things as tax cuts, treaties, and decisions affecting law enforcement practices. Most policy analysis focuses on these "hard" or tangible decisions because such decisions, and their impact, can be studied and conclusions reached as to their effectiveness. Thus the policy analyst concerned with public policy making attempts to measure the specific results of policy being implemented and is much less concerned with the institutional aspects of policy making represented by the "black box." Social scientists are now attempting to broaden their efforts to explain the impact of policy and to develop methods to determine the relative benefits and costs associated with alternative policies while these policies are under active consideration by the appropriate policy-making institutions. Several of the case studies which follow place specific emphasis on considering the impact of the policy under discussion.

Another type of output, often overlooked in the analysis of public policy, is the negative policy response which manifests itself in the failure of decision makers to consider a specific policy alternative or to resolve an issue of importance. For instance, assume there is significant demand for governmental attention to environmental protection, but that for one reason or another government fails to respond or adopts a policy which ignores the desires of a substantial segment of the population. In the former case, there is no policy decision, and in the latter, it may be that specific alternatives have been ignored. The point is that if only overt policies are considered as outputs, an important dimension of policy making may be ignored. As several of the case studies will document, such inaction is quite common in American politics.

Both types of outputs of the decision-making process become part of the *feedback* affecting subsequent action in a political system. The feedback loops are represented by the two long arrows linking outputs with demands and supports. It is reasonable to assume that a specific policy or decision will influence subsequent demands and supports. For instance, a decision to raise or lower income taxes may have a great deal of impact on subsequent demands and supports by those groups most influenced by the decision. Depending on who gains and who loses from such decisions, the sources of demands and supports will vary, and the intensity of the reaction will also vary depending on the number of individuals involved. Thus any analysis of overt policy should take into consideration the impact of that policy on subsequent developments which may affect future demands and supports. Feedback provides public policy with a dynamic quality. Since each output subsequently influences the policy process, it is necessary to consider the results and implications of policy decisions at various points in time.

Related to this point is the fact that failure of the decision-making process to enact policy in a specific area or affecting a particular problem may also influence subsequent demands and support. If there is no tax cut when there is considerable demand for one, it is conceivable that this could result in a lessening of public support and a subsequent demand for change in political leadership. In a democratic system, elections play a uniquely important role in resolving this type of conflict by permitting a change in leadership without requiring a change in the basic governmental structure to bring about the new leadership.

Thus the feedback arrows illustrate the dynamic nature of the political system. Policy making must be viewed as a constantly changing process characterized by uncertainty and complexity. There may be substantial disagreement about the rate or impact of change, but there can be little argument that policy making in a modern society is an ongoing process.

The final component of the systems model, as diagramed in Figure 1.1, is the *environment.* Simply put, the environment is the total set of cultural and ecological factors which influence the policy-making process. It is difficult to assess environmental influence because it is always unique to the particular environment; nevertheless, it is important to understand that environmental factors may influence participants and their actions throughout the policy-making process. An obvious example is the use of force to achieve political demands; in some situations and for some groups of participants, force may be a justified and accepted aspect of political action. The sum of the cultural heritage and individual values, reflected in a political system's environment, will help to determine which strategies are followed and which are not. As the case studies illustrate, environmental factors may create unique opportunities for enlightened political leadership as well as pose major restrictions which limit the flexibility and options available to the decision maker.

This, then, is the systems approach to the study of public policy making. While it may seem a bit overwhelming at this point, the systems approach can in fact be utilized as a way to understand the case studies which follow. By utilizing the component approach represented by the systems model, the reader can break down the cases into manageable parts and isolate the principal participants and decisions of each part. It must be emphasized, however, that other approaches are available for the study of public policy and that they offer other advantages and disadvantages.

THE CASE STUDIES

It may be useful here to describe the emphases of the five case studies. Keep in mind that most prior policy research has concentrated on the institutions involved in policy making, with some recent studies taking a process approach, but few emphasizing the impact and implementation of public policy decisions. The case studies in this volume do all three, but each has a primary emphasis. Table 1.1 summarizes these emphases. As the table indicates, the energy chapter concentrates on the institutional aspects of policy making, the ERA, campaign finance reform, and the Conference on Security and Cooperation in Europe chapters emphasize process, and the community development chapter emphasizes impact.

As the discussion in the earlier part of the chapter suggests, case studies often involve more than one focus, and Table 1.1 shows that all of these cases have at least one and in many cases two secondary emphases. As you complete each case, you are encouraged to review the case to see if you agree or disagree with the editor's decision as to the case study's emphasis, and to consider whether a different approach would have resulted in a different set of conclusions.

It is tempting to begin to discuss the cases, but that temptation will be resisted till the concluding chapter. It is sufficient to conclude this chapter by pointing out that a thorough understanding of the specifics involved in each case study will lead to a fuller understanding of the American political system. While each of the cases deals with a specific policy, the reader should be aware of the generalizations which can be drawn, both from the individual cases and from the five cases together. Specific details are needed to understand each case, but attention should also be directed to the implications of each case and the generalizations that it suggests about public policy making in America.

Table 1.1
Summary of Case Study Emphases

CASE STUDY	INSTITUTIONAL EMPHASIS	PROCESS EMPHASIS	IMPACT EMPHASIS
Equal Rights Amendment	S	M	S
Energy Policy	M	S	—
Campaign Finance Reform	S	M	S
Community Development Act	S	S	M
Conference on Security and Cooperation in Europe	S	M	—

M = Main emphasis; S = Secondary emphasis.

2

The Equal Rights Amendment: Public Policy Making by Means of a Constitutional Amendment

Marcia M. Lee

In the office of the New York Coalition for Equal Rights is a map of the United States. Thirty-five states have been blocked out, indicating their ratification of the proposed Equal Rights Amendment (ERA). The other fifteen remain untouched. Should three of these fifteen states vote for ratification before March 22, 1979, the Twenty-seventh Amendment will be added to the United States Constitution. Whether in fact this will take place is still very much in question.

The Equal Rights Amendment, when proposed in 1972 by both Houses of Congress, received wide support from all sectors of the political community. Within two years twenty-eight state legislatures had voted for its ratification. Since then, however, opposition to the amendment has grown. In 1974 three state legislatures, Nebraska, Tennessee, and Idaho, voted to rescind their previous votes favoring ratification. While there is considerable controversy as to whether a state legislature can legally rescind a vote to ratify an amendment once it has been taken, the re-consideration of their votes by these states has tended to slow down the momentum that was building. An additional setback for proponents of the ERA occurred in November, 1975, when the voters of New York and New Jersey defeated equal rights amendments proposed for their respective state constitutions. The spirits of the proponents were lifted again in 1977, however, when Indiana voted for ratifica-tion and six state legislatures—Kansas, Montana, North Dakota, Oregon, Wyoming, and South Dakota—defeated bills to rescind the ERA.

The next two years, therefore, are crucial in determining whether the amendment will be ratified. Should it be, this amendment, like the other twenty-six amendments that have been added to the Constitution, will have an important impact on public policy making in the United States.

35 States That Have Ratified   **15 States That Have Not Ratified**

Alaska	Maryland	Oregon	Alabama	Missouri
California	Massachusetts	Pennsylvania	Arizona	Nevada
Colorado	Michigan	Rhode Island	Arkansas	North Carolina
Connecticut	Minnesota	South Dakota	Florida	Oklahoma
Delaware	Montana	Tennessee	Georgia	South Carolina
Hawaii	Nebraska	Texas	Illinois	Utah
Idaho	New Hampshire	Vermont	Louisiana	Virginia
Indiana	New Jersey	Washington	Mississippi	
Iowa	New Mexico	West Virginia		
Kansas	New York	Wisconsin		
Kentucky	North Dakota	Wyoming		
Maine	Ohio			

FIGURE 2.1.   States That Have Ratified the Equal Rights Amendment as of January 1977.

THE CONSTITUTIONAL AMENDMENT PROCESS

The proposed Equal Rights Amendment reads as follows:

Section 1. Equality of rights under the law shall not be denied or abridged by the United States or by any State on account of sex.

Section 2. The Congress shall have the power to enforce, by appropriate legislation, the provisions of this article.

Section 3. This amendment shall take effect two years after the date of ratification.

In pursuing the route of a constitutional amendment as the means to change public policy, proponents of the ERA have their work cut out for them. Without a doubt, one of the most, if not the most, arduous methods of changing public policy in the United States is to amend the Constitution. The founding fathers intended it to be so. *While the framers of the Constitution provided an amendment process for changing the Constitution so that its provisions could be made applicable to future generations, they also laid great importance on the need for stability and continuity in the governmental process and hence did not make the amendment process an easy one.*

The constitutional amendment process involves two steps. First, an amendment has to be proposed, either by a two-thirds vote of both houses of Congress, or by a national convention called by Congress at the request of two-thirds of the states. Then it has to be ratified, either by three-fourths of the state legislatures or by a special ratifying convention held in three-fourths of the states.[1] The usual route has been for Congress to propose the amendment and then for the state legislatures to ratify it. No amendment has ever been proposed by a national convention called by Congress, although in the mid-sixties a serious effort was made to utilize this means. Between 1963 and 1970 thirty-three state legislatures—only one short of the required two-thirds—petitioned Congress to call a constitutional convention to propose an amendment which would overturn the Supreme Court's "one person, one vote" decision, a decision which had forced reapportionment of the state legislatures. Even if the required number of states had petitioned, however, there could be no assurance Congress would call a convention. The state legislatures by themselves, no matter how many of them act, cannot officially propose amendments; all they can do is petition. There is no legal way to force Congress to call a national convention even if the necessary two-thirds of the state legislatures petition for it. In the past Congress has always preferred to propose amendments itself instead of calling a convention to do so.

Of the twenty-six amendments ratified by 1976, only the Twenty-first Amendment, repealing Prohibition, was ratified by special state conventions. Congress establishes the ratification process, and in this case the "wets" in Congress believed that the repeal of Prohibition had a better chance of being ratified by state conventions than by rurally dominated state legislatures. History proved them correct.

The arduousness of the amendment process is evidenced by the fact that since the beginning of this nation in 1789 only twenty-six amendments have been added to the Constitution—a modest number compared with the revisions of other national constitutions. These amendments fall into three major time periods. The first twelve, ratified between 1791 and 1804, were remedial amendments designed to perfect the original document. The first ten of these twelve comprise what is called "The Bill of Rights," guaranteeing to American citizens such liberties as freedom of religion, speech, and press (First Amendment), protection against self-incrimination and double jeopardy (Fifth Amendment), the right to a speedy, public trial by a jury of one's peers (Sixth Amendment), and protection against excessive bail and fines or cruel and unusual punishment (Eighth Amendment). The next three, the Thirteenth, Fourteenth, and Fifteenth, grew out of the great upheaval of the Civil War and were designed to deal with the new position of blacks as free men.

The remainder of the amendments were passed in the twentieth century and deal with a wide range of subjects reflecting more recent pressures toward change in American society. The Sixteenth Amendment allowed Congress to pass the graduated individual income tax, the Seventeenth provided for the direct election of senators, and the Eighteenth established Prohibition, an idealistic measure which was later repealed by the Twenty-first Amendment. The remaining amendments concern either the presidency or the right to vote. The Twenty-second Amendment, for example, restricts the number of terms the President can hold office to two, and the Twenty-fifth Amendment stipulates the procedures to be used to remove a President from office in case of mental or physical illness or other disabilities. Provisions of this amendment governed the procedures used to fill the office of the Vice President when Spiro Agnew resigned, and the office of the President when Richard Nixon resigned. Among the amendments pertaining to voting rights are the Nineteenth Amendment, which guaranteed women the right to vote, and the Twenty-sixth Amendment, which extended the right to vote to all citizens eighteen years and older.

There are several factors which explain why it is so difficult to amend the Constitution. The required two-step process of first proposing and then ratifying an amendment is, of course, one of them. The major obstacle has not been ratification, but getting Congress to propose amendments in the first place. Dozens of resolutions proposing amendments are introduced each session, but few make any headway. What Congress proposes, however, is usually ratified. Of the thirty-two amendments proposed since the formation of the Constitution, twenty-six have been ratified. Four of the six unratified amendments were proposed prior to the Civil War; since then, the only amendment that has failed to win the necessary state approval is the child labor amendment proposed in 1924. The ERA is the other proposed amendment which has yet to be ratified.

The fact that the two-step process must be carried out by two different legislative bodies at both the federal and state levels of government further increases the difficulty, since these legislative bodies are composed of people with very different backgrounds, constituencies, and political points of view.

Another difficult hurdle is the large majorities required to propose and ratify. The two-thirds vote needed to propose is particularly difficult to obtain in Congress. The requirement that three-fourths of the state legislatures must vote for ratification also can be a great obstacle, since it takes only thirteen states to block ratification. If these thirteen states should be the least populous states, they might represent less than 4 percent of the total population of the United States.

The fluctuating nature of public opinion coupled with the time it takes to propose and ratify an amendment is another factor that should be mentioned. At the very least it takes one year to ratify an amendment after it has been proposed. Should the American public lose interest in the amendment or turn against it while it is in the process of being ratified, it could fail from lack of public support. The growth of unfavorable public opinion, in fact, is the very problem which the ERA faces, as will be observed later in this study.

Lastly, the strong reverence in which the American public holds the Constitution also adds to the difficulty in changing it. Over the years the Constitution has attained a stature considerably above the other laws of the land. In many respects it has become a symbol of national unity. As a result, a strong public bias now exists against amending the Constitution without considerable justification.

Although amending the Constitution can be a very difficult feat, once accomplished this form of policy making quite clearly has its advantages. *Compared with other methods of policy making such as federal and state legislation executive decisions, amendments to the Constitution are probably least subject to future change.* Once a constitutional amendment has been enacted, there are only two ways by which it can be negated. One, of course, is to pass another amendment which rescinds the previous one, such as was the case with the Twenty-first Amendment, which repealed the Eighteenth Amendment establishing prohibition. As has been pointed out, this method is difficult and seldom successful.

Another way to negate an amendment is for the Supreme Court to interpret the amendment in a way not originally intended by those who proposed it.[2] This in fact has happened, and the Fourteenth Amendment is an excellent example. This amendment was passed shortly after the Civil War specifically for the purpose of making former slaves citizens. It states that no state shall "deprive any person of life, liberty or property, without due process of law," nor deny anyone "the equal protection of the laws." During the latter third of the nineteenth century and the first half of the twentieth, however, the Court interpreted the "equal protection clause" of the Fourteenth Amendment to mean also "separate but equal." In the 1896 landmark decision *Plessy v. Ferguson* the Court held that provision of separate public accommodations for blacks and whites was constitutional if the separate accommodations were equal. Thereafter many states, primarily in the South, passed "Jim Crow" laws which prevented blacks from sharing public accommodations with whites in such places as restaurants, hotels, buses, trains, and even public schools. The separate accommodations for the blacks, however, were rarely, if ever, equal. The Fourteenth Amendment, therefore, instead of promoting racial equality as its proponents had intended, resulted in the segregation of whites and blacks and perpetuated the inferior status of the latter. It was not until 1954 that the original intention of the Fourteenth Amendment was restored when the Supreme Court declared the "separate but equal" doctrine unconstitutional in *Brown v. the Board of Education of Topeka, Kansas.*

A second advantage of the constitutional amendment is that once it is passed it becomes the supreme law of the land, and thereby applies throughout the United States, taking precedence over any conflicting legislation passed by Congress or any of the fifty state legislatures. This means that if the Supreme Court decides by judicial review that a law passed by Congress or a state legislature is not in accord with the Constitution, the law can be declared null and void. Moreover, the Supreme Court can declare any executive act on the part of a President, state governor, or any other elected or appointed official at any level of government, unconstitutional. *A constitutional amendment, therefore, is particularly advantageous as a method of policy making because once it is passed all other laws and all executive acts which a court finds incompatible with it are null and void.*

ANTECEDENTS TO THE ERA

If the proponents of the ERA are successful in gaining the ratification of the amendment, it will mark the culmination of a long drive to give women equal status with men before the law—a drive which goes back further than the founding of the Constitution itself.

At the time of its writing, the Constitution did not grant the same citizenship rights to women as to men. This was no mere oversight on the part of the delegates. The Preamble to the Constitution declares that all *men* are created equal, and, although school children are taught today that the word "men" in this instance is used generically, in fact this was not the intention of the founders. Abigail Adams wrote to her husband, John, while the Constitutional Convention was in session imploring him to include the mention of women as citizens in the Constitution. Her plea, however, went unheeded. Even the great libertarian and statesman Thomas Jefferson later expressed opposition to granting women equal citizenship rights, stating that

> Were our state a pure democracy, there would still be excluded from our deliberations . . . women, who, to prevent depravation of morals and ambiguity of issues, should not mix promiscuously in gatherings of men.[3]

In Jefferson's day such declarations were very much in keeping with the times. At the turn of the eighteenth century most of the states applied the common law doctrine of "femme coverte," under which married women had no legal control over their own earnings, children, or property unless a premarital agreement had been negotiated and their property had been placed in trust. Such prohibitions on property ownership and income did not apply to single women, who were classified as "femme sole." For a married woman, this law meant, among other things, that if she inherited property without a premarital agreement—and most married women did not have such an agreement—the property immediately became her husband's. Should a separation occur, her husband automatically would have custody of the children, and should she wish to go to court to get them back, she might even be denied the right to appear in court on her own behalf. Her husband usually was required to represent her. Moreover, married women could not sign legal contracts, which also meant they could not go into business for themselves. Should their husbands cooperate in signing the contracts, the women still had no legal right to their own earnings. Divorce, when granted at all, was given only for the most flagrant abuses such as adultery, desertion, nonsupport, and extreme cruelty.[4]

By the beginning of the twentieth century, however, many of the legal rights granted to single women had been extended to married women and most of the states had abolished or altered considerably their common law doctrines regarding "femme coverte."[5] As legal beings, therefore, women had made substantial progress since the days of Jefferson, but equality under the law was far from being theirs. The courts still upheld discriminatory practices against women in such areas as education and employment, and only four states had by the turn of the century granted women the right to vote: Wyoming (1869), Colorado (1893), Utah (1896), and Idaho (1896). In all the other states women were prohibited from voting in elections for the state legislature and thus failed to meet a constitutional requirement necessary for voting in federal elections.

A Supreme Court decision handed down in 1875 assured that most of the other states would not extend the franchise to women. In *Minor v. Happersett* the Court ruled unanimously that states could withhold the right to vote from women since voting was not coextensive with citizenship.[6] The denial of the right to vote brought with it the denial of certain other rights, inasmuch as citizens who could not vote could not hold public office or sit on juries.

The result of these abridgments of citizenship was the growth of the women's suffrage movement, which started slowly in the nineteenth century, swelled in the second decade of the twentieth century, and culminated in the passage of the Nineteenth Amendment in 1920. It was the first organized effort by women, and many men as well, to amend the Constitution. In a number of respects this effort was the precursor to the ERA, and many of the arguments for and against the suffrage amendment are being echoed today in the ERA debate.

The first serious attempt to pass a suffrage amendment occurred in the 1830s, when the growth of the factory system began to create a labor force that included women. No longer isolated in their homes, these women joined together to campaign for the right to vote. Later, in 1848, at a small meeting in Seneca Falls, New York, Elizabeth Cady Stanton proposed a resolution calling for the right of women to vote. The measure barely received a majority of support from those who attended, and the public at large generally viewed it as a preposterous measure, but it renewed interest in woman suffrage and attracted many women to the movement. During the next twenty years other women joined the crusade, and in 1869 Mrs. Stanton and Susan B. Anthony founded the National Woman Suffrage Association. The organization advocated a national suffrage amendment and at the same time campaigned against the then proposed Fifteenth Amendment because it specifically gave the vote to black men, but not to women. In the same year Lucy Stone and Julia Ward Howe founded the American Woman Suffrage Association and tried in a more moderate vein to persuade the states, rather than the federal government, to grant women the vote.

For a number of reasons neither approach was successful. The split weakened the movement because it caused efforts to be dispersed on both the state and national levels. The women also were very inexperienced in politics and failed to estimate the extent and complexity of the forces arrayed against them. They were totally unprepared for the opposition of the Republican party politicians and also did not anticipate the desertion of their cause by the abolitionists. Most important was the fact that there existed at the time no intensity of feeling in favor of changing the status of women, even among the women themselves, except in relatively small groups.

In the early 1890s, however, support for woman suffrage began to grow. In 1893 the two groups decided to consolidate their efforts and merged into the National American Woman Suffrage Association. By the turn of the century proponents and opponents of the Woman Suffrage Amendment had solidified their positions. Opponents asserted that women would be corrupted by the political process and that their traditional role as childbearer, child-rearer and homemaker would be destroyed. Senator George Vest of Missouri declared:

> It will unsex our mothers, wives, and sisters, who are today influencing by their gentle caress the action of their husbands toward the good and pure. It will turn our blessed country's domestic peace into ward assemblyrooms. . . .[7]

Many women agreed with Senator Vest and did not favor woman suffrage, arguing that they had their husbands to look after their interests and that they needed no new laws to protect their rights. They were joined in opposition to the amendment by the liquor interests, who feared that woman suffrage would result in the passage of a prohibition amendment. As it happened, the Eighteenth Amendment, which prohibited the sale of alcohol in the United States, was passed in 1919, one year before the Woman Suffrage Amendment was ratified. Also opposed to woman suffrage were the political machines, who were uncertain about the effects that such an addition to the electorate would have on their ability to control the elected officials and the laws that were passed. The Catholic Church also staunchly opposed the amendment in the belief that a woman's place was in the home.

Proponents of the bill argued that politics involves many issues that directly affect the home—issues with which even the most traditionally oriented women are concerned, such as child welfare legislation, pure food and drug acts, kindergartens, and educational innovations. Therefore, they argued, women should be allowed to vote. They also maintained that granting the right to vote to women who were mothers would be very beneficial since, "The ballot will give her prestige equal to that of the father in her boy's mind; and so it will actually lighten her task as chief family teacher."[8] Further, they asserted that female suffrage would result in a social reformation—an argument widely accepted at the time.

While both sides could claim sizable support in the first decade of the twentieth century, after 1910 the forces favoring the passage of the amendment began to win out. In the next four years Washington, Arizona, Kansas, and Oregon granted women the right to vote. By 1914 most women's groups favored the amendment and in that year even the General Federation of Women's Clubs, the last holdout, endorsed the measure.

In 1916 both party platforms professed support of woman suffrage, but only on a state action basis. As a result the more militant suffragettes resorted to more aggressive tactics, such as picketing the White House, burning copies of the President's speeches, and going on hunger strikes when arrested. Even these measures did not bring an immediate victory in Congress. Not until 1919, when fifteen states already had granted full voting privileges to women in all elections and another twelve had granted them the right to vote in presidential elections, did both houses propose the amendment. Once the amendment was proposed, the states acted with unusual speed to ratify it in time for women to vote in the presidential election of 1920. On August 18, 1920, when the state of Tennessee voted for ratification, the Nineteenth Amendment became law.

THE MOVEMENT FOR AN EQUAL RIGHTS AMENDMENT

For a brief period in 1920 a sense of euphoria swept the women's movement. The exhilaration of victory soon subsided, however, and within a few years the feminist coalition broke into factions and the majority of American women turned their attention to other things. For the next fifty years relatively few groups were concerned specifically with furthering women's rights.

Of these, the Woman's Party, founded by Alice Paul in 1916, was one of the most active. In contrast to other women's groups, it decided to concentrate its efforts on attaining an equal rights amendment—a goal which its membership believed would be the surest way to end the many state and national laws that discriminated against women. The amendment, which was first introduced in Congress in 1923, simply read: "Men and women shall have equal rights throughout the United States and every place subject to its jurisdiction." At the time of its initial introduction, the executive secretary explained:

> As we were working for the national suffrage amendment . . . it was borne very emphatically upon us that we were not thereby going to gain full equality for the women of this country, but that we were merely taking a step . . . toward gaining this equality.[9]

The Woman's Party had relatively few members, but the numerous women of wealth and professional eminence who comprised its membership increased its influence considerably. It was not a radical group by any means. Alice Paul, the chairman, consistently fended off attempts to include in its platform demands which were considered at that time to be militant, such as the legalization of birth control, insisting that the Woman's Party's only concern be the passage of the Equal Rights Amendment.

Although the Woman's Party continued to introduce the Equal Rights Amendment in each new Congress throughout the twenties and thirties, support was limited. Such an approach was unacceptable to most other women's groups, including the League of Women Voters, which, during this period, emphasized a program of social reform and political education of women. The League specifically objected to the amendment because it might eliminate laws which gave special protection to women working in factories.

Meanwhile, the average American woman still considered the traditional concepts of home, husband, and the attainment of beauty to be paramount goals.[10] This is not to say women's organizations abandoned their feminist efforts entirely. For a time, in 1936, Mary Anderson, head of the Women's Bureau, worked with women leaders to draw up a charter containing feminist demands for equal rights for women and men in politics, education, law, and employment, and it appeared for a while that the charter would receive widespread support. Few women's organizations, however, actually endorsed it.

World War II had a liberalizing effect on the nation with regard to women's rights. As more and more women took jobs in the labor force vacated by men enlisting in the armed forces, the assumptions about women's capabilities outside the home began to change. In all sectors of the economy women were proving their skills in jobs traditionally performed by men. As a result, in 1940 the Republican party endorsed the Equal Rights Amendment in its platform; in 1943 the General Federation of Women's Clubs announced its support; and in 1944 the Democratic party also included the amendment in its platform.[11]

During the mid-fifties interest in the passage of an Equal Rights Amendment subsided. By the mid-sixties, however, the mood of the nation had changed again, and support for its passage was renewed. Three factors, in particular, were responsible for this. One was the growth of the black civil rights movement. The second was the birth of the women's liberation movement. The third was the dramatic change that had been occurring over the last fifty years in the traditional role of women.

The black civil rights movement, in the process of drawing to the nation's attention the rights denied this minority, also drew to the attention of other groups the rights denied them. One of these groups was women, who increasingly felt that they too must campaign for better job opportunities and better educational opportunities. Their awareness of the similarities between their problems and those of blacks was heightened by reports such as those on employment published in the early sixties by the United States government. One statistic showed, for example, that the average salary for women in the late sixties was about 58 percent of that of men.[12]

This inequity, among others, accounted for the growth of the women's liberation movement—a second factor instrumental in developing renewed support for the Equal Rights Amendment. In addition to the old-line activists, a new group of women feminists emerged in the mid-sixties. More militant in style and demands than their predecessors, they formed loosely structured groups which deemphasized leadership and stressed equality. Many of these groups conducted "consciousness-raising" meetings which employed the techniques of group therapy to heighten their members' sensitivity to the problems of women in America. One of the largest and most active of these groups was formed in 1966 at the Third National Conference of the State Commissions on Women held in Washington, D.C. Dissatisfied with the direction in which the conference was going, Betty Friedan, whose book *The Feminine Mystique* had recently been a best seller, and a number of other women decided to form the National Organization of Women (NOW). With the formation of NOW, the new feminism in the United States was officially launched.

Other organizations soon followed. In 1968 academic and professional women formed the Women's Equity Action League (WEAL) for the purpose of ending sex discrimination in employment, education, and taxation. The Women's Political Caucus, a bipartisan group aimed at pressuring the political parties to consider women's issues and to elect women to office, was organized in 1971.[13]

During this same period a number of women began to express their discontent in print. Kate Millett's *Sexual Politics* (1969) became a best seller. It was followed by Shulamith Firestone's *The Dialetics of Sex* (1970), Robin Morgan's *Sisterhood is Powerful* (1970), and Germaine Greer's *The Female Eunuch* (1971). In 1972 *Ms. Magazine* published its inaugural issue marking the first militant feminist magazine in the history of the nation to attract a sizable circulation.

The factor that was probably most instrumental in advancing the cause of the Equal Rights Amendment, however, was the social change that had been taking place over the last fifty years—the gradual change in the role of women as mothers and home-makers. New advances in medical science had tremendously affected the number of children women were having. The introduction of oral contraceptives in the late fifties and sixties made available a relatively inexpensive and almost foolproof method of birth control. Moreover, at just the time an effective method of birth control became widely available, various organized groups began to encourage women to reduce the number of children they were having because of the threat of overpopulation. These developments and other factors resulted in a drop in the United States fertility rate from 3.69 children per family in 1959 to slightly less than two children (1.86) per family in 1974.[14] The lower fertility rate reduced considerably the number of years the average woman devoted to child rearing.

Medical science also altered the pattern of women's lives by increasing substantially the number of years a woman could expect to live. In 1900 the average life expectancy of women was fifty-one years. The elimination of most communicable diseases and great advances in surgery and the treatment of childbirth complications had by 1974 extended the number of years to seventy-four.[15] The longer life span meant that most women with families had at least thirty years to live after their children had reached adulthood.

Also not to be overlooked is the fact that by the mid-sixties many of the time-consuming responsibilities women had traditionally performed at home could be accomplished in a considerably shorter amount of time. Such labor-saving devices as clothes washers, clothes dryers, and dishwashers revolutionized housekeeping such that the amount of time it took to clean a home no longer filled the average woman's day. The introduction in the fifties and sixties of prepackaged frozen foods also cut down considerably the amount of time a woman spent preparing meals.

The combination of longer life expectancy, fewer children, and labor-saving household devices gave many American women considerably more free time than their mothers or grandmothers had had. The result was that many women decided to work outside the home. National employment figures reflected this increasing demographic trend: in 1950 women comprised only 29 percent of the labor force; by 1970, they comprised 38 percent.[16] Figure 2.2 shows that between 1950 and 1970 the number of women in the labor force almost doubled.

INTEREST-GROUP DEMANDS

The black civil rights movement, the women's liberation movement, and the change in women's role all served to awaken the nation to the issue of women's rights and the ERA. As the decade of the sixties wore on, men and women alike increasingly became aware of and began to sympathize with some of the demands made by the various women's organizations. A Louis Harris poll taken in 1972, for example, showed that women favored efforts to strengthen women's status in society 49 percent to 36 percent, with 15 percent unsure. The same poll conducted only one year earlier showed that a majority of women had opposed such efforts, 42 percent to 40 percent. Significantly, men expressed the same desire to strengthen women's status. Almost half (49) percent favored such action in 1972, while only 44 percent favored it in 1971.[17]

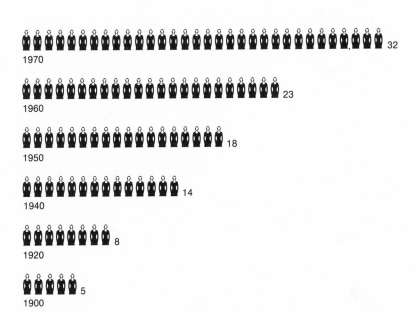

FIGURE 2.2. Women in the Labor Force (Millions). (*Source:* U.S. Department of Labor, Bureau of Labor Statistics; U.S. Department of Commerce, Census Bureau.)

The demands most frequently heard for improving the status of women pertained to the areas of employment, education, politics, marriage rights, and state laws which encouraged differential treatment of men and women. In the area of employment women sought an end to discrimination in certain types of occupations and an end to the practice of paying women less than men for performing the same job. As shown in Figure 2.3, in every category of employment, including professional workers, non-farm managers, clerical workers, operatives (mostly factory workers), service workers, and sale workers, the average annual wages for women in 1970 were substantially below those of men.

In 1972 the 33 million women workers in the United States comprised just under 38 percent of the labor force. Yet women held more than two-thirds of the clerical jobs, reflecting the refusal by most companies to place them in management positions. Moreover, only 7 percent of the working women, but 40 percent of the working men, earned $10,000 or more in 1970.[18] In professional occupations women also were greatly underrepresented, comprising only 3.5 percent of the lawyers in the work force, 6.8 percent of the medical doctors, and 19.0 percent of the college professors and college presidents—percentages which had changed little since the

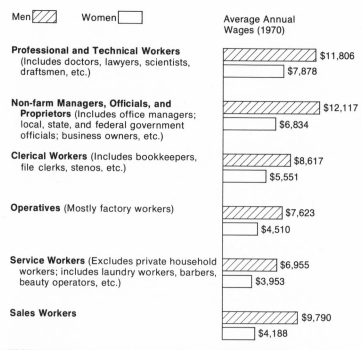

FIGURE 2.3. Average Annual Wages of Men and Women by Occupation, 1970. (*Source:* Women's Bureau, U.S. Department of Labor, *Fact Sheet on the Earnings Gap,* U.S. Government Printing Office, 1972, p. 2.)

1920s.[19] Bias against women also continued in federal governmental employment despite the fact that the last legal barriers to equal employment of women were removed in 1962. In 1971, for example, women comprised 40.1 percent of the federal white-collar workers, excluding most small agencies and the U.S. postal service, but they held only 4 percent of the jobs that paid over $17,000.[20]

In the area of education, demands for change centered primarily on the right of women to be admitted to certain all-male colleges and the right also to be admitted in greater numbers to professional graduate schools, especially in the fields of medicine, law and business, which men have traditionally dominated. Between 1950 and 1972 the number of men receiving medical degrees increased from approximately 5,000 to 8,400, while the number of women only increased from approximately 500 to 800. In law there were approximately 7,900 men receiving degrees in 1950, but by 1972 there were roughly 20,300. In contrast, only 300 women received law degrees in 1950, and only 1,500 received them in 1972.[21] Although many graduate schools have actively sought to increase female enrollment, some even through affimative action programs, the percentage of women in professional graduate schools is still relatively low. The percentage of women in first-year law school classes for the fall of 1974 was 23.7. In the medical schools 22.2 percent of the entering class of 1974 were women.[22] No doubt a number of factors explain this phenomenon, including the lower number of women undergraduates eligible for graduate school, the persistence of less ambitious career expectations on the part of many women, and continued forms of sex discrimination.

In the field of government and politics, the chief demands called for measures which would increase the percentage of women elected to or appointed to public office. In 1974 women held under 7 percent of all the public offices in the United States. Less than 4 percent of the members of the Ninety-fourth Congress were women. The House of Representatives, numbering 435 members, had 19 women members; the Senate had none. No women had ever been appointed to the U.S. Supreme Court, and approximately 1 percent of the federal judges in this country were women—8 women among 675. In 1975 there was one woman governor and one lieutenant governor. In statewide elective and cabinet offices, women held approximately 10 percent of the positions—139 out of an estimated 1,300 offices, and comprised 8 percent of the seats in the state legislatures—611 out of 7,561. Even at the local level representation of women in public office was sparse. Among mayors and city council members in municipalities and townships in 1975 approximately 4 percent were women, and on local school boards women constituted less than 13 percent of the officeholders.[23]

Demands for change in marriage laws have focused on such inequities as personal property rights. The Presidential Commission on the Status of Women noted that matrimonial property tends to be subject to male control in many states.[24] In most states a wife has no legal rights to any part of her husband's earnings, although she does have a legal right to be properly supported. Some states restrict a woman's right to own a business, make contracts, serve as a guarantor or sue or be sued in her own name, if married. Moreover, many women find it difficult to obtain credit or insurance in their own names. Inheritance laws sometimes favor males over females, and the legal domicile, from which many other legal rights flow, is usually held to be the residence of the husband.[25]

Demands for an end to state laws which encourage differential treatment of men and women are aimed at such laws as those which establish different sentencing practices for men and women. For instance, Maine has indeterminate sentencing for both men and women; men, however, can be sentenced under this law only up to age twenty-six, whereas women are subject to it up to age forty. Since the unintentional effect of indeterminate sentencing has been for prisoners to serve longer, not shorter, sentences, this has meant that women between twenty-six and forty end up serving longer sentences than men for the same crime.[26] National statistics also show that girls sent to prison for juvenile deliquency serve longer sentences on the average than do boys, even though girls are sentenced for less serious offenses. Moreover, in some states girls may be convicted under juvenile delinquency laws for acts for which boys are not punished. Connecticut, for example, makes it a crime to be an unmarried girl between sixteen and twenty-one who is in "manifest danger of falling into habits of vice." No boy can be convicted of this.[27]

Other state laws to which proponents of the ERA object include those which allow pregnant women to be fired from public employment, those which bar women from participating in certain school athletic programs, those which provide that prostitution statutes apply only to women, and those which allow retirement plans to be based upon sexual status.

PROPOSED ALTERNATIVES TO THE ERA

While many believed something should be done to change the inequities in the law's treatment of women, not all agreed that a constitutional amendment was the best way to do it.

Revision of State and Local Laws

Some felt that a revision of federal and state legislation would be adequate to achieve the desired goal. They could point to a considerable number of federal and state laws passed during the sixties and early seventies to substantiate their point. In 1963, for example, Congress passed the Equal Pay Act. This act, as its name implies, required equal pay for men and women for equal work. The following year Congress passed the Civil Rights Act of 1964. Title VII of the act makes sex-based discrimination in hiring unlawful. This was a significant advance, for Title VII is a potentially potent weapon against employment discrimination because the Equal Employment Opportunities Commission (EEOC) was established by the act to enforce the law.

In 1972 Congress passed Title IX of the Education Amendments, which banned federal assistance to educational institutions that discriminate on the basis of sex. Exceptions were allowed, however, for admissions to all private and some public undergraduate schools.[28] Also during that same year Congress passed a new and expanded Equal Employment Opportunities Law.

More recently, in 1974, Congress passed two bills designed to prevent discrimination against women seeking to obtain credit and mortgage loans. The Equal Credit Opportunity Act now bars lenders from discriminating on the basis of sex or marital status. The legislation is particularly geared toward preventing discrimination against women with solid employment backgrounds and credit references, who have had trouble opening charge accounts or qualifying for credit cards. The Housing and Community Development Act of 1974 now prohibits mortgage lenders from discounting a women's income in loan approval calculations. Congress also authorized funds that year to enforce a section of Title IX of the Education Amendments which would end sex discrimination in schools and colleges in such areas as vocational and career counseling, sports education, housing, financial aid, and employment. A summary of these legislative measures is contained in Table 2.1.

Less well publicized are the activities at the state level. Many state legislatures are beginning active campaigns to change existing legislation and policies regarding women. Fifteen states, for example, have enacted state equal rights amendments.[29] In complying with these new amendments, most states are changing their laws which give special benefits to one sex, to include the other sex. Examples of such laws are those governing the right to receive pension benefits based on the employment record or occupation of one's spouse, the right to use the surname of one's choice regardless of marriage, the right to receive support or alimony, and the right to be protected from forcible sexual assault.[30]

Certain kinds of discrimination against women, such as special standards for granting unemployment compensation to pregnant women and to women who have left their previous jobs on account of homemaking responsibilities, also have been eliminated in several states, and a number of states have passed laws preventing sex discrimination in parental rights and heads of the household provisions.[31]

Table 2.1

Equal Rights Legislation for Women Passed by Congress Since 1963

ACT	DATE PASSED	PURPOSE
Equal Pay Act	1963	Requires equal pay for men and women for equal work
Title VII of Civil Rights Act	1964	Makes sex bias discrimination in hiring unlawful
Title IX of Education Amendments	1972	Bans federal assistance to educational institutions that discriminate on the basis of sex
Equal Credit Opportunity Act	1974	Bars lenders from discriminating on the basis of sex or marital status
Housing and Community Development Act	1974	Prohibits mortgage lenders from discounting a woman's income in loan approval calculation
Congressional authorization of funds to enforce regulations under Title IX of Education Amendments	1974	Ends sex discrimination in schools and colleges in such areas as vocational training and sports education

Opponents of the legislative route to women's rights do not object, of course, to the passage of these laws and state amendments. They feel, however, that there are serious drawbacks to relying solely on them as a means of guaranteeing women equality. *Basically, ERA proponents believe that in order to eliminate sex discrimination there must exist a single coherent policy on women's equality before the law and a consistent nationwide application of the law.* The state by state "piecemeal" approach would accomplish neither, in their opinion. First, they feel it is unrealistic to expect all fifty states to pass laws which will assure American women the same rights. Instead, the laws will vary from state to state and some states might even fail to pass any laws at all. Moreover, the cost of conducting effective campaigns in each state would be extremely great and the process could not be completed within the lifetime of any woman now alive.

Secondly, they maintain that application of the state laws would not be carried out seriously by many individuals and institutions as long as they believed that the laws were subject to alteration or reversal at the option of the current legislature. Moreover, they argue that neither Congress nor the states can be depended upon to carry out such reform efforts, if their past legislative records are indicative of their performance in the future. Between 1920 and 1963, for example, practically no legislation was passed by Congress in behalf of women's rights. In the future Congress could revert back to its previous performance record, or even worse, reverse legislation already passed. Proponents further note that a recent exhaustive study of sex-based references in federal statutes identified over 800 U.S. code sections containing "gender-based differentials."[32] Congress has a long way to go in putting its own house in order, they maintain, and without the ERA as a reminder, it will be far less likely to do so.

Extension of the Equal Protection Clause

Another group of equal rights advocates, while not supporting the piecemeal legislative approach, believe that equality of the sexes could be achieved through judicial interpretation of the "equal protection" clause contained in the Fourteenth Amendment. This clause provides that no state shall "deny to any person within its jurisdiction the equal protection of the laws." In 1954 the Supreme Court used the "equal protection of the laws" provision as the basis for its landmark decision *Brown v. the Board of Education of Topeka, Kansas,* which outlawed racial segregation in public schools. The decision overturned the "separate but equal doctrine" established a half century earlier in *Plessy v. Ferguson* and set a precedent which basically made racial discrimination in public accommodations unconstitutional.

Many proponents of equal rights for women were encouraged by this decision, believing that since the Court declared discrimination on the basis of race unconstitutional, it would also declare discrimination on the basis of sex unconstitutional. The belief was so strong that in 1963 the President's Commission on the Status of Women held that "the principle of equality [for women could] become firmly established in constitutional doctrine" through the use of the Fourteenth and Fifth Amendments, and that consequently "a constitutional amendment did not need to be sought."[33]

Recent Supreme Court decisions in the early 1970s did signal a new direction in the Court's use of the equal protection clauses to end discrimination on the basis of sex. In *Reed v. Reed,*[34] for example, the Court declared than an Idaho statute that gave preference to males to administer a decedent's estate was unconstitutional, holding that a difference in sex must bear "a rational relationship to a stated objective." The following year, in *Stanley v. Illinois,*[35] the Supreme Court, relying on the due process clause, held that an unwed father wishing to retain custody of his children had to be given a hearing of the kind that would be given to any mother.

Both of these decisions, however, were somewhat unclear as signals to the Court's future course, and it was not until the spring of 1973 that the Court handed down a decision which clearly indicated that sex-discriminatory laws would no longer escape rigorous constitutional review. In *Frontiero v. Richardson*[36] the Court, in an eight to one decision, declared unconstitutional a fringe benefit scheme that awarded male members of the military housing allowances and medical care benefits for their wives regardless of dependency, but authorized these benefits for female members of the military only if they could show that they supported their husbands.[37] In a plurality opinion, four of the justices held that "classifications based upon sex, like classifications based upon race, alienage, or national origin, are inherently suspect, and must therefore be subject to strict judicial scrutiny."

In 1974, however, the majority of the Court backed away from holding that statutory classifications based upon sex are "suspect" under the Fourteenth and Fifth Amendments. In *Kahn v. Shevin*[38] six justices upheld a Florida statute which exempted $500 worth of property from taxation for widows but not for widowers on the grounds that a disproportionate economic burden was created by the death of the male partner. Only three of the justices maintained that the law was in violation of the "equal protection" clause.

In 1976 the Court, in *Craig v. Boren,* further retreated from holding that statutory classifications based on sex are "suspect" under the Fourteenth and Fifteenth Amendments. In this case the Court invalidated by a seven to two vote an Oklahoma "protective" statute that permitted females to buy 3.2 beer at eighteen while boys were not allowed to buy 3.2 beer until age twenty-one. The majority opinion held that "gender-based differential" constituted an invidious discrimination against males, but made no reference to sex as a "suspect" classification.

While these recent decisions and several others described in Table 2.2 were somewhat encouraging to ERA proponents, they remained opposed to relying on this route. They pointed out that over one hundred years elapsed after the passage of the Fourteenth Amendment before the Supreme Court began to interpret the "equal protection" clause in a manner designed to protect women against sex-based discrimination.[39]

During those one hundred years the Court declined to use the "equal protection" clause to guarantee women the right to vote. In 1874 it declared, instead, that such civil rights as voting were not among the "privileges and immunities" of United States citizens and hence were subject to exclusive state regulations. It also maintained that although "women were 'persons' within the meaning of the Fourteenth Amendment, so were children."[40] As a result it took a constitutional amendment, the Nineteenth Amendment, to guarantee to all American women the right to vote. The "equal protection" clause quite obviously had not been adequate.

Table 2.2

*Selected Supreme Court Decisions Concerning
the Rights of Women Since 1970*

DECISION	DATE	EFFECT
Reed v. Reed	1971	State laws giving preference to males in administering a decedent's estate are unconstitutional.
Stanley v. Illinois	1972	An unwed father who wishes to retain custody of his children must be given the same type of hearing a mother would be given.
Frontiero v. Richardson	1973	Military benefits to female personnel must be awarded on the same basis as benefits to male personnel.
Kahn v. Shevin	1974	Widowers need not receive a property-tax exemption granted to widows. Such discrimination is considered reasonable because loss of spouse normally places a greater burden on the woman.
Cleveland Board of Education v. La Fleur	1974	Mandatory maternity leave at a set time in pregnancy violates due process.
Corning Glass v. Brennan	1974	Most employers who have underpaid female workers must not only equalize wages promptly, but make restitution in back payments.
Weinberger v. Wiesenfeld	1975	A widower is entitled to the same social security benefits upon the death of his wife as a widow is upon the death of her husband.
Taylor v. Louisiana	1975	States may not deny women equal opportunity to serve on juries.
General Electric v. Gilbert	1976	Court upheld right of General Electric company to deny disability benefits to women for pregnancies.
Craig v. Boren	1976	An Oklahoma "protective" statute that permitted females to buy 3,2 beer at age 18 and males at age 21 was invalidated.

The Court also declined to use the equal protection clause to declare unconstitutional state laws which excluded women from participating in certain types of employment. In *Bradwell v. Illinois,* for example, the Court approved the exclusion of women from the legal profession, with Justice Bardley stating:

> Man is, or should be, woman's protector and defender. The natural and proper timidity and delicacy which belong to the female sex evidently unfits it for many of the occupations of civil life. The constitution of the family organization, which is founded in the divine ordinance, as well as in the nature of things, indicated the domestic sphere as that which properly belongs to the domain and functions of womenhood.[41]

In *Muller v. Oregon,*[42] a decision handed down in 1908, the Court accepted the argument that women require "protective legislation" in employment, which could not, under the liberty-of-contract doctrine established in a previous Supreme Court case,[43] be extended to men. While the case specifically concerned the fixing of maximum working hours for women by the state, the Court's long recitation on the inferior physical capabilities and social position of women and its subsequent conclusion that "she is properly placed in a class by herself" had far-reaching consequences for "equal protection" law.[44] The *Muller* decision has been widely utilized by federal and state courts to sustain many kinds of sex-based laws against equal protection challenges. More importantly, however, it served to establish as accepted doctrine the belief that women were different and that this justified different treatment under the law.

Later, in *Goesaert v. Cleary* the Court upheld a Michigan statute providing that no female could be licensed as a bartender unless she was "the wife or daughter of a male owner."[45] Justice Frankfurter stated in the decision that "moral and social problems would be less when no females except wives and daughters of male bar owners were permitted to be bartenders." Moreover, in a case as recent   :961, the Court upheld that the right to serve on juries could be reserved to men unless women voluntarily applied and in the same case explicitly refused to apply the "equal protection" clause.[46]

PROPOSAL OF THE ERA BY CONGRESS

Supporters of both approaches to equal rights for women worked actively during the sixties, each group convinced of the merits of its approach. There was little support during this period, however, for an equal rights amendment. Only the National Women's Party, which had sought successfully to have the amendment introduced every year since 1923, the Business and Professional Women, and a few sympathizers supported it.

By 1970, however, the picture had changed. In February, 1970, the Citizens' Advisory Council on the Status of Women, the permanent body of prominent women which replaced the President's Commission on Women in 1963, officially endorsed the ERA and published a definitive legal analysis of it. That same month roughly two dozen National Organization for Women (NOW) members disrupted hearings on the eighteen-year-old right to vote amendment being held by the Senate

Judiciary Subcommittee on Constitutional Amendments, and demanded that hearings be scheduled on the Equal Rights Amendment. As public pressure mounted the Senate Judiciary Subcommittee decided to call hearings on the ERA in early May. At the same time the White House released a task force report with its endorsement of the ERA.

In June the Secretary of Labor designate, James D. Hodgson, added the Labor Department's endorsement of the amendment at an address he gave to the fiftieth-anniversary conference of the Women's Bureau. Later that month Representative Martha Griffiths (Dem., Mich.) filed a petition to discharge the amendment from the House Judiciary Committee, where it had been bottled up for the last twenty years. Using the political power she had accumulated over the years and devoting tremendous energy to the cause, Representative Griffiths obtained the necessary 217 signatures on her discharge petition by July and the House passed the amendment on August 10, 1970, by a vote of 350 to 15.

The Senate, however, failed to follow suit. Instead, opponents delayed further hearings until early September, when fall election campaigns guaranteed the absence of many senators. When the resolution came before the senators in October, it was amended by a vote of 36 to 33 to permit Congress to exempt women from the draft, and a rider was added to permit prayers in public schools. To get around this block, Senator Birch Bayh, (Dem., Ind.) proposed a substitute amendment, but it was opposed by feminist groups as inadequate and the resolution was allowed to die for that year.

The following year the newly convened Ninety-second Congress began consideration of the ERA in the spring. For the most part debate centered on the same question which had arisen on the previous four occasions when Congress had seriously considered the amendment (1946, 1950, 1953, and 1970)—that is, whether the amendment's central principle that "equality of rights shall not be denied or abridged by the United States or by any State on account of sex" should be couched in such absolute terms, or whether, instead, the amendment should explicitly exempt from its coverage such laws as those regarding military service.

The sponsors of the amendment in 1972, Representative Martha Griffiths and Senators Birch Bayh and Marlow Cook (Rep., Ky.) presented the amendment as one calling for uniform treatment of men and women before the law, the principle being absolute and without exceptions.[47] The only qualifications to the principle would be those based on compelling social interests, such as protection of the individual's right to privacy and the need to take into account objective physical differences between the sexes.[48]

In April the House Judiciary Subcommittee Number 4 recommended the ERA, but the full Judiciary Committee chose to amend it as follows:

> This article shall not impair the validity of any law which exempts a person from compulsory military service or any other law of the United States or of any State which reasonably promotes the health and safety of the people.

The full House, however, rejected the Judiciary Committee's attempt to exempt military service and other laws promoting health and safety because it would make the principle of equality less than absolute and thus leave the meaning of the amendment open to future interpretation by the courts. On October 12 the House passed the ERA by a vote of 354 to 23.

The House resolution was sent to the Senate for consideration by the Senate Judiciary Committee, where it awaited the strong opposition of the chairman, Sam Ervin (Dem., N.C.). For years Senator Ervin had prevented the ERA from being reported out of committee through the use of delaying parliamentary tactics. This time, however, the opposition to Senator Ervin's tactics was too great. The full committee reported an unamended ERA out in March by a vote of 15 to 1. On the Senate floor debate was short and uneventful. President Nixon added his support the day after debate began and on March 22, 1972, the Senate voted 84 to 8 for the ERA after rejecting nine amendments offered by Senator Ervin.

INTEREST-GROUP ACTION

At the time Congress proposed the ERA, support for it came from almost every political sector: from men and women of all ages, from people of varying ethnic backgrounds, and from all sections of the country. More than fifty national organizations also endorsed the amendment. Among them were the Republican and Democratic parties, the League of Women Voters, the Federation of Women's Republican Clubs, the American Association of Retired Persons, the American Jewish Congress, Common Cause, the Congress of Italian-American Organizations, the National Council of Negro Women, and the National Council of Senior Citizens. Later the AFL-CIO, which once had been a formidable opponent, also gave its support, when at an October, 1973, convention it voted unanimously for ratification of the amendment.

These organizations did not just give verbal support. The National Ad Hoc Committee for the ERA, a group formed by governmental employees, became the nucleus of the lobbying activity for the ERA. This committee sent out innumerable mailings to organizations and individuals requesting them to wire their representatives. Over 40,000 letters were sent to presidents of various organizations.[49] It also initiated a telephone campaign aimed at the House members, and instituted lobbying of the Senate Judiciary Committee.

Common Cause, a public interest group headed by former Secretary of Health, Education, and Welfare, John Gardner, sent letters to all its 215,000 members requesting them to call their representatives. Shortly thereafter a battery of their volunteers made over 51,000 phone calls on Common Cause's WATS lines. The Business and Professional Women's Clubs also sent at least 100,000 letters to state officers and local club presidents, and spearheaded many pass-ERA drives in locales where feminist organizations were unpopular. The result was that some members of Congress received over 1,500 letters a month and Congressman Tip O'Neill of Massachusetts was quoted as saying that the ERA generated more mail than the Vietnam war.[50]

Proponents did considerably more than write letters, however. At one point twenty to thirty-five full-time and part-time volunteers were literally living in the halls of Congress. The lobbying efforts of the National Women's Party also were very direct. Over its forty-seven years of lobbying for the ERA it had secured the sponsorship of the ERA by 248 members of the House and 81 members of the Senate. Most of these people agreed to sponsor the amendment thinking they would never have to vote for it. When they were finally put to the test, they either had to vote for it or appear hypocrites. They chose the former.

Getting Congress to propose the ERA, therefore, involved intensive lobbying efforts by volunteers at both the national and grassroots level. The quick success which the interest groups had had with Congress, however, was not to be duplicated in all the states. For the first year the amendment appeared to have smooth sailing as twenty-eight states quickly ratified, it, but in January, 1973, a national "Stop ERA" campaign was begun by arch-conservative Phyllis Schlafly. She was joined in support by such groups as the John Birch Society, Pro-America Incorporated, the Christian Crusade, the Young Americans for Freedom, and the National Council of Catholic Women. Since then the popularity of her cause has grown considerably and other organizations have aligned themselves with her, among them the Daughters of the American Revolution (DAR), the Federation of Republican Women's Clubs in twenty-five states, the Rabbinical Alliance of America, the Southern Baptist Association, WUNDER (Women United to Defend Existing Rights), and the American party.

The Schlafly forces have directed most of their energy toward influencing the votes of legislators in southern and rural areas, where latent opposition to the ERA existed. Among other things they have organized mass mailings to the legislators, bused in women to lobby, and testified at ratification hearings. In Illinois the women even baked apple pies for the state legislators.

The effectiveness of Mrs. Schlafly's campaign is evidenced by the small number of states that have ratified the amendment since her forces took action. By the end of 1974 only five more states had ratified the amendment and two others—Nebraska and Tennessee—had voted to rescind their ratification. In 1975 the Stop ERA coalition also decided to direct its efforts against the passage of the state equal rights amendments before the electorates in New York and New Jersey. Figure 2.4, which is a handout distributed by Operation Wake Up, a coalition of organizations opposed to the New York State amendment, is a good example of the presentation of arguments against the amendment made by Mrs. Schlafly and others.

The tactic was successful. In both states the amendments to the state constitutions were defeated. The defeats were a tremendous psychological blow to the ERA proponents and were taken by many in the public at large as a signal that public opinion was turning against the amendment.

The effectiveness of the anti-ERA lobbying can be attributed largely to Phyllis Schlafly herself. An attractive, articulate mother of six who has written six books and has degrees from Washington University and Radcliffe College, she has traveled extensively throughout the United States speaking in behalf of her cause. Maintaining that women will be drafted, wives will lose the support of their husbands, and mothers will lose custody of their children, she asserts that the ERA will not give women any new benefits they do not already have under existing state and federal legislation, and that it will take away special benefits already granted to them. She argues further that

> The claim that American women are downtrodden and unfairly treated is the fraud of the century. . . . The truth is that American women have never had it so good. Why should we lower ourselves to "equal rights" when we already have the status of special privilege?[51]

EQUAL RIGHTS AMENDMENT
IS DANGEROUS
TO WOMEN–DAMAGING TO MEN
DEVASTING TO CHILDREN– AN ATTACK ON THE FAMILY

Most people think the Equal Rights Amendment (ERA) means equal pay, jobs, credit and education for women, but these areas are already covered by existing laws and the ERA will have NO EFFECT on them! Instead, under the guise of "equality," the ERA, at either a state or federal level, seeks to strip from women the many privileges traditionally granted to women by law. The ERA should really be termed a Loss of Rights Amendment. See questions on the other side.

"COULD BE RUINATION OF AMERICA – CHOICE IS UP TO YOU IN NOVEMBER"

ONLY twenty-six little words...that can revolutionize your lifestyle, the STATE ERA says: "EQUALITY OF RIGHTS UNDER THE LAW SHALL NOT BE DENIED OR ABRIDGED BY THE STATE OF NEW YORK, OR ANY SUBDIVISION THEREOF ON ACCOUNT OF SEX."

The National ERA is almost identical in wording to the N.Y. State ERA. ASK YOUR STATE SENATOR AND ASSEMBLYMAN TO REPEAL (RESCIND) RATIFICATION OF THE NATIONAL ERA WHICH IS ONLY A FEW STATES AWAY FROM BECOMING RATIFIED.

WHAT THE ERA WILL DO . . . .

ERA WILL INVALIDATE ALL STATE LAWS WHICH REQUIRE A HUSBAND TO SUPPORT HIS WIFE. Women will be equally liable for financial responsibilities. The stability of families will be undermined by this drastic change in wives' legal status.

ERA WILL WIPE OUT STATE LAWS THAT EXEMPT A WIFE FROM HER HUSBAND'S DEBTS even if the husband has deserted her and she has children to support.

ERA WILL HARM DIVORCED WOMEN BY WIPING OUT ANY PRESUMPTION OF CHILD CUSTODY – OR ALIMONY – EVEN FOR SENIOR WOMEN. Orders for child support will be even harder to enforce.

ERA WILL WIPE OUT STATE LABOR LAWS AND GUIDE-LINES WHICH BENEFIT WOMEN IN INDUSTRY who do heavy, manual work.

ERA WILL TAKE FROM WIDOWS ALL SPECIAL BENEFITS AND MONIES they now receive.

ERA WILL ELIMINATE PRESENT LOWER LIFE AND AUTO INSURANCE RATES FOR WOMEN because they are determined by actuarial tables that are based on sex.

WHAT THE ERA WILL NOT DO . . . .

ERA WILL NOT GIVE WOMEN "EQUAL PAY FOR EQUAL WORK." ERA can add nothing to the Civil Rights Act of 1964, The Equal Employment Opportunity Act of 1972, The New York State Human Rights Law of 1974, and a multitude of Federal and State laws and Executive orders in regard to employment.

ERA WILL NOT IMPROVE PRESENT EDUCATION OPPOR-TUNITIES FOR WOMEN which have already been man-dated by Title IX of the Education Amendments of 1972, and H.E.W. regulations.

ERA WILL NOT WIPE OUT DISCRIMINATION AGAINST WOMEN IN GETTING CREDIT. This has recently been ordered by the Depository Institutions Amendments of 1974 and the Extension of Credit Amendment of 1974 to the New York State Human Rights Law.

ERA WILL NOT AUTOMATICALLY EXTEND WOMEN'S BENEFITS TO MEN. Courts do not write laws, but they do strike them down.

ERA WILL NOT ADD ANY FURTHER RIGHTS IN THE AREAS OF EMPLOYMENT, CREDIT, PUBLIC ACCOMMODATION AND HOUSING. These are already guaranteed in this state by the Human Rights Law.

FIGURE 2.4. Anti-ERA Handout Distributed by Operation Wake Up. (*Source:* Operation Wake Up, P.O. Box 466, Harrison, New York, 10528.)

The basic thrust of her attack, and that of other ERA opponents, has been to predict a number of undesirable results that will occur if the principle of women's equality before the law is incorporated into the Constitution. The arguments have raised questions in many listeners' minds. The conflicting claims of the opponents and proponents have created so much confusion that many are taking the attitude that it is better to keep what we have than to risk the unknown. In fact, misunderstandings about what impact the ERA will have on women's role may well cause its defeat. It is important, therefore, that we turn our attention to this topic.

THE PROJECTED IMPACT OF THE ERA ON PUBLIC POLICY

In the eyes of the proponents of the ERA, including its sponsors in Congress, the basic legal principle established by this amendment is that "sex is not a permissible factor in determining the legal rights of women, or men."[52] This does not mean that differentiation in treatment of people by the law may not be based on other characteristics such as strength, intelligence, and the like. It does mean, however, that differentiation may not be based solely on the fact that a person is of one sex or the other.

Under the ERA, therefore, the existence of a characteristic or trait to a greater degree in one sex than the other does not justify classification by sex rather than by the particular characteristic or trait. The fact, for example, that the average man's arms tend to be more muscular and therefore able to hit a baseball farther than the average woman's, is not sufficient grounds for precluding all women from playing professional baseball. Exclusions from this sport must be based on some other classification, such as the ability to hit the ball. Consequently, if a female Babe Ruth comes along, under the ERA she would be entitled to play ball.

Similarly, the fact that in our present society members of one sex are more likely than those of the other sex to be found in a particular activity or perform a particular function does not allow the law to base legal rights on membership in that sex. For example, although there was a time when women were denied the right to practice law because of their sex, such a restriction would be unconstitutional under the ERA since admission to the bar should depend upon bona fide qualifications such as legal training and competence in the law, rather than sex. Similarly, sex would be an inadmissable category by which to determine the right to a minimum wage and the custody of children since, here again, these decisions should be based on relevant criteria such as the right to earn a living wage and the welfare of the children, not on a wholesale classification by sex. By the same right, men could not be prevented because of their sex from assuming roles traditionally given to women. Airline companies, for example, could not discriminate against men who wanted to be stewards, and hospitals could not discriminate against men who wanted to be nurses.

In short, the fundamental legal principle underlying the Equal Rights Amendment is that the law must deal with particular attributes of the individual, not the sex of the individual. What will this mean in terms of the ERA's impact on women's lives and on public policy? This will depend on a number of factors, foremost among them how the courts interpret the amendment and rule on its implementation.

Many of the policy changes required, however, are easy to predict and noncontroversial.[53] The amendment will guarantee, for example, equality of treatment for women and men in the labor market, and require that men and women be considered for admission to all state universities on an equal basis. Government benefit programs which currently discriminate on the basis of sex will be made available on the same terms to men and women alike, and manpower training programs will be required to accept young women on an equal basis with young men. The age at which one can legally marry will be made the same for men and women, and child labor laws and juvenile court laws will cover all young people until the same age. Similarly, legal retirement ages will be equalized for men and women and social security will be required to provide the family of a working woman with the same benefits it provides to the families of working men.

There are a number of areas of the law, however, in which the impact of the ERA is less predictable. Questions have been raised most frequently about the areas of domestic relations, protective labor policies for women, military service, and the right to privacy.

Domestic Relations

Domestic relations—that is, the laws governing the rights of partners in marriage—include such items as alimony, custody of children, duty of family support, ownership of property, and the legal requirement of women to change their names upon marriage. Opponents of the amendment maintain that the ERA would end a woman's right to alimony and her usual right to have custody of the children. They also maintain that it would terminate the husband's legal obligation to provide family support. The ERA, says opposition leader Phyllis Schlafly, "will make a wife equally responsible to provide a home for her family and to provide 50 percent of the financial support of her family."[54] A number of these assertions are misleading or incorrect, but the opposition is correct in maintaining that the ERA will change laws regarding these items.

Alimony would not be abolished by the ERA. A married woman who has devoted her life or even part of it to raising children and taking care of the home would still be entitled to alimony should her husband divorce her. What the ERA will do, however, is to make alimony available to either spouse—not just the wife. If, for example, a husband has stayed home to keep house and raise the children (a role pattern which is uncommon but not unheard of) then a working wife seeking divorce would pay him alimony, especially if he had never worked outside the home. It should be noted that granting alimony payments to both spouses would not be a new development under the ERA. Already one-third of the states authorize courts to grant such payments to either spouse.

Custody of the children, should a divorce occur, is another issue that has raised considerable concern. Under common law, which still exists to some degree in eight states, the children would be awarded to the father after a divorce since they were considered his property. In most states today, however, such preference is archaic and the courts now give custody of the children to the mother, if the children are young or teen-age girls. Preference is usually given to the father, however, in the case of a teen-age boy. The ERA would prohibit such automatic preferences, and would require the courts to consider, among other things, which parent is better suited to take care of the child. Such a change, of course, would expand the role of the court. The presiding judge would have to listen to testimony from both parties before deciding which spouse would gain custody of the children.

The allocation of responsibility for *family support* between husbands and wives also would be affected by the ERA. As things currently stand, all but three states have criminal statutes which penalize a man for desertion or nonsupport of his wife. In many states the wife may be liable for support of her husband, but generally only if the husband is incapacitated or indigent. All American jurisdictions set criminal penalties for nonsupport of young children by the father.[55] These same laws typically penalize, as well, the mother who fails to provide support for a minor child, but normally only if the father refuses or fails to provide for child support. For both child support and interspousal support, therefore, the husband has the prime responsibility in most states, and the wife, only if the husband fails to meet this responsibility.

Under the ERA the child-support sections of the criminal nonsupport laws would continue to be valid in any jurisdiction where responsibility applies equally to the mother and father. Where it does not, the practice would have to be terminated. The sections of the law dealing with interspousal support also could not be sustained where only the male is liable for support. Courts would have to strike down non-support laws which impose the duty of support only on men. The ERA, however, would not require mathematically equal contributions to family support from the husband and wife in any given family. Support obligations could be based on current resources, earning power, and nonmonetary contributions to the family welfare. If, for example, one spouse was the wage earner and the other performed uncompensated domestic labor for the family, the wage-earning spouse would owe a duty of support to the spouse who worked in the home. If the husband and wife had equal resources and earning capacity, however, neither would have a claim for support against the other. In the civil enforcement of support laws,[56] as well as the criminal enforcement, the ERA would bar a state from imposing greater liability for support on a husband than on a wife merely because of sex. The courts would probably equalize the civil law by extending the duty of support to women as well as men.

Property ownership raises other questions about the ERA. In the United States two different systems exist governing property rights within a family: the community property system and the common law system. Both systems contain discriminatory aspects which would be changed under the ERA. The community property system, which stipulates that property acquired by either spouse during the marriage is owned in common by the husband and wife, applies in eight states: Arizona, California, Idaho, Louisiana, Nevada, New Mexico, Texas, and Washington. In all these states, except Texas, however, the husband has the power of management and control over the community property, and in some states he can sell the property without his wife's consent. Under the Equal Rights Amendment, laws which favor the husband as manager of community property would not be valid. The courts or new legislation would have to provide that community property be managed jointly by husband and wife.

In the other forty-two states the common law ownership system applies, which, until the Married Women's Property Acts were passed in each state, gave the husband complete control over his wife's property and the products of her labors. The Married Women's Property Acts, however, generally give a wife the right to control property she owned before marriage as well as property she earns or receives by gift or work during marriage. In other words, each spouse owns his or her separate property free of legal control by the other spouse. The ERA would affect this system, particularly in the case of laws governing the right of a surviving spouse to inherit his or her spouse's estate. All states except North Dakota and South Dakota give the wife legal rights to a share in her husband's estate, but a number of states fail to give the husband a corresponding legal claim to his wife's estate. Other devices such as widows' allowances or family allowances which protect a surviving wife against complete disinheritance probably also would have to apply in the same manner to men. In these states where the wife has a protected position, the discriminatory laws would either be invalidated or extended to the husband.

As regards to the *change of a woman's name upon marriage,* the ERA would not permit this to be a legal requirement. A married woman would still be free to adopt her husband's name if she wished, but no longer would this measure be legally obligatory. For purposes of identification or other reasons a state legislature could pass legislation stipulating that spouses use the same last name. The states could conform to the ERA by requiring the couples to pick the same last name, but allowing selection of the name of either spouse, or of a third name agreeable to both. In the case of children, the ERA also would not permit laws which stipulated that the children's last name be the same as the father's, or for that matter, the same as the mother's. If a state had no requirement that a husband and wife must pick the same last name, it could comply with the ERA by having no rule at all or by requiring the parents to choose one of their names for their children.

The net effect of the ERA on domestic relations laws would be basically to make men and women equal partners in the eyes of the law, both with regard to privileges and responsibilities. Those laws which discriminate against women would not be permissible, and likewise, those which discriminate against men would not be permissible either.

Protective Labor Laws

At the beginning of this century, many women and men campaigned for passage of protective labor laws for women, and their success was heralded by many as a major victory in the cause of women's rights. Many people who oppose the ERA, therefore, do so on the grounds that the amendment would deprive women of gains made by previous generations who worked hard to achieve them.

Proponents of the ERA argue, however, that despite the original intention of such legislation, on the whole it has proved to be more repressive than protective of women. In support of their position they point to the number of women's lawsuits challenging these restrictions under the provision of Title VII of the Equal Rights Act of 1964. Title VII provides that for employers engaged in an industry affecting interstate commerce, with twenty-five employees or more, it shall be an "unlawful employment practice" to "discriminate against any individual with respect to his compensation, terms, conditions or privileges of employment, because of such individual's race, color, religion, sex, or national origin."[57] While the courts have not completed the task of interpreting the prohibitions upon sex discrimination embodied in Title VII, the decisions made so far give a preview of how the courts will treat protective labor legislation under the ERA.[58]

Basically the laws involved can be grouped into three broad categories: (1) those conferring special benefits to women, (2) those excluding women from certain jobs, and (3) those restricting women's employment under certain conditions.

In the case of laws conferring special benefits to women, such as minimum wages and required rest periods, these benefits probably would be extended to men. Title VII cases which have considered such laws have held that by extending the benefits to workers of both sexes, the employer could conform to both state and Title VII requirements.

Laws that plainly exclude women from certain occupations such as bartending or mining, and laws which exclude women from employment under certain circumstances, such as those which require pregnant employees to take a leave of absence for a specified period before and after childbirth without providing job security or retention of accrued benefits, would be invalidated.[59]

Laws that restrict or regulate women's employment, such as those preventing women from working at night and those setting the maximum number of hours a woman can work a day, would probably be invalidated, leaving the process of general functional regulation to the legislatures. Beginning in 1969 the EEOC, the agency that enforces Title VII of the Civil Rights Act of 1964, took a strong position against labor laws that impose restrictions only on women's employment, and the trend of court decisions under Title VII is to invalidate such laws.

Since the courts already have been active in the field of labor laws regarding women, the effect of the ERA will not be so much to change the laws as to accelerate the trend already underway. It would also provide an additional incentive to unions and legislatures to develop and implement programs of genuine protection to workers of both sexes.

The Question of Privacy

Another argument frequently made against the ERA concerns the right of privacy. Opponents maintain that the amendment would strip women of their right to privacy, requiring them to share toilet toilet facilities in public places, hospital rooms, and prison facilities with men. It is highly unlikely, however that this will be the case. The Supreme Court, in *Griswold v. Connecticut*[60] and subsequent cases, has already recognized an independent constitutional right to privacy, based on a combination of rights embodied in the First, Third, Fourth, Fifth, and Ninth Amendments.

The Griswold case specifically concerned a Connecticut statute which prohibited the use of contraceptives even by married couples. The Court invalidated the statute on the grounds that it infringed upon intimate relationships in marriage and the home. Although the exact scope of the right of privacy was not completely spelled out by the Court, the decision did make clear that one important part of the right to privacy is freedom from official coercion in sexual relations.

No one can say in advance the precise boundaries that the courts will eventually fix in accommodating the ERA and the right to privacy, but it can be said that the privacy concept based on this court decision is applicable to situations which involve disrobing, sleeping, and performing personal bodily functions in the presence of the other sex. Consequently, under the ERA it is unlikely that men and women would have to be concerned about infringement of their rights to privacy in such matters.

The Military

In the case of military service, opponents of the ERA maintain that women will be subject to the draft and to active combat duty. The ERA, says Phyllis Schlafly, will

Positively, absolutely, and without the slightest shadow of a doubt make women subject to military draft on the same basis with men. Women will be sent into combat and onto warships with men and will be required to carry the same forty- or fifty-pound packs. Mothers will have to be drafted on the same basis as fathers.[61]

The amendment, as envisioned by its proponents and most of its Congressional sponsors,[62] indeed will mean that women as well as men will be subject to the draft, should Congress reinstate it, and to combat duty on the same basis as men.[63] For a number of reasons, however, proponents do not object.

First, they point out that combat soldiers make up only a small percentage of the military personnel. Moreover, many of the jobs performed in combat zones such as logistics and administrative support are the same as those performed in noncombat duty. The issue of assigning women to actual combat duty, therefore, involves a relatively small segment of the total military assignments.

Secondly, while many people view the restrictions placed on women's military service as relieving them of a highly undesirable burden, proponents maintain that there are many benefits afforded to those who serve. The armed forces furnish in-service vocational and specialist training, medical care, and many benefits for dependents. Moreover, veterans receive educational scholarships and loans, preferences in government employment, pensions, insurance, and medical treatment.

Since only a small percentage of women are taken into the military (until 1973 women comprised less than 2 percent of the full strength of the services) few are eligible to receive these benefits and training. The ERA very likely would change this and require that standards for enlistment and eligibility for benefits be the same for men and women. Currently women who enlist must meet higher standards than men in some areas. Enlisted women have to be high school graduates while men do not, and until 1974 women had to make higher scores on the educational tests. A man may enlist at age seventeen and a half, a woman at eighteen. A man needs parents' consent if he is under eighteen, a woman if she is under twenty-one, unless she lives in a state that has lowered the age of majority.[64]

Deferments and exemptions from military service also would have to be granted on the same basis to both sexes. Where there are, for example, certain special draft exemptions such as exempting from combat the sole surviving son of a family which has lost another son in combat duty, such exemptions would have to apply to women as well.

In addition, the grounds for discharge would have to apply equally to both sexes (unmarried women could no longer be discharged for having a child unless unmarried men were). Moreover, both sexes probably would be eligible for the same four- to six-month basic training, and, upon completion, be assigned on an equal basis to the same five broad areas of duty in the military: administration, intelligence, training and tactics, supply, and combat.

Third, although opponents of the ERA claim that women are physically incapable of performing combat duty, proponents disagree. It is true, they admit, that in the past physical strength was essential to military success. Weapons were heavy, hand to hand fighting was common, and long marches on foot were frequent. Today, however, the success of the modern soldier is due more to equipment and training than to individual strength, and most American women, they maintain, are capable of fulfilling these modern combat requirements.

Finally, another frequent objection to women in combat service concerns problems that might arise with regard to discipline and sexual activity. However, there have apparently been no serious problems of this sort in modern armies in which women have been used extensively, such as the armies of Israel and North Vietnam. Nor have such problems arisen when women have been used in the United States armed forces. In commenting about the use of women in World War II, General Dwight D. Eisenhower observed:

> Like most old soldiers I was violently against women soldiers. I thought a tremendous number of difficulties would occur, not only of an administrative nature, but others of a more personal type that would get us into trouble. None of that occurred . . . In the disciplinary field they were . . . a model for the Army. More than this their influence throughout the whole command was good. I am convinced that in another war they have got to be drafted just like the men.[65]

Should the ERA be ratified, therefore, it will result in substantial change for both the military and the role women play in it. Proponents of the ERA feel these changes are necessary, however, on the grounds that women cannot expect to have the full benefits and privileges of citizenship unless they also are willing to assume the full responsibilities.

There are a number of other areas of public policy that will be affected, although the extent to which they will be affected is difficult to tell at this time. The amendment, for example, mandates that the states, as well as the federal government, must enforce the ERA, thus raising the question of how far into the private sectors of our lives the states will go in applying it. Some activities such as voting and employment are clearly "public" activities and the state would be required to assume extensive enforcement responsibility. Others, such as social, recreational, and fraternal associations, usually are considered "private" activities and the scope of "state action" would be limited. In some areas, however, the line between "public" and "private" is not clear. Education is one of these areas. There is no doubt the ERA would eliminate discrimination on the basis of sex in public schools and public university systems. How the amendment would affect private schools and universities is another question. Although the courts could rule differently at a later date, under present court decisions regarding state action it appears that private educational institutions would remain within the private sector, not subject to the constitutional requirements of the ERA.[66]

In these areas, and many others, therefore, ratification of the ERA will necessitate many changes. Whether or not these changes will be brought about is the topic to which we now turn.

THE PROSPECTS FOR RATIFICATION

Two more years remain in which three more states must ratify the amendment. It is very difficult at this time to predict whether this goal will be achieved. On the one hand, the defeat of the state equal rights amendments in New Jersey and New York could slow the already dragging momentum for national passage enough to make the 1979 deadline impossible. On the other hand, these defeats and previous failures to win ratification in state legislatures have caused proponents to reorganize themselves and to seek new strategies. These changes may be effective.

In 1973 and 1974, for example, the ERA proponents decided to pool their efforts and form a coalition of over two dozen organizations. The coalition, called the ERA Ratification Council, is concentrating its efforts in the states which have not passed the amendment but which appear to have the greatest chances of doing so. The National Federation of Business and Professional Women's Clubs has raised $250,000 to aid ratification and has even hired a political consulting firm—Bailey, Deafdourf, and Eyre—to help formulate strategy in the key states. In 1974 and early 1975 these states were North Dakota, Missouri, Illinois, and North Carolina. Other targeted states include Arizona, South Carolina, Florida, Indiana, and Nevada. So far only North Dakota, in February, 1975, and Indiana, in January, 1977, have voted for ratification.

The approach used in each state has basically been twofold. First, efforts have been directed toward electing state legislators who are favorable to the ERA. This effort has met with some success. In nine of the key states thirty anti-ERA incumbents were replaced by amendment backers, and only one pro-ERA legislator lost to an anti-amendment challenger.[67] In Arizona, alone, six anti-ERA legislators were defeated by challengers who favor the ERA.

Secondly, supporters of the ERA are directing their efforts to the voters especially women, in an attempt to clear up the confusion which exists about the ERA. To this end equal rights proponents are arranging for speakers to address local organizations and are attempting to get the press to present what they feel is fair coverage of their arguments. In the fall of 1975, Jill Ruckelshaus, presiding officer of the National Commission on Observance of International Women's Year, scored the press for unbalanced and misleading coverage of the ERA. The result was that the National Press Club called a luncheon in which Phyllis Schlafly and Ruth Robbins, former president of the New York League of Women Voters, debated the pros and cons of the amendment. "Any similarity between my interpretation of the ERA and Mrs. Schlafly's," warned Mrs. Robbins, "is purely coincidental. In fact, after hearing us, you'll wonder if we're talking about the same amendment."[68]

Proponents are hopeful that their efforts will prove fruitful. A Gallup poll taken in March, 1975, showed that 58 percent of those questioned favored the ERA. But it also indicated that support was weakest in the Midwest and South, where most nonratifying states are located.[69]

This does not augur well for the ERA. Of the fifteen states that have not voted for ratification, at least one legislative chamber in each state has rejected the amendment since it passed Congress in 1972. These states include Alabama, Arizona, Arkansas, Florida, Georgia, Illinois, Louisiana, Mississippi, Missouri, Nevada, North Carolina, Oklahoma, South Carolina, Utah, and Virgina.

In addition to the opposition which may prevent the required three states from ratifying the amendment, there is the question of whether the three states which have rescinded their votes for ratification—Nebraska, Tennessee and Idaho, legally can do so. The Supreme Court ruled in *Coleman v. Miller*,[70] the only case to come before it regarding the ability of a state to rescind such a vote, that the question was a political one, and, therefore, only Congress could decide whether to accept or reject the recision. In prior instances in which states have rescinded their ratifications, Congress has ignored their attempts. In 1868, for example, Ohio and New

Jersey first ratified and then rescinded their ratification of the Fourteenth Amendment. In 1869 New York also rescinded its ratification of the Fifteenth Amendment. In the congressional proclamations that declared these amendments part of the Constitution, however, the rescinding states were included.

Proponents of the ERA are still hopeful about its ratification. President Ford, in mid-April, 1975, came out strongly for the ERA and backers are counting on this to have some effect. President Carter also has given his support in favor of ratification. New efforts to push the ERA also are being made, including a fund-raising drive. The momentum, however, that had earlier been built up for the ERA has diminished. Winning a twenty-seventh amendment will be a difficult job to accomplish by the 1979 deadline.

IMPLICATIONS FOR AMERICAN POLICY MAKING

Effecting a change in public policy by means of a constitutional amendment can be a long and arduous process, as demonstrated by this account of the drive for the ERA.

The procedures required to pass an amendment necessitate that there be widespread support for the amendment throughout the United States. If opposition is well placed, it is possible for the thirteen least populated states with a total population of less than 4 percent of the whole country to prevent the passage of an amendment. In fact, the population can be even smaller, given the realities of state legislative politics.

This situation closely approximates the circumstances of the ERA. With the exception of Illinois, most of the highly populated urban states have ratified the amendment, while the less populated rural states have failed to do so. The thirty-five states which have voted for its ratification comprise 73 percent of the United States population.

Not only do the procedures required to pass an amendment necessitate widespread support, but they require that the support continue in strength for at least a period of several years. This can involve a tremendous financial commitment as well as a great personal commitment on the part of a large number of people.

Proponents of the ERA now face organized opposition which threatens to reverse the growth of public support for the amendment to the extent that the three states still needed for ratification may never give it. With regard to public opinion, therefore, timing is important. Support can easily wane, and once it begins to do so it may be extremely difficult to reverse the process.

Moreover, even constitutional amendments are subject to alteration. The courts, especially the Supreme Court, are likely to assert considerable influence in determining the meaning and application of the amendment. Where there is disagreement as to what was originally intended by passage of the amendment, the courts will use their own judgment. It is possible that their decisions may take a direction different from what the original advocates had in mind. No form of public policy, therefore, not even one incorporated into the Constitution, can be considered permanent.

3

Energy Policy and the Ford Administration: The First Year

David Howard Davis

Three days after assuming the presidency in the wake of Richard Nixon's post-Watergate resignation in August, 1974, President Gerald Ford set forth his new administration's goals in a televised address to Congress. With respect to energy he pledged a vigorous policy:

> The nation needs action, not words . . . We must not let last winter's energy crisis happen again. I will push Project Independence for our own good and the good of others.[1]

Yet despite this call for action, a year later the Ford administration had achieved little in its energy program. The ringing rhetoric of the 1974 speech had given way to the drift and contradiction of 1975. This year of inaction serves as a case study for analysis of policy making in the field of energy.

Policy, as political scientists use the term, has at least two definitions. One is the equilibrium within an issue area after all political forces, nongovernmental as well as governmental, have come to bear. The other is a narrower governmental input, usually emphasizing a goal to be sought. The first definition recognizes that some sort of political array always exists on an issue. In this sense there is always some policy in effect even though many observers may be unaware of it or deny its existence. The coupling of the term laissez-faire with policy to describe the federal government's relation with business in the late nineteenth century is a quintessential example. As the words imply, the laissez-faire policy was a governmental policy of not having a governmental policy. But to speak of a governmental policy at all indicates a shift to the second definition: policy as a goal. This is the way in which the word will be used in this chapter. It is the way President Ford, executive branch officials, members of Congress, oil company executives, and other participants in the energy field commonly define the term.

In his August 12 television speech President Ford summarized his administration's energy policy as promoting Project Independence. A week later at a New York conference John Sawhill, the Administrator of the Federal Energy Agency, defined it, in part, as freedom from foreign coercion. Senator James Buckley of New York said the policy was, or should be, support for the traditional privately owned industries. Environmentalist Barry Commoner said just the opposite—that industry had failed and the government should take over.[2] What were, and still are, the basic energy problems facing the United States?

THE ENERGY QUESTION

An economist would say that America's energy problems are simply a question of supply and demand. In 1974 the U.S. economy required 200 trillion Btu's of energy a day. In terms of primary sources, 46 percent came from oil, 18 percent from coal, 30 percent from natural gas, 2 percent from nuclear fuels, and 4 percent from other sources, chiefly falling water. A quarter of this was transformed into a secondary form, electricity, for utilization. The pattern of energy consumption in this country in 1974 is depicted in Figure 3.1, along with available energy resources.

Oil was the chief problem in August, 1974. The United States needed 17 million barrels per day and the amount had been growing at the rate of 4½ percent a year. While domestic wells produced 65 percent of the oil, 35 percent came from abroad. Except for a small quantity Alberta shipped to the Pacific Northwest, virtually all of the imported oil came from the OPEC countries,* which after boycotting the United States in 1973, were now charging an official price of $10.46 a barrel. This was a fourfold increase from January, 1973, and a sixfold increase from 1970. With domestic production no longer increasing, the amount being imported was growing rapidly, 4.2 percent a year.[3] Virtually all of the additional oil came from Moslem countries in the Persian Gulf. Supply was entirely in the hands of privately owned corporations. Seven "majors" (Exxon, Texaco, Mobil, Standard of California, Gulf, Standard of Indiana, Shell) predominated, but numerous "independents" participated as well. Having produced the crude oil (domestically or abroad) and refined it, the private companies distributed it to meet consumer demand. Typically one company handled all phases of the process. These vertically integrated companies completely controlled the fuel from the well to the gasoline station. A few small "independents," however, only refined or distributed the petroleum. Since many had depended on imported crude oil the 1973 OPEC boycott had hurt them particularly badly.

While the economist would see America's energy problems in terms of supply and demand, the policy maker or policy analyst would focus on other aspects of the question, namely, security, cost, and allocation. Even though this focus does not deny the validity of the economist's focus on supply and demand, the two points of view are not analytically compatible. Resource allocation is the balancing of supply and demand domestically. Security is the reduction of uncertainty in supply. While these are basically economic problems, they are not treated as such. Why not?

This tension between economic and political solutions to economic problems has characterized American society throughout the twentieth century. (Indeed this conflict is not solely a twentieth century or an American phenomenon.) American history,

---

*Organization of Petroleum Exporting Countries: Saudi Arabia, Iran, Venezuela, Libya, Kuwait, Nigeria, Iraq, United Arab Emirates, Algeria, Indonesia, Qatar, Ecuador, and Gabon.

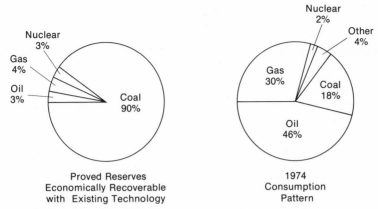

FIGURE 3.1. U.S. Energy Consumption and Reserves. (*Source: 1976 National Energy Outlook, F.E.A.*)

particularly since the election of Franklin D. Roosevelt in 1932, has displayed a continuing tendency toward government intervention in economic matters. Great national crises such as the depression of 1929 and World War II brought dramatic intervention in the economy by agencies of the government such as the National Industrial Recovery Act and the War Mobilization Board. Quieter times have brought more subtle influences like oil import quotas and the National Environmental Policy Act. The tendency for political solutions to prevail over economic solutions is referred to as the *primacy of politics.*

What form does this primacy of politics take? Chiefly it manifests itself as governmental action, for although politics is not, strictly speaking, synonymous with government, the overlap is evident. While policy formulation occurs to some extent outside of government, policy implementation virtually always requires government, if only for the shadowy background presence of its ultimate sanction of coercion. In the case of energy, the national governmental role has long been dominant. *Governmental participants, such as the President, the Department of the Interior, the Federal Power Commission, and the Federal Energy Administration, have traditionally formulated, as well as implemented energy policy.*

When President Ford articulated those brave words about energy in his first televised address, he was setting forth his administration's energy goals. Likewise, FEA Administrator Sawhill, Senator Buckley, and environmentalist Barry Commoner, speaking at the New York conference on energy, were all advancing their own, somewhat different sets of energy policy goals.

ENERGY POLICY GOALS

Granting that all participants in the policy-making process articulate differing solutions, what are the common issues which the government should address? What goals should it seek? Three seem paramount. (1) security, (2) low cost, and (3) efficient allocation.

Security

Security is the most legitimate issue in terms of the traditional function of government. Defense of the realm is a time-honored duty of a national government. In times past, defense and domestic peace keeping were the only functions of government. Today security is more complex. The first tier continues to be military. Airplanes, ships, and tanks require fuel. Without petroleum the billions of dollars worth of warcraft would be useless. Granted, petroleum is not the only energy source for the armed forces: ICBM's burn chemical propellants, some ships are nuclear powered, coal and uranium can generate electricity to run radar and communications, and coal heats the Pentagon. But in any military action lasting longer than the fifteen minutes necessary for ICBM's to deliver the thermonuclear overkill of World War III, shortage of petroleum would deprive the military of its most mobile forces. Fuel for airplanes, ships, and tanks is only part of the military's defense needs. Combat craft must be backed up with their immediate logistical support, which in turn must be backed up by a civilian economy manufacturing and delivering the engines of war. All of this demands energy, much of it petroleum. Thus an economy short of energy cannot long support its armed forces. Since governments tend to grant the military their highest priority, however, diminished resources are not likely to lead immediately to diminished war-making capabilities. A shortage of energy would show up last in the armed forces, not first.

The second tier of the security issue is the security of the national economy. Since Franklin D. Roosevelt's New Deal the federal government has sought to ameliorate the hardships wrought by the business cycle. The Employment Act of 1946 explicitly set full employment and a stable economy as national goals. At a rather naive level this means that no person, firm, or industry should ever become worse off financially. This naive viewpoint is widely held, judging from the rhetoric venting forth from those persons, firms, or industries who from time to time find themselves threatened. An economic status, once gained, is presumed to be an inviolate right regardless of changing markets, technology, or consumer preferences. The same seems true of tax loopholes, tariff preferences, and an assortment of other concessions as well. Hence when economic conditions change (as they inevitably do) those disadvantaged besiege Congress with demands for help. Congress usually obliges. The executive branch is nearly as accommodating. The result is a panoply of privileges such as price supports for farmers based on "parity" with 1917–1920 crop prices (a record high period), natural gas prices dating back to an era when it was cheaper to burn gas at the well head than to ship it to northern cities, and a regulated price for "old oil" set at half the world price.

At a more sophisticated level this concern with the security of the economy means that the economy should not be subjected to inordinate shocks. Being a rather delicate creature, the American economy requires insulation from the buffeting of sudden changes, particularly artificial ones. Petroleum is a pervasive factor in production, at many points. Hence the 1973 OPEC embargo and price hike were major causes of the 1973–74 recession. If the new higher price were legitimate and long-term it would be appropriate for the economy to face up to this stark new reality and make the necessary adjustments. But in fact the OPEC price was artificial and provisional. It was set and maintained by a thirteen-nation cartel under the strong leadership of Saudi Arabia. Were the United States to adjust to the high price by developing oil shale extraction, synthetic gasoline from coal, and so forth, OPEC could arbitrarily cut its price, thereby making the new alternatives noncompetitive. The new equipment and plants would become white elephants. With billions of dollars invested in this futile venture, the economy would once more be shocked out of balance.

Insulating the American economy from direct OPEC manipulation is not enough to insure its security. The economies of the United States's major trading partners must be protected as well. An economic disaster in a major European country or Japan will affect the American economy in turn. America is not immune to foreign problems, for inflation and recession are contagious.

Cost

Cost is the second issue in governmental policy goals. Put simply: cheaper is better. Lower costs for energy, whether domestic or foreign, are an economic advantage. Assuring inexpensive inputs is not, however, a traditional function of government, as is security. If cost is a true reflection of market forces there should be no role for government. The intervention of government implies market distortion. With respect to foreign petroleum, imperialism used to be a frequent manifestation of government entry into the normal market. An economically advanced country would coerce a less developed country to supply crude oil at a lower price than a competitive situation would yield. This, indeed, is what many of the OPEC countries accuse the United States, Britain, France, and the Netherlands of doing throughout much of the twentieth century. A number of specific instances support this, such as the American insistence that the Shah of Iran grant American petroleum companies access to Iranian oil fields after the CIA aided the Shah in regaining power in 1953.

After 1973, however, the situation was reversed. Rather than the consuming nations coercing the producing nations, the producers coerced the consumers. The tightly united and ably led OPEC cartel imposed its will on the divided and disorganized industrial nations of Europe, Japan, and the United States. OPEC's success in maintaining the cartel derived from (1) its small size, (2) the united goals of its Arab core, and (3) strong leadership. OPEC's membership includes only thirteen countries. This gives it the cohesiveness of a small group; each member easily sees the value of its contribution and the potential penalties the group would suffer were it to break ranks.[4] The political and religious unity of the seven Arab states at the core of OPEC enhanced this small-group cohesiveness. It was the 1973 Yom Kippur War which was the catalyst for the boycott. The boycott was in part an attempt to get the United States and Europe to exert pressure on Israel. Hence hatred of Israel reinforced the financial benefits to be gained. Saudi Arabian leadership was the third factor accounting for OPEC's strength. This feudal, theocratic kingdom possessed vast quantities of cheaply produced oil and a small, subservient population. The combination gave its government great freedom to act. Being so fortunately endowed it could afford to forgo income during the boycott and even subsidize other countries. It needed income less than the industrial nations needed oil. Thus the oil imperialism gave way to the new monopoly. American desire to obtain cheap oil could not stand up to the OPEC desire for political influence and financial gain.

The cost of oil is logically a policy issue only for imports. It may make sense for a government to use coercion against a foreign state to influence prices, since the cost is not borne at home; however, domestic coercion is pointless, since benefits for parts of the population are gained at the expense of others. Worse still, since this means less than maximum efficiency, the whole nation will end up in a less beneficial aggregate situation. But for an importer like the United States, coercion to reduce prices paid overseas is a desirable economic policy, just as coercion to raise prices is a desirable policy for an exporter like Saudi Arabia. Whether or not these policy goals are morally sound, they are economically sound.

Allocation

Allocation of the fuel available is the third issue. Again this is not a traditional government function. Indeed much of the essence of American politics in the twentieth century has centered on the issue of how resources should be allocated. The two poles are the price system and central planning. As a capitalist nation the United States pays lip service to price as a means of coordination. Buyers seek the cheapest goods and sellers seek the greatest return. Competition on both sides leads to the most efficient allocation as if guided by a "hidden hand," to use Adam Smith's classic phrase. While paying homage to the price system as a means of coordination, the American economy often opts for central planning rather than a free market. Virtually always this means government planning. One rationale is that conditions such as natural monopolies make competition impossible. Another frequent rationale is a crisis such as war or depression. The result is a mixed economy combining both. Once institutionalized, usually in the form of a federal government agency, the central planning mechanism tends to remain even when the original situation changes. Wartime arrangements continue in peacetime. Antimonopoly procedures remain even when expanded competition and new technologies lessen the monopolistic features.

The issue of resource allocation is one of the chief ones dividing the two political parties. Although American parties may generally agree on the first two issues of security and cost, they disagree on this third issue. The Republicans favor coordination via price, while the Democrats favor coordination via planning. The differences are far from absolute. Republicans have long supported some government role in the economy, and the Democrats have never sought to abolish the price system. Nevertheless this dimension is perhaps the most notable and consistent difference between the two parties.

The rationale for the price system is efficiency. The consumer is sovereign. He spends his dollars to satisfy his wants, thus signaling business to provide the desired goods and services. The most efficient producers, being able to supply goods and services most cheaply, prosper, whereas the inefficient are driven out of the market. In contrast, the rationale for central planning is social justice. Its premise is that wealth is maldistributed in the first place, and that the price system perpetuates this condition. To give the consumer the right to "vote" with his dollars is unfair since some have more dollars than others. Therefore the government's aim should be to intervene to promote equality, even at the cost of efficiency.

When translated into specific proposals, the positions of the two political parties often converge. Republicans favor market (price system) solutions only slightly more than Democrats. To a large degree Democratic preference for government intervention derives from its New Deal experience. With the Republican economic policies of the 1920s discredited by the Great Depression, the Democrats embarked on a course of federal government control and electoral success. The legacy remains. Rightly or wrongly, the Democratic party sees federal economic intervention as the road to electoral victory.

Analyzing America's energy situation in terms of three issues—security, cost, and allocation—this chapter asks: how successfully did the nation's political system cope with energy problems during President Ford's first year in office? In order to assess the Ford administration's first year of making energy policy this chapter will examine seven major proposals with respect to the three general goals of security, cost, and allocation. Although the entire energy problem is rightly recognized as interconnected, for heuristic purposes the exposition will first examine international issues, next national executive branch organizational issues, and finally legislative issues.

INTERNATIONAL PROPOSALS

The September Energy Offensive

The Ford administration came in like a lion. Its energy hard line began with the new President's speech to the United Nations on September 18, 1974, in which he threatened retaliation against the OPEC nations withholding oil:

> The attempt by any country to use one commodity for political purposes will inevitably tempt other countries to use their commodities for their own purposes.[5]

The following week in an address to the World Energy Conference sprinkled with words such as "political weapons," "conflict," and "war," Ford declared:

> Sovereign nations cannot allow their policies to be dictated or their fate decided by artificial rigging and distortion of world commodity markets.[6]

Simultaneously Secretary of State Kissinger conveyed the same bellicose message to the United Nations. His threat was to make food a quid pro quo for oil. If OPEC were to persist in manipulation of petroleum, the United States would manipulate food. This could be done either directly, as by withholding grain shipments, or indirectly, as by withholding fertilizer or advanced agricultural technology.

Behind President Ford's veiled references to the horrors of war and Secretary Kissinger's unveiled threat to starve OPEC stood the specter of military action. Venezuela was the country most convenient to invade. It was close to the United States and far from the Soviet Union. America had a long history of invading Caribbean islands and Central American banana republics. Venezuela would be only an incremental move south. Arguing against such an untoward move, however, were the facts that Venezuela produced only a moderate amount of crude oil, its offshore wells were easily sabotaged and hard to restore, and its mountains and forests would be hard to secure against guerrilla counterattack. More serious, the United States had long professed friendship for Venezuela as a Pan-American neighbor. An invasion would alienate Latin America and Canada as well as many Americans.

Completely opposite conditions would exist were the United States to invade an Arab oil-producing country. Geographically the Persian Gulf is remote from the United States and close to the Soviet Union. Military action would require a forward base such as Diego Garcia, an Indian Ocean island which the U.S. Navy was coincidently seeking to develop as a logistical center. The United States had no history of military activity in the region, having left that domain to the British prior to their withdrawal in the late 1960s. America had few friends to alienate in the area. Indeed domestic public opinion tended to be hostile to the Arabs both for the oil boycott and their opposition to Israel.

The predominant scenario envisioned seizing the western coast of the Persian Gulf, 400 miles from Kuwait through Saudi territory to Qatar.[7] This sector accounted for 40 percent of OPEC production and 50 percent of world reserves. Furthermore, sabotaged wells could be easily repaired, and the desert terrain made conquest easy and guerrilla counterattack difficult. The oil tankers, however, would not sail the comparatively secure Caribbean but faced the perils of the Strait of Hormuz and many miles of the Indian and Atlantic Oceans, where they would be subject to submarine attack.

While the idea of a direct American invasion was farfetched, some variations were not. The United States might find surrogates to undertake the conquest of the Middle East oil fields. Thanks to twenty years of American military aid, Iran had a strong military force, particularly well equipped for amphibious landings. It also had unsatisfied territorial claims against its neighbors on the west of the Gulf. Though a member of OPEC, Iran was not so generously endowed with oil and in the past had been more willing to cooperate with the United States, Europe, Japan, and even Israel. Israel, itself, was a second possible surrogate for an American conquest of Arab oil lands. The Jewish state captured the Abu Rudays fields from Egypt in the 1973 war and held them for two years. Since the Israelis and the Arabs have fought four wars since 1948, a fifth war which would include capturing major petroleum fields was a logical possibility.

In suggesting a possibility of military action, the Ford administration was not making a specific threat but a vague one. Likewise the warning of withholding food in exchange for oil was deliberately vague. The message was subtle. Direct warmongering (or starvation mongering) would produce a backlash of righteous indignation. OPEC understood the implication well enough to counter with denunciations of America's "economic imperialism" and a defense of oil as a "legitimate weapon."

How did the September belligerance vis-à-vis OPEC measure up against the three goals of a national energy policy? To make such an evaluation requires the assumption of success, for were the stern policy to fail the goals could not possibly be achieved. Assuming success, then, would the goals be realized? An assured supply of oil would certainly improve national security in terms of fueling airplanes, tanks, and ships and powering an economy to back up these warcraft logistically. But could such a policy really assure a dependable supply? If achieved by an ultimatum short of military invasion, the certainty of supply would be tenuous for the OPEC nations might renege. If achieved by actual conquest of foreign territory, the oil fields and the shipping lanes would require constant defense. Hence the United States would be expending a certain amount of military effort to maintain its military position. Whether this would be efficient would depend on exactly how much military force yielded how much petroleum. If the scheme is unpredictable in the military security it would provide, it is also unpredictable in protecting the United States economy from the shocks of sudden changes in the petroleum supply. Other economies with which the United States trades extensively would likewise be liable to sudden shocks.

Low-cost petroleum would be the goal clearly achieved. The coerced price drop would benefit all users. The price, however, would not be lower than that existing prior to the 1973 boycott since even crude oil from captured wells would cost something to pump and ship. Some price reductions might be possible since the preboycott price included royalties to the foreign governments and, for American buyers, were artificially higher than the free market to protect domestic producers. But the Texas and Louisiana producers who raised the pre-1973 price with an import quota and fee system have no more reason to welcome really cheap oil now than before. Hence a reestablished import quota would be a foregone conclusion. The September policy offensive to coerce a greater and cheaper supply of petroleum implied no consequences with respect to internal allocation. Its target was foreign, not domestic.

To summarize, the goal of a cheap supply of oil is the only one to which September's tough talk could contribute. It would have no impact on allocation. Security would not be enhanced since the nature of coercion, whether by threat or actual military invasion, would produce an extremely uncertain supply. The issue was thus the balance between the cheapness of the petroleum and the risks and costs of obtaining it.

In contrast to the rather slight net gain to be achieved, the September energy offensive is better understood in terms of the policy process. In addressing the United Nations and the World Energy Conference, Ford and Kissinger were setting forth a policy position. The particular needs expressed were not new, for the United States had stated them many times before. What was new was the intensity. The United States had decided to take a hard line, threatening a food boycott and hinting at war. OPEC's problem was to decide to what extent the energy offensive was a bluff. This meant assessing the American ability to make good on its threats. With respect to food the United States was far from a monopolist. Although America is a major exporter of food, especially wheat, many other countries produce food which could be substituted if the United States were to embargo food. Furthermore American food exporters are private, decentralized, and not eager to forego profits. Merely to stop wheat exports would require the federal government to overcome the resistance of politically powerful farmers, railroads, and shippers. In contrast, the OPEC members, particularly those surrounding the Persian Gulf, have small populations needing comparatively little food. The United States would have to starve most of the world before these countries would begin to go hungry.

The food embargo seemed to be a bluff, but what about a military action? This too seemed to be a pretense. In the region where the United States was strongest militarily, Venezuela, the foreign relations costs were highest. The Colossus of the North was unlikely to alienate all of Latin America and domestic public opinion as well by invading a generally friendly neighbor. Yet in the region where the foreign relations costs were lowest, the Persian Gulf, the United States was weakest militarily. The forward logistical base at Diego Garcia was only a gleam in the

Navy's eye, not an actual jumping-off point. The United States had fewer ships in the Indian Ocean than the Soviet Union did. There, too, the foreign relations costs would be high, though lower than for a Western hemisphere invasion. Saudi Arabia, the most likely target, had been over the years America's best friend among the Arabs. Use of Israel or Iran as a surrogate was not easy. A thousand miles of desert stood between Israel and the major oil fields. Iran was closer, but was itself an oil exporter. While it was comparatively less well endowed than the Arab states on the western side of the Gulf, nevertheless its incentive for an extensive military invasion to serve American interests was small. Its own goals were more related to marginal operations to gain rights to disputed islands, offshore sites, and control of the Strait of Hormuz.

The International Energy Agency

Clearly, the United States could do little acting alone. This situation led the Ford administration to a second major foreign policy proposal to resolve the oil shortage. This was an organization of the oil-consuming nations of Western Europe. Secretary Kissinger maintained that it was foolish for the industrial nations to try to bargain with OPEC individually. Only in presenting a united front could they counter the producers monopoly. In mid-November the United States joined fifteen other industrial countries to establish the International Energy Agency under the auspices of the Organization for Economic Cooperation and Development. Among the first plans to come before the IEA was a Kissinger proposal to set a minimum price for oil. While most people were concerned with the high cost of crude oil, the Secretary of State was concerned that the price not drop too low, for if the consuming countries developed expensive alternative sources like tar sands, shale, or synthetic forms, OPEC could wipe out the value of their investments simply by dropping its price back to the old $3-a-barrel level. Thus it was necessary for the International Energy Agency to establish a floor price that would guarantee such investments. Kissinger spoke of a floor of $7.

The goal of such a scheme was clearly economic security. It would insulate economies of the United States and other industrial nations from sudden and arbitrary OPEC price manipulation. Alternate sources which would be worth developing at the then current world price would not be driven out of the market by a fall in price provided they were profitable at $7. The sixteen member nations of the IEA would insulate their economies via subsidies, tariffs, or direct investment. Achievement of this goal of economic security would, however, do little to enhance military security. In a crisis, first priority would go to the military anyway. Only if the oil shortage were to be so extended as to crimp the manufacture of war matériel would the IEA plan be beneficial.

In terms of cost, Kissinger's proposal for an International Energy Agency price floor would have a mixed impact. On the one hand, $7 per barrel is more expensive than the pre-1973 $3 per barrel. On the other hand, it would be less than the $11-per-barrel OPEC price. Both the IEA and the OPEC prices were artificially high. The choice lay between a self-controlled $7 or an outside controlled $11. The choice, however, was hypothetical for no one could guarantee the IEA nations' willingness to continue to support the $7 floor were OPEC apparently permanently to drop its prices below that level. Were that to happen the United States would either have to subsidize an inefficient system or renege on its commitment. Like the administration's September energy offensive, the IEA price floor would have no impact on the internal allocation of oil.

Kissinger's plan for an IEA price floor is an example of building agreement on policy. The industrial nations shared a common need for security, particularly economic security. The 1973 boycott and the subsequent price jump aggravated a worldwide recession, turning a minor slowdown into the worst slump since the Great Depression. While all the major industrial nations were victimized, each felt the effects differently. Japan, which produced virtually no petroleum, capitulated immediately. France believed its historic ties to many Arab states would give it a comparative advantage, hence struck a series of its own deals. European countries bordering on the North Sea reacted according to the extent of their new-found oil fields. Norway, the most blessed with offshore oil, held back, expecting soon to join the ranks of the major exporters. Its illiberality soon earned its people the sobriquet of "the blue-eyed Arabs." As the United States is a major producer (though not a net exporter) of petroleum, its stake was, to a large extent, indirect. However, even if it were self-sufficient, the United States could not have its major trading partners and military allies vulnerable to OPEC. *Thus it was necessary to unite the industrial countries in order to take a strong bargaining position vis-à-vis OPEC.* Kissinger's consensus building met with limited success. Meeting at Paris in late March the IEA members agreed "in principle" to keep oil prices high enough to encourage the development of alternate sources. What the minimum was to be, however, was not decided.

EXECUTIVE BRANCH PROPOSALS

Project Independence and the Energy Independence Authority

One Ford administration proposal straddled the fence between its international and domestic aspects: Project Independence. President Ford inherited its ill-defined outline when he assumed office. Immediately he seized on the amorphous scheme, mentioning it frequently in his early speeches as President. In the succeeding year Project Independence took many incarnations, culminating a year later as an elaborate proposal to establish a $100 billion Energy Independence Authority, a quasi-public corporation designed by Vice President Rockefeller.

When the new President pledged on August 12, 1974, to "push Project Independence for our own good and the good of others," he acknowledged the built-in contradiction of the concept. On the one hand its goal was to make the United States independent of foreign energy sources, and on the other it implied economic and political isolation.

> As you know, a theme of the foreign policy of this Administration is "international cooperation in an interdependent world." Stressing interdependence, you may ask why is our domestic energy program called Project Independence?[8]

Ford's answer to his rhetorical question was an outpouring of doublespeak worthy of George Orwell's novel *1984:*

> This will reduce the growing dependence on foreign petroleum. . . . As I see it, especially with regard to energy, national sufficiency and international

interdependence fit together and actually work together. . . . Independence
cannot mean isolation. . . .[9]

Rather than ask how independence can mean interdependence, the President
should have asked what Project Independence was in the first place. At the time he
assumed office it was a series of unintegrated draft proposals aimed at reducing
American vulnerability in case of a second OPEC embargo. At that point it was a
target rather than a plan. While the formal mandate included all forms of energy,
in fact the problem was oil, for oil was the most vulnerable fuel. Natural gas was
nearly all domestically produced. Coal was plentiful. It, along with uranium and
falling water, could be substituted for oil to generate electricity. It was the shortage
of oil that was felt so sharply. The public wanted gasoline for its automobiles and
kerosene for its jet planes. The military wanted the same for its vehicles and aircraft.

Project Independence took its final form in November when the Federal Energy
Administration submitted its report. While Project Independence had once given
the illusion of being an integrated program, the report belied this. It was a catchall
encompassing a range of alternatives. The FEA report was an assessment rather
than a plan of action. To the surprise of those who had followed its early stages
the report came down more on the side of conservation than development. It argued
that certain petroleum sources could not be developed economically. Massive recovery of oil from shale was impractical because of shortage of water in the Rocky
Mountains. Drilling on the outer continental shelf was more feasible but still imposed heavy costs in production and environmental safety. A world market price
of $11 per barrel would be necessary for the United States to come close to inde-
pendence. Conservation seemed to be the most efficient way in which the United
States could lessen its dependence on foreign sources. But this, the report noted,
would mean extensive government intervention in the market and changes in
lifestyle which many Americans would resist. Mandatory conservation was needed
but was unacceptable. First of all it was unacceptable from the convenience point
of view. Americans were fond of their fast automobiles, warm houses, and jet airplanes. More importantly, it was unacceptable for the economy. The report calculated that at $7 per barrel the national growth rate would drop from 4.5 percent
a year to 3.2 percent, at $11 it would drop to 2.7 percent, and if the nation adhered
to a truly rigorous policy of energy independence it would drop to 2.0 percent.[10]

President Ford incorporated a number of the report's recommendations for
energy independence into the State of the Union speech he delivered to Congress
on January 15. For the short run he proposed to reduce imports one million barrels
by the end of 1975 and two million barrels by the end of 1977. For the middle run
he proposed ending "vulnerability to economic disruption by foreign suppliers by
1985." And for the long run he proposed that the United States be able to supply
a significant share of the non-Communist world's energy needs by the year 2000.[11]

Brave words—were they possible? Were they desirable? Reaching independence
by 1985 demanded rapid exploitation of outer continental shelf and Alaskan oil
fields. The administration proposed prompt leasing of outer continental shelf tracts
along the east coast and the opening of Naval Petroleum Reserve Number 4 in
Alaska. It also proposed to exploit the one fuel in which the United States had an
abundant supply: coal. Within ten years it envisioned the opening of 250 major

new coal mines and 150 major new coal-fired power plants. Acknowledging that the bright star of nuclear power was waning, it recommended revivifying the industry with 200 major nuclear plants. It also foresaw 20 major new synthetic fuel plants (which would for example, convert coal into gasoline).

The nation took issue with the wisdom and practicality of building all the mines, plants, and wells the President had proposed. Governors of western states opposed massive development which would destroy their states' lands and lifestyles. Meanwhile those convinced that a massive construction effort would solve the energy independence problem were stymied by where to find the capital to invest in it.

One solution came from Vice President Rockefeller, whose Domestic Council developed plans for a quasi-public corporation to channel up to $100 billion in loans and loan guarantees into energy projects which would make the United States independent of foreign supplies. Besides indirect financing, the corporation might choose to establish subsidiaries which would invest directly. While the corporation would be financed by the Treasury it would be autonomous in its undertakings. It would be exempt from Civil Service Commission regulations, from annual congressional review, and from federal, state, and local taxes. When Rockefeller presented the plan in August, financial conservatives within the administration opposed it as incompatible with the free market system. Nevertheless Ford adopted the concept, christening it the Energy Independence Authority. The similarity in name to the Tennessee Valley Authority was deliberate. The administration saw it as a "crash program" to solve the 1970s energy demands as TVA had solved those of the 1930s.

In first presenting the EIA publicly on September 22 in a speech to AFL-CIO trade unionists meeting in San Francisco, Ford compared it to the Manhattan Project to develop the atomic bomb and President Kennedy's fulfilled pledge of 1960 to land a man on the moon within the decade.[12] In these comparisons to three previous heroic national programs President Ford sought to inspire his audience with the drama and excitement of making America energy independent.

As in Kissinger's policy of organizing the industrial nations into a consumers' cartel to counter OPEC, the chief goal of Project Independence was security. Military security demands dependable fuel supplies. So does economic security. An American economy independent of energy imports is free from OPEC threats and boycotts. As outlined in the President's State of the Union speech, the Ford administration foresaw even more than protecting the American economy. In setting a goal of net exporting of energy by the year 2000, it envisioned the United States being the bulwark of the non-Communist economies as well. This would have returned the United States to the position it enjoyed during World War I and II when its oil exports fueled the British and other allied nations' navies, armies, and air forces.

When Project Independence realities made their appearance alongside its goals, cost proved to be the crucial issue. *The United States could be energy independent, but at what price?* The November FEA report estimated that achievement of the goal of zero imports would result in cutting the real economic growth rate to less than half—from 4.5 percent to 2.0 percent. Mammoth new plants can crush the oil out of Colorado shale or turn coal into synthetic gas, but at what cost? Even oil from the new frontiers of Alaska and the outer continental shelf would require prices of about $11 per barrel to be economically feasible. This was as high as the "usurious" price OPEC demanded. Indeed this is one reason why the OPEC price was $11. The cartel must keep its prices below that of alternate sources, otherwise the industrial consumers would start using those sources.

Even OPEC had some misgivings about the effect of its high prices. When the exporting countries met at their Vienna headquarters to determine the price to go into effect on October 1, 1975, Saudi Arabia argued that any price increase be minimal. The Saudi petroleum minister, Sheik Yamani, argued for no increase or at most a 5 percent rise. He pointed out that the 400 percent increase since 1973 had worked extreme hardship on the underdeveloped countries and was contributing to a global recession among the industrial countries. In fact it was the general softness of the market that concerned him. The Saudis could afford to sit tight for their reserves were extensive and their needs slight. Iran, in contrast, had fewer oil reserves and more need for cash to support the massive development program the Shah had promised his larger and more restive population. Iran asked for a 28 percent increase. After four days of heated debate, which featured Sheik Yamani flying off to London in a fit of pique, the OPEC ministers compromised on a 10 percent increase, from $10.46 to $11.51. Skeptical observers viewed the meeting as a sham staged to mollify the consumers, who were thus led to believe that OPEC had been generous. They saw the real cause for the moderation of the price rise (about equal to the inflation rate) to be slackened demand, not OPEC kindness.

Even at $11.51 per barrel, imported oil was still a good buy. Whereas the Ford administration's goal of opening new coal mines, nuclear plants, and oil wells had clear advantages in terms of security, these advantages were cloudy in terms of cost. Had they been economically competitive they would already have been put into production. The basic premise of the Energy Independence Authority was that the government had to make the investment because private capital would not. The reasons were several. The most damning was that the projects were inefficient. A business could not earn as good a rate of return as it could elsewhere. If this were the case there was no justification for the federal government to squander the nation's resources. An alternate reason was that the projects were efficient but required large accumulations of capital, which only the government could aggregate. A project might be potentially profitable yet of too great a scope for a single corporation to manage. A related rationale was that the time span necessary to bring these projects to fruition was too long for private business, which needed to start generating a return within a few years. A third reason was that private business was overly cautious. The federal government, supposedly being shrewder, would recognize the true worth of these projects and surmount the excessive timidity of the private sector. A fourth rationale was an analogue to the government's social welfare responsibilities. Just as the government has the duty to aid blind, disabled, and helpless people, so it has the duty, the EIA seemed to be saying, to aid blind, disabled, and helpless corporations. If an industry were ailing, the government should doctor it. Although the analogue was patently specious, its popular appeal was strong. In the twentieth century the federal government has frequently come to the aid of sick industries. Agriculture is a prime example. As the industry's importance to the American economy declined, government subsidies increased. Energy industries have furnished their share of horrible examples. Coal's decline from the end of World War I through the 1960s brought forth a series of federal acts of charity such as the NRA, the Guffy Coal Act, and Coal Mine Health and

Safety Act of 1969. The relative decline of Oklahoma and Texas oil fields was ameliorated by the Interstate Oil and Gas Compact and the Connally "Hot Oil" Act. The decline of domestic (in comparison to foreign) production brought forth the import quota system of the Eisenhower administration.

Albeit low-cost energy is the proper goal, there is no guarantee that the federal government will actually seek it. It is too easy to go astray. The low costs Project Independence contemplated were often illusory. If the price to the consumer were really a subsidized price, the total economy would not benefit. Rather it would be led to make an inefficient allocation of its resources. So it was that Project Independence impinged on the goal of resource allocation.

The naming of the Energy Independence Authority so as to recall the Tennessee Valley Authority suggests comparing the two. To the extent to which the TVA succeeded economically, much of the success was attributable to the backwardness of the middle South in the early 1930s. The ignorance, poverty, and defeatism of the region dated back to the Civil War. TVA's success came from importing proven hydroelectric engineering technology into a valley with untapped natural resources. The Energy Independence Authority did not appear to enjoy this advantage of an unexploited natural situation to develop. Instead it faced the much more onerous task of trying to develop marginal energy sources—those currently considered below par. Its success would have to come from new technologies and the rising costs of alternative supplies.

In choosing to promote the EIA as the vehicle for gaining energy independence the Ford administration implicitly chose to change resource allocation in several ways. The first, just discussed, was to artifically and inefficiently shift resources into energy production. If the purpose were to increase the nation's military and economic security, the immediate maldistribution might be rational. If, however, the shift were made in the mistaken belief that it was efficient, then the result would be a net sacrifice on the part of the American people. The November, 1974, FEA report noted this when it calculated the degree to which the quest for energy independence would decrease growth in the GNP. This warning seemed to have gone unheeded nine months later when the administration made final its plans for the Energy Independence Authority.

The second change in resource allocation which the EIA implied was a shift toward government control. It is ironic that a Republican administration should choose this policy, for Republican party doctrine traditionally glorifies the role of private ownership in contrast to the Democratic doctrine of government ownership. After forty years of denigrating the New Deal it seemed incongruous to imitate it. At least President Ford, perhaps inadvertently, had forewarned of the policy chosen when he compared it to President Roosevelt's 1942 pledge to produce 60,000 airplanes in 1943, the Manhattan Project, and President Kennedy's man on the moon effort—all programs of Democratic Presidents. The administration's EIA proposal, however, was far from a total abandonment of pro-business Republican ideology. In discussions during the summer of 1975 prior to its unveiling, Secretary of the Treasury William E. Simon, Budget Director James T. Lynn, and Council of Economic Advisors Chairman Alan Greenspan opposed the program precisely because it gave government too big a role. The final form was less like TVA than another New Deal agency, the Reconstruction Finance Corporation. The Authority's major role was foreseen to be indirect. The EIA would give loans and loan guarantees to private corporations as its major activity. Direct programs would be secondary.

The evolution of Project Independence from Ford's ringing endorsement in the first days of his presidency to the stillborn EIA a year later teaches some lessons about policy making. These lessons emphasize the pitfalls, however, rather than the successes. For example the FEA, in its November report, was unable to bring together an integrated program. Where it had intended to present one solution, it ended up presenting multiple solutions. Ford learned some of the difficulties of creating a unified policy during a February trip thoughout the Great Plains states to drum up support for Project Independence. Under pressure from local interests, the President tailored his speeches to mollify parochial criticism. In Kansas he promised farmers the government would compensate them for high fuel prices. In Texas he told oilmen the proposed windfall profits tax would not apply if they reinvested their profits in further exploration.[13]

The protean nature of Project Independence during the first year of the Ford administration suggests what may be considered its true purpose—to be a symbol. The words themselves connote this. "Project Independence" evokes an image of action. There was a challenge and the administration was doing something. Independence is indubitably a virtue; after all the nation began with a Declaration of Independence. The EIA again played upon these inspiring words, adding an echo of the TVA éclat to the quest. When the domestic ebullience proved discordant to America's European allies Secretary Kissinger tried to restore the harmony by deliberately interplaying "Independence" and "Interdependence." So the world was treated to convoluted doublespeak proposing that the word meant its opposite. The analogies Ford, Kissinger, and other high administration officials used in describing Project Independence added to the impression that its main purpose was symbolic. They compared it to wartime mobilization, the space race with Russia, and New Deal crusading.

Murray Edelman says politicians' first reason for manipulating symbols is to maintain their positions of leadership.[14] This would explain why President Ford dwelt on Project Independence so frequently in his public addresses in the first month after assuming the presidency. Coming into office in the wake of Richard Nixon's disgrace and lacking even the legitimacy of having been elected Vice President, Ford especially needed to assert his claim to leadership. The new President took this route with a vengeance. He did not stop with the American television viewers, the U.N. General Assembly, and the World Energy Conference as audiences for his exhortation. On October 15 he preempted national television for prime-time coverage of his Kansas City lecture to the Future Farmers of America annual meeting in which he offered tomorrow's agribusinessmen and the television audiences such energy-saving tips as these: turn off lights, turn down the thermostat, ride a bicycle for errands, walk instead of riding, and buy warmer clothing for winter. This proved to be the high-water mark for symbol manipulation as widespread criticism ridiculed the vacuity of the telecast.

Edelman says the second reason politicians engage in symbol manipulation is to assure the naive public that they are protecting its interests while they are actually providing a sheltered arena in which business may conduct inside bargaining. Such analysis would point to the EIA as a prime shelter. Outwardly the EIA is a government agency, presumably dedicated to the public good. Yet closer examination reveals limitless opportunities for abuse. The Authority would be exempt from

Civil Service regulation, Congressional review, and taxation. It would raise capital through issuing government bonds, then turn the money over to private companies. That Nelson Rockefeller was its principal architect did little to allay suspicions that the Authority was a $100 billion boondoggle for business.

The Federal Energy Agency

The nation already had several agencies responsible for energy policy. The chief one was the Federal Energy Administration. President Nixon had assembled an ad hoc Federal Energy Office in December, 1973, in order to better coordinate energy policy making to counter the then ongoing OPEC oil embargo. Prior to this time energy responsibility was spread widely throughout the federal government. The Interior Department was concerned with oil and coal production. The Federal Power Commission's responsibility was natural gas and electricity transmission. The Department of Defense was heavily involved both because it was a major consumer and because it had civil defense responsibilities. Civil defense, everyone's stepchild, was then represented in the White House by the Office of Emergency Preparedness. It was the tangled lines of jurisdiction between these agencies that led President Nixon first to set up the temporary Federal Energy Office and then to ask Congress to make it the permanent Federal Energy Administration. Congress did so and the FEA officially came into being in July, 1974, led by John Sawhill, the former deputy director of the FEO and prior to that an associate director of the Office of Management and Budget.

Sawhill's tenure as FEA head was to be brief and stormy. President Ford had barely made the acquaintance of his "energy czar" when he announced his forced resignation on October 29. The issue was the degree to which the federal government should opt for mandatory controls to lessen dependence on foreign oil imports. During September and October the FEA's recommendations were taking their final form for the publication of the Project Independence report. As the final drafts were reviewed it became apparent that Ford and Sawhill were diametrically opposed in policy. Sawhill recommended the major emphasis be on conservation. A key feature was to be a steep federal tax on gasoline; twenty cents a gallon was a likely figure. The FEA preferred to tax gasoline rather than crude oil because it was a more elastic commodity. The homeowner has little flexibility in heating. Reducing the temperature to sixty-eight degrees saves little fuel. And it is a one-time saving; no matter what the price is, the home owner still has to maintain a livable temperature. The automobile driver has much more flexibility. He can take a train or bus, join a car pool, or forego a Sunday drive in the country. Boosting the price in a gallon of gasoline twenty cents encourages these alternatives without rigid coercion. The FEA draft contained stronger measures for industrial users in order to shift them away from oil back to coal. It recommended the government establish mandatory standards for energy efficiency for automobiles, appliances, and buildings, maintaining a maximum price of $5.25 per barrel for old oil and restricting the amount of crude oil imported. Such suggestions proved anathema to President Ford and his economic advisors, particularly Treasury Secretary Simon, and CEA Chairman Greenspan.

Ford's opposition stemmed from partisan concerns. In general, Republican party ideology opposed mandatory government controls like those the FEA was about to publish. More immediately, Ford feared the rumored twenty cent gasoline tax would cost Republican congressional candidates votes in the November election. Sawhill tried to reconcile his policy differences with the rest of the Ford administration. He claimed he no longer supported the gasoline tax and an import quota. This backtracking was not enough, however. On October 8 Ford established a new cabinet-level Energy Resources Council, chaired by Interior Secretary Rogers Morton, to oversee the FEA. This was still not enough to eclipse the FEA proposals, so at the end of the month Ford requested and received Sawhill's resignation.

Ford's nomination of Andrew E. Gibson to succeed Sawhill as FEA Administrator served only to further the administration's appearance of confusion and inconstancy with respect to developing a coherent energy policy. While the FEA had sought to restrain demand with mandatory taxes, standards, and quotas, the President's Citizen Action Committee callowly suggested that consumers sign pledge cards promising to be "energy savers." Gibson's nomination proved equally embarrassing. Unbeknownst to Ford his nominee had a ten-year severance contract with a former employer, the Interstate Oil Transport Company, which paid him $88,000 annually.

Frank G. Zarb was the president's next nominee to head the FEA. Zarb prudently kept a low profile. He praised the emasculated *Project Independence Report* issued November 14 as a useful source of information and ideas without committing himself to its orientation toward mandatory conservation. During the ensuing months, Zarb quietly worked at developing (and redeveloping) the many energy proposals which the President sent to Congress in late January. In the process he found the right balance within the administration. Whereas Sawhill had envisioned an activist role for the FEA in developing and promoting programs, many of which strained the traditional Republican reluctance to intervene in the economy, Zarb saw a less prominent role for the agency. It would gather information. It would recommend programs more compatible with Republican ideology.

Besides a change of leadership, the FEA underwent a change of its political environment. The "energy crisis" receded. Sawhill had been with the organization since its founding as the ad hoc FEO in the stressful days of the oil boycott. The frenetic style of the FEO was no longer suitable for a less concerned nation and a different President. In the winter of 1973-74 long lines at gasoline stations and a sense of impending doom made extreme measures such as state allocations and printing ration coupons a reality. The next winter political and supply conditions differed, but Sawhill's sense of urgency did not. Zarb, coming to the FEA without the earlier crisis heritage, could blend in better with the subdued FEA Ford wanted. Zarb's combination of political sensitivity and technical knowledge enhanced his influence in the policy process so that by the end of Ford's first year in office Zarb and the FEA had regained the leadership role lost the previous October.

Measuring the FEA's performance against the national goals centers primarily on allocation and secondarily on cost. The security issue was largely ignored or rejected. Sawhill had tried to confront the security goal but got little thanks for playing Cassandra. The boycott was over and the winter had been mild, so the danger seemed remote. The Ford administration, and the country as a whole, preferred business as usual. Furthermore Sawhill offered no means of increasing supplies significantly. The FEA's conclusion that a strenuous conservation effort was the only answer did not match the "can do" rhetoric of the President. The defeatism of restraining consumption was unattractive. Disregarding security was the simplest tactic.

The FEA gave better consideration to the cost issue. Indeed this was one of its chief foci. The agency brought some rationality to the information disarray. Its economists analyzed the impact on the economy of various world prices. An $11-per-barrel price would make energy self-sufficiency easier to accomplish since marginal sources would become profitable. It would also make it easier to withstand another boycott. One problem, however, was that even the $11 price was too low to cause a shift away from oil. Eleven-dollar oil was still a good buy. But though the expensive oil would encourage energy self-sufficiency, it would be better for the economy to have cheaper sources even if this meant depending on imports.

Allocation was the essence of FEA's responsibility. In its FEO infancy it allocated petroleum to each state and set up a rationing scheme. Sawhill's concern, and his Waterloo, was allocation. He favored the various mandatory programs discussed above while the President and the rest of his administration favored market allocation. By early 1975, however, the administration was not so confident that market forces would do the job. In particular the economic recession had worsened. Hence the administration embarked on a series of its own alternatives and of ultimatums to Congress to resolve the problem. The FEA, once again ascendant, served as a clearinghouse. The Energy Resources Council, chaired by Secretary Morton, no longer superintended the process. Ford had created it to tame Sawhill. With his departure and Ford's growing confidence that Zarb was ideologically safe, the council's raison d'être waned.

The FEA serves as a good example of bureaucratic policy making. Traditional political science theory sees *private* groups as the breeding ground for ideas, but in rapidly evolving issue arenas the *government* bureaucracy is a more common source of innovation (or at least articulation). In 1974 and 1975 the desires of private groups were essentially conservative. They wanted the least change possible. The petroleum companies, which were making huge profits during the period, did not want to see the rules changed. Motorists wanted their usual amount of gasoline at the old, cheap price. Home owners and industrial users wanted their same amounts of fuel oil. To some extent FEA fostered the maintainance of the status quo. Its allocation program required oil companies to supply the same buyers as they had previously. This froze the market, blocking the normal dynamics. Thus FEA caused inefficient rigidity. For example, a company which was in the process of consolidating its market in a certain region was stuck with supplying old customers it wished to eliminate even before the 1973 "crisis." Another FEA rigidity was to institutionalize the official ratio between imported and domestic supplies. East coast refiners use mostly imported oil and mid-continent refiners use mostly domestic oil. To equalize the hardship of the fourfold increase in the OPEC price, FEA decreed that all refiners should earn profits according to the national average of 40 percent of the oil being imported. One absurd result was that each month the comparatively small Cities Service Corporation sent a check from Oklahoma to the Exxon Corporation, because Exxon's refineries were in the Northeast. The irony of Citgo subsidizing the world's biggest corporation did little to compensate the public for removing Exxon's incentive to find cheaper sources of crude oil.

FEA, of course, did not intend to discourage efficiency when it established state allocations or decreed Exxon be subsidized. Its aim was to spread the burden. The agency meant to protect the consumer. If everyone wanted plenty of cheap petroleum, what could FEA do? It is ironic that Ford's conservative Republican Administration repeatedly rejected the conservative Republican answer, which was to allow market forces to find a new equilibrium. Higher prices would have allocated the gasoline more efficiently than FEA's quotas and would have given Exxon the incentive to find the cheapest supplies available. To the extent to which it increases the gasoline price to the consumer, it also signals him to find alternative modes of transportation. Sawhill's advocacy of a twenty-cents-per-gallon tax represented a middle ground between signaling to motorists to use less gasoline and freezing the northern home owner with only enough insulation for the bygone days of cheap fuel oil. Yet Ford found this to be the most objectionable of all the FEA recommendations.

The FEA served some of the symbolic functions previously discussed with respect to the EIA. In particular, Edelman's allegation that regulatory agencies serve as façades behind which transpires the real bargaining among narrow special interests seems applicable. Liberal congressmen frequently decried the large numbers of FEA employees recruited from energy corporations. One example was the short-lived nomination of Andrew Gibson to replace Sawhill as Administrator. Another was the nomination of former Exxon executive Melvin A. Conant to be an assistant administrator. Even Ford's own Justice Department had reservations about the $90,000 Exxon gave Conant when he left the company. The preponderance of personnel recruited from energy businesses extended throughout the agency. Defenders rebutted this, pointing out that FEA needed expertise and the only place to find it was in the energy companies. Even granting the necessity of such hiring, the result was an agency environment conducive to just the sort of coziness Edelman warned against.

President Ford was not able to use the creation of FEA as a sign that he was taking action to resolve the "energy crisis" since President Nixon had preempted that possibility the previous winter when he organized FEO. In the Ford administration this sort of symbol manipulation was better applied to the establishment of the Energy Research and Development Administration (ERDA).

In distinction to FEA, which was essentially a regulatory and policy-making agency, ERDA had a technical mission. It combined the Atomic Energy Commission (minus its regulatory functions) with the Office of Coal Research and other research programs from the Department of the Interior, geothermal and solar heating programs from the National Science Foundation, and the automobile-alternative research program from the Environmental Protection Agency. Since it aimed at inventing and developing new technologies on the frontiers of science, ERDA's potential was as great as the imagination. Hence it made an appealing symbol of future hope. To the more skeptical ERDA was just the same old Atomic Energy Commission with all its flaws. (The AEC supplied 85 percent of its personnel and 84 percent of its funds.) To remedy some of these flaws AEC critics in Congress insisted on certain provisions. One was that the incumbent AEC Chairman not head ERDA. This necessitated finding a new position for Dixy Lee Ray, the eccentric marine biologist from the University of Washington, who headed the Commission. To do so Congress created the position of Assistant Secretary of State for Oceans and International Environmental and Scientific Affairs. After serving only briefly in her sinecure Dr. Ray decided the post was meaningless, and resigned to return home to Seattle. President Ford named Robert C. Seamans, former deputy director of NASA and Secretary of the Air Force and a man untainted by prior association with atomic energy, to head ERDA.

Other provisions of the ERDA law sought to prevent undue emphasis on atomic power. The act directed that "no unwarranted priority" be given any one energy technology. The administrator must be a civilian (since ERDA inherited the AEC's job of building bombs) and must be broadly qualified to manage all forms of energy. There was to be an assistant administrator for conservation as well as one for environment and safety.

ERDA's mission to develop nonpolluting power such as solar and geothermal power projects an environmentally clean image. The fast breeder reactor will generate more nuclear fuel than it burns, promising unlimited power. Fusion power will literally run on water, since the deuterium fuel (a radioactive isotope of hydrogen) comes from heavy water (D_2O). However, this happy vision of the future is clouded. The large initial investment for solar power makes it too costly. Suitable geothermal sites are rare and, when found, vent steam which may be polluting. The plutonium of the fast breeder reactor is the most toxic substance known and must be safeguarded for thousands of years before its radiation decays. Fusion power has yet to be invented.

LEGISLATIVE ENERGY POLICY PROPOSALS

Much of the Ford energy policy emerged, not out of international deliberations or executive agency proposals, but out of interaction with Congress. The White House–Capitol Hill tug of war was fought to a stalemate in the Ford administration's first year, though some resolution came later, in December, 1975, when Congress passed and the President signed the Energy Policy and Conservation Act— a 270 page omnibus law incorporating provisions ranging from a forty month deregulation schedule to permission for motorists to turn right after stopping at a red light. In dealing with Congress, Ford showed a preference for negative sanctions. He vetoed a law challenging his authority to impose import fees and twice vetoed strip mining control laws. Deadlines for congressional action and threats to impose import fees and to abruptly end oil price controls marked the year-long conflict over the Energy Act.

Coal Mining

The Ninety-third Congress had already passed house and Senate versions of a strip mining control law by the time Gerald Ford took the oath of office on August 9, 1974. The legislation effected a major environmental reform in surface mining practices. Sponsored by Congressman Morris Udall of Arizona, the bill required the operators to restore the land to its approximate original contours, banned mining in mountains too steep to be reclaimed, and generated funds to repair long abandoned "orphan" spoil banks. The Senate had passed its version in 1973 and the House passed its in July, 1974. The two versions went to conference on August 1, languishing there until the conferees resolved the differences in early December. The Ford administration did not reveal its final stance until December 13, when FEA chief Zarb announced the President would veto the bill because it would hamper coal production at a time when energy was vitally needed. Since Congress had adjourned, the President's "pocket veto" could not be overridden.

The new, more liberal Ninety-fourth Congress promptly passed a new version: The Surface Mining Control and Reclamation Act of 1975. The 1975 bill went to the White House in early May. Ford vetoed it on May 20, adding the dangers of increased unemployment to his previous criticism of decreased energy. Three weeks later the House fell three votes short of overriding the veto.

Assessing the surface mining bills presents a different problem from that of the proposals mentioned previously since the strip mining bills were designed not to increase energy supplies but to protect the environment. It was their potential reduction in the amount of fuel available that caused the President to veto both versions. But was this assumption valid?

In terms of security coal is nowhere as important as oil. Its military applications are slight. The U.S. Navy has not fueled its ships with coal for years. No American airplane or tank ever burned the soft black mineral. To the extent that coal plays a role in military security, it is indirectly through the total economy. It was the general health of the economy which Ford cited in both his vetoes. At one point when the administration was urging the Ninety-third Congress to soften the operators' burden, the administration claimed the 1974 bill would reduce production 187 million tons. The next year in similarly urging the Ninety-fourth Congress to soften the replacement bill's requirements, the administration also asserted that enactment would cost 40,000 jobs. While many rejected this particular figure, the unemployment risks weighed heavily.[15]

In the case of oil, the security rationale was based on insulating the economy from sudden and untimely shocks. This line of reasoning was less appropriate in the case of coal. All of this fuel is mined domestically. There are no foreign sources which could suddenly cut off supplies. The implementation of the act was to have been phased over several years so there would have been no interruption in operations. Thus the economy's security was not a valid concern. Neither was the economic security of the United State's major trading partners a valid issue. To the extent to which other countries like Japan import American coal, *their* security is at stake, but not that of the United States.

Cost was a more legitimate concern. The surface mining bills would have raised the price of coal. Proponents said this was only fair. Coal operators were not bearing the true cost of their product since despoiling the land shifted to society a cost rightfully the responsibility of the mining company. The Interior Department and the Environmental Protection Agency advanced this line of reasoning in urging Ford to sign the bill. The people should not be expected to subsidize the coal industry. Besides, they noted, some of the jobs lost because marginally efficient mines would have to close would be recouped in restoration of the strip mined land. FEA's argument, which Ford adopted, focused more narrowly on the energy problem. The "crisis" was of energy, not land. Since coal could substitute for oil and natural gas in generating electricity and heating buildings, cheaper coal would reduce demand for petroleum.

Implicitly, the surface mining bills pointed to a shift in allocation between the private and public sectors. Forcing the operators to restore the land they dug up placed the burden on them rather than society. Mining companies would have to internalize some of the production costs they had hitherto externalized. The shift was subtle and, in comparison to FEA's allocation of petroleum, its impact would have been slight. Even though Republican ideology supports the theory of private ownership as preferable, the Ford administration did not adhere to it consistently in this case, for that would have meant a shift of *costs,* not benefits.

The passage and vetoes of the surface mining bills were classic instances of interest groups engaged in the policy-making process.[16] As is usually true, business was well organized. The coal industry, led by its trade association (the National Coal Association), promoted its position with both Congress and the executive branch. This ranged from engineers providing information, to lobbyists blatantly threatening congressmen. The United Mine Workers union was ambivalent. The national UMW endorsed the bills, believing it was just as beneficial to be paid to fill in an abandoned mine as it was to dig the coal out in the first place. But some union locals opposed the bills, fearing that their mines might be the marginal ones that would have to close. Electric utility companies were effective in organizing their customers to voice their objections to their congressmen. The utilities noted that more expensive coal would mean more expensive electricity. This feature was unusual because consumers are usually the unorganized victims. In this instance the public played two roles: energy consumer and environmentalist. The consumer role dominated, thanks to the organizing role of the utility companies. Cheap electricity won out over a restored landscape.

The Oil Import Fee

President Ford successfully used the veto to defeat the oil import fee bill as well. In his State of the Union speech on January 15, the President challenged Congress to produce an energy program within ninety days. To spur the legislators to act, Ford imposed a fee of $1.00 on each barrel of oil imported. Outraged at what it considered high-pressure tactics, Congress immediately passed a bill suspending the President's authority to impose such fees for ninety days. But Ford vetoed the bill. In order to let tempers cool the President and Congress compromised. Ford withdrew his ninety-day deadline in return for Congress not voting on whether to override the veto. Passion cooled to the point of inaction. Congress did not pass the energy program the administration sought, so on June 1 the President raised the import fee to $2 per barrel.

Meanwhile Ford's fees were under challenge in federal court. In August the court ruled that the President did not have the authority to impose the fee in the first place. Thus a year after assuming office and eight months after issuing Congress a ninety-day ultimatum, Ford was back where he started on this aspect of his energy program.

Although the President imposed the import fee partly for bargaining with Congress, the scheme deserves analysis on its merits. By making OPEC oil more expensive the import fee would enhance national security insofar as it shifted dependence to domestic oil and alternative fuels. Adding $2 to the price of foreign oil would stimulate exploration for new fields and secondary and tertiary recovery. More domestic sources would make the military less vulnerable to a future boycott and would help insulate the economy. On the other hand, the 400 percent increase of the world price to over $11 had done the same thing. Raising it an additional $2 was unlikely to have much effect. Only a few more wells would be profitable at

$13 than at $11. Furthermore if the high price of imported oil were already contributing to the recession, would not a $2 fee only compound the effect? The increased
cost contravened the advantages of security.

The Energy Policy and Conservation Act

Just after Christman, 1974, the President's energy and economic lieutenants rendez-
voused at Ford's Vail, Colorado, ski lodge to regroup and to revise the administration's strategy. One tactic adopted was the tough talk of the State of the Union
message threatening to impose import fees if Congress did not act within ninety
days. As just discussed, this route helped neither the administration nor the public.
Ford proposed a number of other petroleum measures on this occasion. Unlike the
oil import fee, these proposals did not spark an immediate confrontation with
Congress. Rather the opposite occurred—inaction. At least this was the administration's characterization of the congressional response.

As Ford completed his first year in office in August 1975, Congress had not passed
any of his legislative proposals, though it had rejected the $2 import fee. In the
State of the Union address Ford had asked for laws both to increase and to conserve
oil. Removing the price controls on "old oil" was the first way he put forward to
boost the supply. "Old oil" was domestic oil already in production when President
Nixon ended Phase IV of his New Economic Policy begun in 1971. At that time the
Nixon administration economists believed that although most controls could be
removed without kindling excessive inflation, oil was an exception. Therefore they
recommended continued control of oil at $5.25 per barrel. So as not to discourage
new exploration, drilling, and production, the administration decreed that new oil
would not be controlled. Producers could sell it at the world price. Decontrol of old
oil excited contention because of the potential for windfall profits. Since the oil was
already in production the new high price would not serve as an incentive. It was
already profitable at the old price. The petroleum companies would enjoy a much
greater income for nothing. To counteract this, Ford urged that a windfall profits
tax accompany decontrol. The President put forward two other measures to increase
domestic supplies: prompt drilling on the outer continental shelf and in Naval
Petroleum Reserve Number 4 in Alaska.

To conserve petroleum Ford suggested mandatory federal thermal efficiency
requirements for all new buildings, amending the Clean Air Act to postpone the
antipollution deadlines five years, and requiring automobile manufacturers to
improve mileage.

In challenging Congress to enact his legislative package Ford's strategy differed
from the strategies of recent Presidents. Rather than merely insisting that Congress
vote on the specific bills he sent to the Hill, President Ford sought to spur Congress
to develop its own alternatives. The Ford proposals were as much a threat as a
program. Ford believed that only when the Democratic majorities in the House and
Senate had agreed upon their own position could the administration negotiate a
compromise which would become the final program.

The Democratic response lacked unity. The regular committee structure splin-
tered responsibility many ways. No committee had the leadership role. Recognizing
this disunity Democrats in each house set up special energy task forces. Senator
John O. Pastore of Rhode Island headed one and Representative Jim Wright of

Texas headed the other. The two task forces announced their alternatives on February 27. They included a five cents per gallon tax on gasoline, a tax on automobiles with poor mileage, a tax on windfall profits by large oil companies, controls on old oil, and a National Production and Conservation Board to give nonpartisan advice to the President. Al Ullman of Oregon, chairman of the House Ways and Means Committee, found these alternatives to be far too weak, especially the Senate provisions, which he scoffed at as "a milk-toast program." He responded with a tougher program featuring a gasoline tax beginning at 10 cents per gallon and rising to fifty cents, quotas on oil imports, and incentives to switch from oil to coal.

Oil was a difficult issue for Congress, especially Democrats. Many referred to it as a "party-splitter." Critics of the House task force said the party leadership chose Wright as chairman because he was safe. As a Texan he represented a major oil-producing state. Speaker Carl Albert of Oklahoma, the party's leader in the House, came from another oil state. Yet because House representation is based directly on population, the House tends to be less favorable to oil producers than the Senate. The Senate overrepresents sparsely populated states, and hence shows partiality toward natural resource industries. Oil is a prime example but mining and forestry fit the same mold. The interests of these industries are promoted more vigorously in the Senate than those of the consumers, the majority of whom are crowded into a few states with correspondingly few senators. Thus the oil consumer is at a disadvantage in Congress. In addition, the Democratic party, generally more consumer oriented, finds the issue divisive. Whatever force unites the Democrats, it is certainly not oil. Texas, Louisiana, and Oklahoma Democrats are natural adversaries of their brethren from northern consuming states.

The Senate acted on the Ford administration's energy challenge in the spring, passing a comprehensive bill reported by the Interior Committee, chaired by Henry Jackson. Senator Jackson had emerged as a leading Democratic spokesman on energy matters a year before when he castigated the major oil companies for making excessive profits during the OPEC embargo at the expense of the American public. In the January, 1974, hearings Jackson had gained headlines for expressing widely felt indignation at an 81 percent increase in Exxon's profits and a 91 percent increase in Gulf's profits. The nineteen largest oil companies had boosted their profits an average of 76 percent. Jackson had chosen energy issues as part of his quest for the 1976 Democratic presidential nomination. Since energy seemed destined to be an important issue to the voters it behooved him to develop his expertise and establish his authority. The key features of Jackson's energy bill were standby authority under which the President could order rationing, fuel allocations, and import quotas in an emergency, continuation of price controls on old oil, and a series of energy conservation standards.

The House did not act so expeditiously. In July it began debate on a similar bill, which it did not pass until September 23. The House version was broader in scope. For example it "rolled back" the price of new oil from the free market price to $7.50, provided for congressional review of presidential implementation of emergency authority, and required the President to reduce gasoline consumption through efficiency standards.

A theme of the congressional debate was the series of Ford administration deadlines. The President pressured Congress with the threat of decontrolling the price of old oil, which accounted for two-thirds of domestic production. The Emergency Petroleum Allocation Act of 1973 expired automatically on August 31. Congress voted a six-month extension, which Ford vetoed September 9 and the Senate sustained September 10. Though oil was legally decontrolled, the nation held its breath, as if unbelieving. Old oil could now soar in price. Confronted with the awesomeness of the prospect Ford said he would continue controls temporarily until a compromise could be worked out. A new November 15 deadline was set and again passed without a resolution as a conference committee debated the differences between the House and Senate versions. Another deadline was set—December 15. The third deadline expired with no law passed. Senator Jackson called the deadlock "a dangerous game of economic brinksmanship." The bill originally passed by the Senate in April and the House in September did not go to the White House until December 17. On December 22 the President signed the Energy Policy and Conservation Act of 1973.

The 1975 Energy Act was a potpourri. *Since every geographical region produced or used a different mix of fuels, the new energy law was a series of awkward trade-offs.* Few provisions were without controversy. Perhaps the only provision universally supported was the creation of a one billion barrel civilian and military reserve to cushion the impact of a future boycott. Besides this the law authorized the president to allocate fuel in both emergency and normal conditions, set efficiency standards for automobiles and appliances, and authorized the U.S. General Accounting Office to audit energy companies, which had heretofore been extremely secretive. The most contrived provision of the law established a new price control scheme for oil which would immediately roll back all domestic prices to an average of $7.66. This drop of over a dollar a barrel was designed to reduce the price of gasoline three cents a gallon in 1976. But after the initial decrease the price would creep back up over the succeeding forty months. Thus voters in 1976 would enjoy the benefits of the temporary reduction price before the prices began to rise in 1977, 1978, and 1979. But even as the law was passed, FEA head Frank Zarb conceded that inflation would eat away the three cent reduction so the result would only be no increase.

Despite all its internal contradiction the Energy Policy and Conservation Act did meet a number of the nation's goals. The security issue was dealt with directly. The act provided for a oil stockpile that would insulate the economy for six months during an embargo like that of 1973–74. The eventual higher price scheduled to follow the 1976 election year gift to the voters would stimulate marginal domestic sources otherwise below the level of profitability and would encourage consumers to switch to more efficient uses or to other fuels. The forty-month transition period, denounced as a cynical manipulation of the ignorant voter, might alternatively be viewed as a salutary transition period in which business and the public could shift to less energy intensive production and lifestyles. To artificially prolong the era of cheap oil would lead to just as great a shock in some future year as to suddenly decontrol oil on August 31 or November 15 or December 15 of 1975.

No one observing Congress and the administration in conflict over an oil law from January through December of 1975 could deny cost was being considered. The problem was not to keep the goal foremost in the debate, but to accomplish it. This issue illuminated the philosophical differences between the Republican administration and the Democratic congressional leadership. Republican party ideology holds that the free play of the market yields the lowest costs. Democratic ideology, on the other hand, still holds, true to its New Deal heritage, that the market is distorted and thus government must intervene to assure the greatest efficiency. Monopolies, oligopolies, lack of information, and other imperfections make a truly free market a myth. In addition Democrats believe that even if this market did work with full efficiency some people would always be disadvantaged and deserve compensation. Old people living only on Social Security (itself a New Deal creation) should get heat stamps just as the poor get food stamps. Yet while Ford pushed hard for decontrol, he was not so doctrinaire as to work unnecessary hardship. He was sometimes too lenient. In his February trip to Kansas and Texas to build public support for his program his advisors thought him too quick to promise more gasoline for tractors or a reinvestment tax credit. One of the major shifts in administration policy from the fall of 1974 to the spring of 1975 was attributable to rising concern about consumption. The White House worried that the stringent conservation measures it was advocating were deepening the recession and so eased up on them.

The 1975 Energy Act Ford pushed Congress so hard to pass gave him extensive powers to allocate resources—considerably more authority than he sought. He and his economic advisors like Treasury Secretary Simon and CEA Chairman Greenspan wanted allocation through the market. The 1975 act gave a wide range of nonmarket means. Many of these were standby powers only to be used in an emergency (such as gasoline rationing). Given the administration's economic predispositions Ford was unlikely to invoke them. He said repeatedly that he did not believe in rationing or even a steep gasoline tax. Yet President Nixon said similar things before instituting his New Economic Policy with the price and wage freeze of 1971. Even if Ford or some future President chose not to exercise such standby authority, its nonuse could be a political weapon for his critics or election opponent, who might charge the President with failing to serve the public interest in not invoking such powers.

The year-long debate leading up to the Energy Act illustrated the classic lessons of policy making. Republicans, both in the administration and in Congress, stood for more freedom for business so that the market could work its will. Ford's year-long aim (and sanction) was decontrol. In the end he accepted a plan for gradual decontrol, perhaps frightened himself at the inflationary prospect of immediate decontrol. His staunch advocacy of decontrol echoed his unequivocal opposition of the gasoline tax FEA Administrator Sawhill urged. The practical positions showed up as the regional conflicts. The major producing states of Texas, Louisiana, Oklahoma, and Alaska wanted to favor the producers. The middle South, served by TVA, and the Pacific northwest, served by the Bonneville Power Authority and cheap natural gas, were at odds with New England, which produced virtually no energy.

While party and regional differences may explain the basic conflicts they do not explain why it took so long to resolve the issues. The parties' economic preferences and the various states' energy endowments were clearly established before debate began. The Republicans did not suddenly realize they preferred market solutions, and New England did not suddenly realize it was short of fuel. Indeed the debate itself consumed only a few weeks time in each chamber. The Senate passed its version in April and the House, in September. Why did the whole process take until December?

Edward C. Banfield suggests a variety of reasons why governments cannot make and implement rational decisions.[17] Several apply here. One is the uncertainty of the future. Since neither Congress nor the administration knew how OPEC would behave, how America's European allies would respond, or whether the winter would be warmer or colder than usual, they were loath to make a decision, for any one decision is likely to be wrong.

A second point Banfield makes it that policy goals are never clear. The three analytic goals of security, low cost, and efficient allocation are heuristic, not necessarily those to which politicians subscribe. The Ford administration and the Ninety-fourth Congress had difficulty agreeing to a law because they could not agree what that law was supposed to do. Banfield points out the value of vagueness in this situation. Ambiguity masks unresolved problems.

A third reason is the stronger pull of present concerns than of future ones. President Ford and Congress, voting on the bill in 1975, were highly concerned about the 1976 election. Hence the law was designed to keep prices low in 1976 and raise them afterward. All the participants were concerned with maintaining themselves in office (or seeking a higher one). They did not really want long-term commitments, or any commitments. It seemed better politics for the President to blame Congress, and vice versa, than to resolve the issue.

Related to this is Banfield's observation that government tends to focus on the immediate crisis at the expense of longer-term problems. The Energy Act's aim was to get the United States safely through the 1970s, not to plan for the 1980s. Even the term "energy crisis" accentuated this mentality. The crisis was, to a large degree, a false crisis. It was not an *energy* crisis but a narrower *oil* crisis. The United States had more coal than coal buyers. The much publicized natural gas shortages derived directly from the Federal Power Commission's artificial suppression of the price prior to 1976. The problems with nuclear power came from the lethalness of the radioactive fuel, not lack of uranium. Falling water for hydroelectric plants was as common as it ever was. Coal, natural gas, uranium, and falling water might not have been as cheap as users would like, but this was far from a crisis. The crisis, to the extent there was one, derived from the OPEC cartel and from the United States's near hysterical reaction to it. The FEO allocation program during the 1973–74 embargo created severe regional shortages. New Jersey lacked gasoline while Pennsylvania had enough. The District of Columbia was desperately short, Virginia had more, and Georgia had plenty.

Ford sought to invoke a crisis atmosphere as a strategy for prodding Congress. His January State of the Union speech and the subsequent message accompanying his own legislative proposals set a ninety-day deadline. He imposed a $1 import fee on February 1 and vowed to impose another if Congress failed to act before his deadline. Though he extended the deadline, he lost patience and raised the fee to $2 on June 1. Also as threatened, he allowed controls on old oil to lapse on August 31 and vetoed the law granting a six-month extension. In return for promises to act quickly he set new deadlines of November 15 and December 15.

Ford's deadlines to Congress share many of the aspects of symbol manipulation expounded by Edelman. The threats to impose import fees or to decontrol oil prices were highly visible symbols designed to provide a cover for bargaining. But in Ford's case the threats were part of the bargaining, not mere facades. The administration actually did impose the fees and came close to decontrolling oil.

Definitely in the case of the fees, and probably in the case of decontrol, Ford did not really want to take the action. Though these were strong policies in their own right, the President put them forward more in order to force other action. In this they resembled Kissinger's hints of military capture of an OPEC oil field. The extreme policies might work but they were not the administration's first choices.

THE OUTCOME OF THE FORD ADMINISTRATION'S ENERGY POLICIES

Examining the Ford administration's policies on energy during its first year yields a number of small insights for the policy analyst but only a few major ones. This itself is an insight. The inconclusiveness of the policy analysis mirrors the inconclusiveness of the politics. As mentioned in the introduction, Gerald Ford began his presidency with a call for action on energy issues, yet a year later there had been little action. This holds true even when the Energy Policy and Conservation Act's final passage and signing in December 1975 is included. While Congress had passed a massive (270 page) law as Ford had been exhorting it to do for a year, the law gave the President little of what he wanted. To a large extent it froze the status quo.

Little progress had been made in achieving the goals of security, low cost, and efficient allocation. Secretary Kissinger's attempts to organize the oil-consuming nations into a counter-OPEC cartel had come to naught. The International Energy Agency remained a hope rather than a reality. The United States had not invaded Venezuela or the Persian Gulf to seize oil fields. Nor had the insinuations that it might do so worked. OPEC recognized it as a bluff. In September, 1975, OPEC even raised the price 10 percent. OPEC, it turned out, faced more armed danger from six allegedly pro-Palestinian thugs than from the American army, navy, and air force, for a few months later five men and a woman invaded the OPEC head-quarters in Vienna killing three men and menacing the lives of Sheik Yamani and Iranian Interior Minister Amouzegar. After a week of suspense the six flew the OPEC leaders to Algeria, where the terrorists eventually surrendered.

Project Independence brought no more economic and military security to the United States than did threatening OPEC with starvation, invasion, or unified bargaining. This ambiguous scheme dropped from sight, as did its offspring, the Energy Independence Authority designed by Vice President Rockefeller. The one creation that promised to do the most for economic and military security was the one billion barrel oil reserve authorized in the Energy Policy and Conservation Act.

The goal of low-cost energy was not achieved either. To a large extent such a goal is beyond the capacity of government since cost reflects the economic realities. Only when government is artificially inflating the price does it have the capacity to lower it. To do so otherwise would involve subsidizing the cost of fuel at the expense of something else. In the case of oil, a cartel of foreign governments was artificially inflating the price, and the American government was not in control of the situation. Its attempts to counter the foreign cartel met with no success because it could not secure the cooperation of other oil-consuming nations. Domestically the United States government did seek to reduce cost and did so, but in a false way. The Energy Act provided for lower prices in 1976 in return for higher prices later. The October, 1974, establishment of the Energy Research and Development

Administration promised a more valid means to lower energy costs. ERDA's prospects of lowering energy costs depend, however, on its luck in inventing and developing new technologies. Congress cannot legislate the laws of physics.

Despite a major effort the Ford administration was unable to make much of a change in the system of allocating energy supplies. The President had continually sought deregulation of old oil, yet the Energy Act kept the basic regulatory system in place. Although the law provided for a forty-month phase-out, it also expanded price controls to new oil in the interim. And there was no guarantee that Congress would not extend the controls before the May, 1979, expiration date. The administration's single gain in this area was that the President got authority to raise the price of oil up to 10 percent a year—7 percent to adjust for inflation and 3 percent to increase the incentives to explore and drill.

Oil is not the only fuel, even though the Ford administration neglected the others during its first year in office. The President did demonstrate his commitment to increase coal's availability by twice vetoing strip mining bills in December, 1974, and May, 1975. In September, 1975, the Interior Department moved to resume the sale of coal from government-owned land in the West. The department had imposed a moratorium two and a half years before because of public objections.

The administration's campaign to deregulate old oil had a counterpart in its campaign to deregulate the price of natural gas. The Federal Power Commission sets the price for natural gas shipped interstate. The controlled price of fifty-two cents per thousand cubic feet was only a third of the price of unregulated intrastate gas. The fifty-two cents price was a boon to the consumers only if there was gas available. Since the price was so low, producers refused to sell to the interstate pipelines. The consequence was shortages in the northern consuming states. In the summer of 1975 many realized that the shortages the following winter might be so severe that factories would close. Not until a year later did the Federal Power Commission raise the price of new gas to $1.42.

Nuclear power did not occupy a key role in Ford's energy program. The commercial plants in operation were proving more expensive than planned. Breakdowns were frequent and dangerous. In March a fire at TVA's Browns Ferry reactor revealed a danger that would cost billions of dollars in rebuilding the fifty-six reactors then in operation to insure their safety. A fire beneath the control room deactivated the pumps needed to cool the reactor just as the uranium pile was heating up uncontrollably. Fortunately there was just enough water in reserve to prevent a melt-down that would have destroyed the plant and released radioactive gases into the atmosphere. By eight o'clock that night seven of the plant's twelve emergency systems had failed.

Such technical failures push light water nuclear plants further into the future as a major source of power. ERDA may hold the key to twenty-first century energy from fast breeder reactors, fusion, and solar and gas thermal energy, but these futuristic forms offered no aid for Ford's more immediate problems.

IMPLICATIONS FOR AMERICAN POLICY MAKING

Energy was a particularly difficult issue. Domestic needs conflicted with international ones. One state's needs conflicted with another's. Short-term needs conflicted with long-term needs. Partisan conflicts overlaid the basic issues. Republican ideology of market freedom conflicted with Democratic ideology of market supervision. Institutionally, a Republican administration faced a Democratic Congress. Energy was not an issue suitable for logrolling. On many issues a small group has an intense interest while the vast majority care little. This makes a series of trade-offs possible whereby everyone gets the one item most important. Energy is different. There no one is disinterested. Giving to one means taking from another.

While President Ford had called for action, his own action was negative, aimed at negating the problems. He sought to negate the oil shortage through decontrol. If the FEA stopped holding down the price of old oil there would be more oil used more efficiently. He acted to negate unreasonable land restoration demands which would prevent the needed mining of coal. His Project Independence was intended to negate America's dependence on insecure foreign sources of oil and thus also negate the power of OPEC to rig the price of oil. Yet although the Ford administration sought to negate the evils causing energy shortages, this was a hard policy to convey. It is easier to exhort the Congress and the public to support something more positive.

Even a good negative style was hard to maintain. Kissinger wanted to organize the International Energy Agency. Rockefeller wanted the Energy Independence Authority. Sawhill wanted a high gasoline tax. Ford, himself, found it easy to slip into calls for action, proposals for new programs, and advocacy of new agencies. The public and congressional expectation of leadership demanded that the President initiate new activity, not restrain his administration and himself.

Ford's negative approach showed in his relations with Congress. He used the veto more frequently than previous Presidents. He vetoed two strip mining bills, the six-month oil price control extension, and the oil import fee suspension. Threats were another manifestation of the President's negative style. Many of these were threats to veto laws. One threat, which he carried out twice, was to impose a dollar import fee if Congress did not act within ninety days. The first fee went on February 1, and the second, June 1. During the summer and fall of 1975 Ford threatened to abruptly decontrol old oil if Congress did not pass a comprehensive oil law.

The Ford administration threatened foreign nations as well. International protocol demanded more circumlocution than when dealing with Congress but the messages got through. During the September 1974 "get tough" period, Ford and Kissinger politely threatened to starve or invade the oil-exporting countries.

The administration's negative style was not the President's alone but extended to his key advisors. Much of the internal politics within the White House and Cabinet may be understood in these terms. When a resolution came, the victors were usually those disposed toward negative solutions. Treasury Secretary Simon and CEA Chairman Greenspan fit this mold. The more positive members of the official family lost out in these struggles. Ford first demoted Sawhill, then forced him to resign, for continued advocacy of strong government action. Rockefeller's Energy Independence Authority faded quietly almost as soon as the Vice President put it forward. Shortly thereafter Rockefeller recognized that his predisposition to government activity was not welcome and bowed out of consideration for the vice-presidential nomination in 1976.

Evaluation of energy policy in the first year of the Ford administration reveals both substantive and procedural conclusions. Substantively, the nation made little progress in achieving the three goals of security, low cost, and efficient allocation. In part this was because the goals were beyond the scope of any government to achieve and in part this was because the Ford administration could not secure the agreement of foreign allies, the executive branch bureaucracy, or Congress to achieve the goals in the manner it wished. When the goals could not be achieved, symbol manipulation became a substitute.

Procedurally, energy has proved to be an especially intractable problem since it deeply concerns all fifty states, as well as the other industrial and energy-producing nations of the world. It is important to everyone and there is little room for bargaining. Political party ideology splits on the extent to which the government should enter into the market by controlling prices or loaning capital. When one party controls the White House and the other Congress prompt enactment of laws is especially difficult for Republicans and Democrats do not agree what those laws should be. The Ford administration's negative policies, in its first year, may well have been the proper course for relieving the nation's energy ills, but it made the President's leadership role more difficult.

4

The Politics of Campaign Finance Reform in America

David A. Caputo

Few things are as typically American as American political campaigns. Building on a variety of time-honored campaigning techniques such as fund raisers, endorsements, and political rallies, recent political candidates have sought to increase their impact on the voters by adding sophisticated new techniques such as statistical analyses of voting behavior, mass media spot advertisements, and directed regional appeals. In all of the hoopla and often seeming chaos accompanying American political campaigns, whether for the presidency or for a lower office, one ingredient—seldom discussed and rarely understood—is always present: money.

Regardless of what it is called, or how it is raised or spent, money remains a major factor in political campaigns in the United States. Even in the 1976 presidential contest between Jimmy Carter and Gerald Ford, the first presidential election to be regulated by the public funding provisions of the 1974 Federal Election Campaign Act, money played an important role throughout the campaign, just as it did in the 1976 congressional elections. A review of the journalistic accounts of the Carter-Ford campaign reveals their emphasis on, and even preoccupation with, campaign decisions involving fund raising and expenditures. While such revelations are not unimportant, they may sometimes obscure the larger issue: the question of what role money plays in a democracy and whether regulating its use in political campaigns is possible or even desirable. Considered in this light the politics of campaign finance becomes much more interesting and assumes greater importance.

While it is impossible in one case study to consider all aspects of these questions, it is possible to consider several major implications of the movement for campaign finance reform and to draw certain generalizations about the American political process. In this case study, a variety of legislation will be considered, and the relationship between policy-making institutions and the general public will be explored, along with the significance of the findings for a democratic society. From the outset, it should be kept in mind that the policy-making process responsible for

71

political finance decisions is not very different from the policy-making process in other areas and that the lessons learned from this case may be useful in understanding other policy decisions.

In any event, emphasis will not be on which candidate spent what amount for what purpose, or on the negative influence money has had on American politics. Rather, this chapter will focus on the specifics of the campaign finance reform legislation in the 1970s and the complex set of events and decisions which influenced its development, consideration, and implementation. As this case involves more than one particular decision, it clearly illustrates the complexities involved in public policy making in the United States. It is these general observations which are important to an increased understanding of the American political system.

Finally, the reader is cautioned to avoid overemphasizing the significance of money or its role as a political resource. While money is obviously important to any political campaign, it is not the only resource available to potential candidates and actual participants.[1] Money cannot assure voter allegiance, buy large numbers of volunteer workers, or guarantee positive media coverage. In many cases, money may even be detrimental to these and other campaign objectives. Money should be seen as a means to an end rather than as an end in and of itself. If it is viewed this way, its influence can be studied objectively rather than simply decried as a threat to the electoral process.

Thus it is now time to explore the course of recent campaign finance reform in the United States and its impact on American politics in general. Interested readers may consult any of the sources listed in the notes section if they desire a more detailed account of the specific decisions or events reviewed here.[2]

THE CALL FOR REFORM

Federal regulation of campaign financing in the United States is not new. In fact, such regulation has often been proposed and discussed at both the national and state levels of government. As with any public policy issue, however, campaign finance regulation becomes quite complicated, and proposals for change need to be clearly understood. Any attempt to regulate the use of money and its impact during a campaign usually concerns itself with the following set of questions.

1. Should there be individual contribution limits? By limiting the total amounts of individual contributions, it may be possible to limit the influence that an individual contributer will have over the candidate. It is generally assumed that an individual who contributes $250,000 to a candidate's campaign will have greater influence than the individual who contributes $250 or $25. Thus the rationale for limiting individual contributions is that it limits undue individual influence, as well as equalizing financial resources. Particularly large contributions are feared to have inordinate influence on the candidate's specific policy decisions. Those favoring limiting contributions argue that by doing so the election process becomes more open and responsive to more people and therefore more democratic. As the upcoming discussion indicates, debate over the desirability and legality of individual contribution limits, as well as the specific amounts involved, is frequent and lively.

Large contributors are common in American politics and especially in presidential politics. Contrary to popular belief, not all are Republicans. In 1972 eighteen individuals officially contributed more than $100,000 to Senator George

McGovern's campaign. Stewart Mott led all reported contributors with his $724,000 contribution to McGovern's campaign.[3]

2. What role should contributions of corporations, labor unions, and other large organizations be permitted to play in financing political campaigns? The role of such groups is of crucial importance in the United States, where groups of all types provide a variety of political and financial support for candidates. This support can take a variety of forms, but almost always involves some sort of endorsement which is communicated to the group's membership in the hopes they will vote accordingly. In addition, these organizations, whether labor unions or big firms, can muster significant financial resources, which are important to any political candidate. The financial resources of a corporation or a labor union are usually greater than the resources of a single individual. If the candidate who receives such support then feels obligated to support policy beneficial to the groups which provided financial support, what will be the impact on the public?

The philosophical question behind this issue is whether these large organizations should have such great potential for influencing the electoral process. Labor unions and business corporations are seldom controlled in a democratic fashion, and certainly the leaders in these organizations are interested in increasing their power as well as strengthening the organization's position vis-à-vis the political process. For all of these reasons, and others more practical, such as the influence of labor unions in the Democratic party and of large corporations in the Republican party, considerable attention has been given to discussions of ways to control or regulate group and organizational activity.

3. What is the proper expenditure level for campaigns for different political offices? In recent years the general public and political leaders themselves have become concerned with the staggering cost of running for public office. It has been estimated that the McGovern-Nixon presidential contest in 1972 involved over $100 million in campaign expenditures and that the 1976 presidential contest between Jimmy Carter and Gerald Ford resulted in expenditures of over $40 million.[4] It is not unusual for a U.S. Senate race in a large state to cost the candidate more than $1 million, and in some competitive House districts candidates often spend over $150,000 in seeking election. These figures represent expenditures only and not the value of time spent by staff or volunteers; if these were included, the total expenditures would probably be several times greater. Because of these very high costs and increases due to technological developments, those interested in financial regulation often consider imposing a ceiling on the total costs which can be incurred in any campaign by any one candidate.

Once again the theoretical rationale for such limitations is easily explained. *If there are no limits on what can be spent, isn't it realistic to assume that elections in the United States will be dominated by those candidates who can raise large amounts of funds and that the "average" person will be effectively prevented from seeking nomination and election?* This argument has considerable appeal for American politics with its myth of the dominance of the "common man." Proponents of limiting expenditures argue that such a practice would limit the actual ability of money to determine election outcomes, with the net result that American politics would become more democratic.

An important counter-argument to this position maintains that limiting expenditures clearly favors the incumbent or the well-known individual since such a limitation will restrict the exposure a challenger can obtain. Thus it could be argued that the limitation of expenditures does not open the system up, but actually helps to insure the continued domination of those already in power or those with well-known names (such as sports or movie figures). Final resolution of this point is impossible, but its complexities need to be fully understood.

4. Should there be restrictions on how campaign funds can be spent? The issue of permissible and not permissible campaign expenditures often evokes lengthy debate. While there may be general agreement that campaign funds should not be used to bribe voters or to disrupt the opponent's campaign, there often is considerable disagreement over whether the funds can legitimately be used to raise other funds or to provide travel for the press corps which may accompany a candidate. An example involving the former case illustrates this point.

In recent years the direct mail approach to raising money has become more popular with many candidates pursuing public office.[5] A private firm is hired to raise money by supervising the direct solicitation of individuals. Thus individuals receive personal letters requesting funds and may respond to them with contributions. Expenses cover obtaining the names, preparing and processing the letters and returns, and then keeping track of who has contributed what amount. This is done at a cost, and for each dollar received via direct mail, twenty-five to seventy-five cents may have to be spent. One might well question whether it is legitimate to use campaign funds to raise other campaign funds in this manner. Nevertheless, direct mail campaigns can be quite productive and can broaden the base of support by tapping many small contributors and thus increasing individual involvement.

The point is that it is indeed difficult to reach agreement on what is and what is not an acceptable campaign expenditure. Despite this difficulty, the question of how campaign funds should be spent inevitably arises as a major point whenever financial regulation is discussed Once again, as in usually the case in politics, a series of trade-offs has occurred. Policy makers must decide which are acceptable.

5. Finally, what methods of regulation should be employed to enforce the provisions which are adopted, and what penalties should be exacted for violations? *Enforcement is a crucial part of policy because no matter how strict the law may be, if enforcement is weak or lacking, it will have little or no effect on behavior.*

Self-enforcement has been a popular option, but is it realistic to expect those involved in such a high-risk undertaking as elections to adequately police their own behavior? In many cases self-enforcement is tantamount to asking the wolf to guard the chickens. Though advocacy of self-enforcement has given way to some extent to recognition of the need for regulatory bodies, there is still considerable disagreement and discussion over the composition and role the regulatory and enforcing bodies should have. For instance, should enforcement be carried out by an independent regulatory commission or by a group composed of those being regulated? Should violations of the law be defined in terms of specific penalties or should punishment be up to the discretion of the authority responsible for administering the regulations? These are not easy questions to answer since complex regulations may require complex enforcement procedures. Without such procedures, enforcement may be so ineffective as to make the entire set of regulations and rules obsolete and impossible to enforce. Thus the end result may be the lack of a well-functioning regulatory system and the greater likelihood of frequent abuse of the regulations.

These five points provide the basis for a systematic consideration of campaign reform in general and the 1974 Federal Election Campaign Act in particular. What follows is such an account with specific emphasis on the relationships among the various institutions and actors comprising American politics. In order for the ensuing discussion to be understood, it is important to place the legislation in its proper political perspective.

To begin with, the 1974 legislation was an attempt to strengthen earlier legislative efforts to bring tighter control to the nominating and election processes in the United States. The 1971 Campaign Reform Act, which will be discussed in depth in the next section, was the most comprehénsive approach to campaign regulation and reform since the Corrupt Practices Act of 1925.[6] The 1971 legislation (formally signed into law in early 1972) was the result of extensive political debate and conflict. The shortcomings of the 1971 legislation were made obvious by the major domestic events of the early 1970s and the furor over Watergate and its implications for campaign finance.

Watergate

Watergate turned out to be more than a "third rate burglary attempt." Not only were individual lives and reputations badly damaged, but the stability of the American political system itself was threatened. Though space does not permit a full discussion of Watergate and all of its implications, it is necessary to specify the areas in which Watergate exposed the need for campaign finance reform.[7] Perhaps the most damaging piece of evidence was the following tape-recorded exchange between President Nixon and H. R. Haldeman, his chief of staff, concerning the money paid to the Watergate burglars:

> *Nixon:* . . . They've traced the money? Who'd they trace it to? . . . It isn't from the committee though, from Starr?
>
> *Haldeman:* Yeah, it is. It's directly traceable and there's some money through some Texas people that went to the Mexican bank which can also be traced to the Mexican bank. . . .[8]

Not only was the Committee to Reelect the President directly linked to the burglary attempt, further evidence indicates that illegal contributions were common, that campaign funds were used for illegal break-ins as well as disruptive tactics aimed at opponents, and that promises of future appointments and favorable policy decisions were made in exchange for campaign contributions.[9] In short, the Watergate affair revealed the inadequacy of campaign finance legislation and sounded a rallying cry for those advocating reform.

Coupled with public demand for change was the determination of a variety of individuals and interest groups to insure the enactment of legislation designed to regulate and control campaign finances. Most notable among these was Common Cause, which was founded in the 1960s by John Gardner as an organization pledged to develop grassroots participation in politics and to increase the responsiveness of the national government to the needs of the populace. Emphasis was to be on reform through public accountability.[10] As will be shown later, Common Cause exerted considerable influence and had substantial impact during the legislative debate and subsequent judicial review of the campaign reform legislation.

While the revelations of Watergate and the dedication of a cadre of individual groups committed to change were important impetuses, the national "mood" was what ultimately set in motion the drive to change campaign finance legislation.

Inertia and entrenched power often make it difficult to bring about major changes in this country. Individuals interested in change must be prepared to wait for the proper conditions and time if significant success is to be obtained. Such was the case with campaign reform—Watergate was the catalyst needed to increase public demand for reform and to provide the reformers with the opportunity they needed to enact major changes. This experience suggests that reformers may have to wait till a national crisis creates the environmental conditions which permit the consideration and possible adoption of their reform measures. *In other words, the policy-making system may not be open to a major change until a crisis has developed, and that change is more likely to be a response to the crisis than an anticipation of the need to change.* The significance of this for orderly change in a democratic state should not be overlooked. If in fact the policy-making system is truly responsive only to crisis, one may logically question how well elected leaders will be able to lead—to avert crises—and ultimately how well the country will be able to adapt to a rapidly changing world.

LEGISLATION PRIOR TO 1974

Prior to the 1974 Federal Election Campaign Act there were several attempts to regulate campaign financing and expenditures. In the early 1900s, an era characterized by extensive reform measures, reformers and even some political candidates actively sought campaign finance reform. In 1905 President Theodore Roosevelt used his State of the Union message to call for major campaign reforms.[11] His proposal was a far-reaching one and specifically stated that "all contributions by corporations to any political committee or for any political purpose should be forbidden by law."[12] Federal legislation was passed as early as 1907, and more was passed in 1910 and 1911; however, the Federal Corrupt Practices Act of 1925 was the first major federal legislation of its kind prior to 1971.[13]

The Corrupt Practices Act of 1925

The 1925 Corrupt Practices Act set expenditure limits of $10,000 per candidate for Senate general elections and $2,500 for House elections, or an amount equal to three cents for each vote cast in the last election for that office but not more than $25,000 for the Senate and $5,000 for the House. Thus states with more than 833,000 voters in the last Senate race were subject to the $25,000 upper limit. The legislation contained several provisions which were to remain essential aspects of campaign reform, among them the different limits on House and Senate campaign expenditures and increased allowances for more populous states. No expenditure limits were placed on presidential contests.

In addition to these expenditure limits, the 1925 legislation also ruled out campaign contributions by national banks, corporations, or federal employees. The assumption was that, by controlling the sources of donations to political campaigns, corruption or undue influence could be kept to a minimum. The 1925 legislation also specified regular reporting of gifts over $100. Again, the assumption was that such reporting, which was to be done with the Secretary of the Senate and the Clerk of the House of Representatives, would provide the public with the information it needed to discern who was providing the financial resources to various candidates. Once this information was available to the public, it could then decide its own reaction and course of action.

Most people are surprised to learn that these specific regulations were enacted as early as 1925. What is more, the Hatch Act (the Clean Politics Act of 1939) added several other important restrictions on campaign activities.[14] This legislation regulated the political activities of federal employees and, as amended in 1940, gave Congress the right to regulate primary elections when federal offices were involved, placed a ceiling of $3 million on the expenditures of any political committee acting in more than one state, and limited contributions to $5,000 by any individual during any particular calendar year or particular election for a federal office.

To many observers it appeared that federal elections, in fact, were well regulated and that the pernicious influence of "big money" was thoroughly restricted by combining outright restrictions with public disclosure. History proved that this was not the case and that abuses of the statutes were both flagrant and widespread. The abuses were so obvious and pervasive that Congressman Wayne Hays, in a statement made during congressional consideration of campaign finance reform legislation in 1971, remarked:

> I think everybody knows that the Federal Corrupt Practices Act of 1925 . . . is more honored in the breach than it is in the enforcement of it because there are so many loopholes . . . and consequently there is no real limitation and no real enforcement.[15]

Evasions of Campaign Finance Restrictions

Ingenious methods were devised to avoid meeting the legal requirements for campaign finance. It is worth noting here the most typical means utilized to avoid both the spirit and the letter of the legislation. Plays were developed for all three areas of legislation: contributions, expenditures, and enforcement.

In the area of *contributions,* the restrictions on who could contribute and what amounts were permissible were avoided or circumvented in a variety of ways, but three are most important. In the first place, wealthy individuals were limited to a maximum $5,000 contribution, but other members of the family were also entitled to the same $5,000 contribution. Thus a wealthy family, assuming it had a large number of sons and daughters or other close relatives, could contribute a significant amount of funds to a favored candidate. This tactic permitted wealthy individuals to tap their family resources in order to gain access to public office.

A second variation was that the contributions could go to state or local campaign committees and not be subject to the $5,000 limitation. Thus a contributor could donate $25,000 or any amount desired to the committee to elect candidate X if that committee was organized at the state or local level. The state or local committee was then permitted to contribute those funds to a national committee working for candidate X. Very effective and very legal, but obviously a violation of the spirit of the legislation, which was intended to regulate the total amount of funds involved.

Perhaps the strongest admonition against this type of practice was offered by Senator Edmund S. Muskie in 1971 before a Senate subcommittee dealing with campaign reform. Muskie stated:

Now the belief that all citizens, regardless of wealth, should have an equal opportunity to participate in politics is an axiom of our political system. . . . But as our practices of equality in voting have grown, our opportunities for equality in seeking office have shrunk. Once again, wealth is a barrier to democratic practice. . . . Certainly great wealth or the ability to solicit that wealth is not a proper prerequisite for office in a democracy. Nor is it healthy to have elected officials making decisions about the common good knowing that they will depend upon wealthy interests to survive reelection.[16]

A third method of circumventing the law was practiced by corporations, which were prohibited from making cash contributions. They could effectively evade the law by giving large bonuses to their employees, who just by coincidence donated a sum of money about the size of the bonus to a political candidate or party. In addition, the services or products which a corporation might have to offer, such as office space, transportation, or equipment, could be utilized by a political party or candidate and the bill for them never collected. Thus, while direct cash contributions were forbidden, it was possible to contribute indirectly to a campaign.

These three examples clearly show how any law designed to control campaign finance can easily be evaded if the actual legislative restrictions are not made clear and enforcement procedures not clearly established. This becomes even more apparent when the other two aspects of the legislation in effect prior to 1971 are considered.

Though the 1925 act and subsequent amendments were specific on the *expenditure* amounts allowed in federal elections, they also specified that money expended without the candidate's knowledge or consent was not subject to the expenditure restrictions. Thus, if a candidate was not informed of where campaign funds were coming from or how they were being used, it was possible to claim that the expenditure requirements were not applicable. The result of this was that campaign treasurers often became central figures as both fund raisers and planners and were reluctant to publicly discuss campaign finance with the candidate. To do so would jeopardize the candidate's later claim of ignorance.

In addition, since the expenditure limits applied to each specific committee, candidates and parties were quick to organize multiple committees, which were then each entitled to spend the legal limit. By organizing in this fashion and by developing techniques to take advantage of other provisions in the laws, it was possible for candidates and their supporters to spend whatever amounts of money they could raise. The situation was so offensive that Senator Mike Gravel testified before a 1971 Senate subcommittee that

under the present system of financing campaigns exclusively from private funds, the candidate who does not have great personal wealth must raise these large sums by relying on large contributors—a fact that understandably tends to foster compromising obligations. This potential of large contributions for corruption is aggravated by the secrecy and subterfuge surrounding present campaign-financing practices.[17]

Despite the fact that several candidates have been denied their seats because of alleged violations of the 1925 act and its amendments, *enforcement* practices have usually aided those interested in working around instead of complying with the law.[18] Prior to the 1971 legislation, it was common practice to simply ignore the various provisions in campaign finance legislation and to attempt to restrict their enforcement. The earlier comment by Representative Hays is indicative of the prevailing attitude towards enforcement practices under the 1925 legislation. Certainly one of the main reasons for violations of the legislation was the realization that enforcement was unlikely.

The news media and a few members of Congress regularly embarrassed other congressmen by making public their failure to file complete contribution and expenditure records. The usual result was a flurry of public indignation and subsequent inaction by either the House or the Senate. As late as 1964 several Senators reported zero receipts and zero expenditures in their campaigns even though they were involved in major contested elections.[19] In similar fashion, the Justice Department during Eisenhower's presidency and Attorney General Herbert Brownell's tenure refused to prosecute possible violations, claiming that the initiative for such action had to come from the respective congressional body.[20]

The result of this unwillingness to apply and enforce the law was increased unwillingness to abide by it. After all, if violations were to be tolerated, why should a candidate put himself at a potential electoral disadvantage by obeying the law? Thus campaign reform was largely rhetoric and individual candidates and committees were able to ignore the legal requirements with little fear of public disfavor and even less fear of formal action against them. Instead of legal restrictions, what one had was a series of legal loopholes which were to be ignored and evaded in as many different ways as possible.

While it is easy to blame the politicians and the individuals responsible for abusing both the letter and the spirit of the legislation, it should be pointed out that the public did not demand strict enforcement. In fact, violators of the campaign regulations were regularly reelected to public office. This raises an interesting question about the relationship between the general public and the regulatory process. Why didn't the public react more strongly? Was it ignorant of the abuses or simply indifferent? On the one hand, it could be argued that the campaign finance laws are too complex to be fully understood by the general public. In that case the elected leaders and news media should be held responsible for preventing abuses. On the other hand, it could be argued that the public is indifferent because of its acceptance of widespread corruption and dishonesty in government. Why should the public become aroused when action will only lead to changes which sound and look good but which will do little to change a basic character defect common to political candidates? The implications of the two positions are different. In the former, increased disclosure should be able to bring about reform; in the latter, alienation from the system will be much more difficult to combat. In any case, there was no sustained and widespread public indignation over the abuses of campaign legislation till the late 1960s. This public indignation led to the Federal Election Campaign Act of 1971, which was signed into law in February of 1972. The next section considers that piece of legislation and its unique approach to campaign reform.

The 1971 Federal Election Campaign Act

Abuses of campaign finance and expenditure statutes prior to 1971 were quite common. Their flagrancy ired advocates of reform and adequate enforcement of the existing statutes. But the factor which was most important in bringing about discussion and ultimately new legislation was the rapid increase in campaign costs and expenditures. For instance, *Congressional Quarterly* reported that nonpresidential radio and television spending for campaigns grew from $20 million in 1962 to $30 million in 1966 and nearly $60 million in 1970.[21] This tripling in eight years was a dramatic example of the surging campaign costs associated with more extensive use of the electronic media. Figure 4.1 presents an even more dramatic view of the tremendous increase in campaign spending since 1960. As that figure indicates, the largest increases in direct campaign expenditures since 1912 occurred in 1960, 1964, and 1968; the figure also indicates that the cost per voter increased dramatically during that same time period. Thus it is clear that the campaign committees were simply spending more money in general and that costs had increased.

The actual dollar amounts involved are no less impressive. Dr. Herbert Alexander, director of the Citizen's Research Foundation, commented on these amounts in Senate testimony in 1971:

> I estimate that $300 million was spent in 1968. . . . This represents a 50 percent increase from 1964 . . . and an increase of more than 100 percent since 1952. . . .[22]

Alexander, however, went on to place these costs in perspective.

> Considered in the aggregate, politics is not overpriced. . . . $300 million is just about one-tenth of one percent of the amounts spent by governments at all levels . . . $300 million is hardly more than the amount spent in 1968 by the largest commercial advertiser in the U.S. which . . . had a $270 million advertising budget in 1968.[23]

Regardless of whether you think political campaign costs are a bargain or not, they do represent large amounts of money and they did increase substantially in the 1960s.

An important aspect of this problem which is often overlooked is the fact that the increased costs of campaigning are even more burdensome to the challenger than they are to the incumbent since the challenger is usually less well known than the incumbent and usually has less of an opportunity to raise funds. This discrepancy introduces an ironic note into the discussion of campaign reform. Keep in mind that Congress is responsible for enacting campaign finance and expenditure legislation. State laws apply only to candidates in that state for a state office; federal statutes are needed for federal offices. *Is it realistic to expect a partisan group to enact legislation which may make challenges to its members more easily financed and perhaps more successful?* Put another way, isn't it more likely to assume that a representative's or senator's perception of his own self-interest will have considerable importance in influencing the final position he or she takes? If one accepts these points, then it is easy to understand why Congress has been reluctant to enact far-reaching legislation which would have the tendency to influence the outcome of the reelection campaigns of its membership. Carried a step farther, it becomes even easier to understand why members of Congress, despite the importance of partisan party affiliations, may be more likely to enact legislation influencing presidential campaigns than to reach decisions affecting themselves. This is not meant to say that nonpartisan motives are totally ignored or to argue that the sole motivation for

Campaign Spending

Indexes of Direct Campaign Expenditures
by National-Level Committees, Number of Votes
Cast, and Consumer Prices

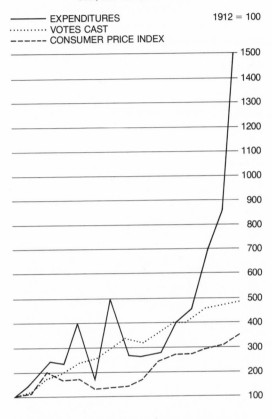

FIGURE 4.1. Campaign Spending Increases: 1912–1968. (*Source:* Statement of Representative Wayne L. Hays to Subcommittee on Elections of the Committee on House Administration of the U.S. House of Representatives, U.S. Government Printing Office, 1971, p. 8. Data from Citizens' Research Foundation, Elections Research Century Fund.)

congressional action is individual self-interest. It is meant only to suggest that such factors need to be placed in their proper perspective and that their influence needs to be fully considered. This is true not only for the Federal Election Campaign Act of 1971, but for any legislation intended to control an elected political leader's behavior.

Despite these tendencies, the 1971 legislation was important for a variety of reasons. First of all, it replaced the Corrupt Practices Act of 1925 with a new set of regulations and rules. A summary of the 1971 legislation follows.

In the area of *individual contributions,* the legislation placed an upper limit of $50,000 on the amount any candidate or his immediate family could donate to his presidential or vice-presidential campaign, and limits of $35,000 and $25,000 respectively, for Senate and House campaigns. Individual contributions of $100 or more also had to be reported. However, there was no provision limiting the maximum an individual outside the candidate's family could contribute.[24]

Even more important were the provisions governing *corporation and labor union contributions.* Of these, three provisions gave greater freedom for increased political action on the part of corporations and unions.[25] The legislation permitted:

> communications by a corporation to its stockholders and their families or by a labor organization to its members and their families on any subject; non-partisan registration and get-out-the-vote campaigns by a corporation aimed at its stockholders . . . or by a labor organization aimed at its members and their families . . . and the establishment, administration, and solicitation of contributions to a separate segregated fund to be utilized for political purposes by a corporation or labor organization. . . .[26]

Thus corporations and labor unions could effectively be major participants and contributors in any political campaign under this legislation. The practical result of these provisions was to broaden the overall role of corporations and labor unions in the campaign process.

There were no general *expenditure limits,* but there was the provision that expenditures for advertising in communications media be limited to $50,000 or ten cents per eligible voter, whichever was greater.[27] These and the following provisions were made as amendments to the Communications Act of 1935. Thus a state with a voting age population over 500,000 would have a substantially higher limit and in reality the total cost involved could be much higher than $50,000. These provisions also applied to presidential candidates in the respective states. This point is closely related to another point dealing with restrictions in the *use of expenditures.*

The 1971 legislation capped a long and often bitter struggle between proponents of campaign reform, the White House, and the electronic media. The 1971 act specifically defined communication media to include billboard advertising, radio and television, newspapers, and even some form of telephone solicitations. It was agreed that 60 percent of the total for communications spending could be used for broadcast costs.[28] Thus if a candidate was entitled to expend $50,000, $30,000 was the maximum that could be used for radio and television time. The 1971 legislation also included the provision that broadcasters sell candidates advertising at the lowest unit rate in effect for the time used.[29] What this in fact meant was that political candidates, in many cases, would receive lower rates than if the candidates purchased time under usual circumstances. The National Association of Broadcasters strenuously opposed this provision and attempted to have it deleted, but unsuccessfully.[30] These provisions clearly attempted to control the costs associated with political advertising.

In addition to the expenditure limitations, the legislation specifically included primary elections and required that any expenditure incurred by an agent of the candidate would be charged against the total of funds allowed to the candidate. Promises of employment or appointments in exchange for political support were specifically forbidden. While on the surface these changes appeared far-reaching and comprehensive, the provisions dealing with enforcement practices indicated that regulation and enforcement patterns were not going to be dramatically different from prior legislation.

In its provisions for *regulation and enforcement*, the 1971 legislation required all campaign committees which anticipated receipts over $1,000 to register with the appropriate election officials, to report all income on a regular basis, to report any contribution exceeding $5,000 within forty-eight hours, and to report all contributions, including the name and address of the contributor, within forty-eight hours.[31]

The Clerk of the House of Representatives and the Secretary of the Senate were responsible for overseeing the campaign finance administrative details and general compliance with regulations. In addition, the General Accounting Office was designated as the supervising agency for presidential candidates.[32] There were attempts to authorize the creation of a separate organization to oversee the administration of the legislation, but these were unsuccessful.[33] Thus a pattern similar to the one established by the 1925 act remained; regulation and enforcement of campaign finance codes were entrusted to those being regulated. As a review of the legislation indicates, prompt and accurate public disclosure was again seen as the way to control campaign finance abuses.

Given these provisions, it was very clear that Congress had indeed failed to alter its basic approach to campaign finance and expenditure regulation—an approach which repeatedly had been shown to be ineffective, widely abused, and often so complicated that legal loopholes and personal interpretations dominated. Campaign finance reform was still needed, a fact underscored by Deputy Attorney General Richard B. Kleindienst's testimony before the 1971 House Subcommittee on Elections:

> There are no dissenters to the proposition that (election law) reform is badly needed. A democracy functions largely on trust—trust on the part of its citizens in their representatives and the means by which they are selected. In this country, that trust is being eroded by cynicism and the causes of the erosion are apparent. Our so-called election laws are archaic, unrealistic, and unenforceable; therefore, they are ignored, to the dismay of the public. . . . The problem now is to agree upon effective means to restore that confidence.[34]

Despite such statements, it took the 1972 election and the trauma of Watergate to bring about major change in the legislation regulating campaign finance.

THE 1974 FEDERAL ELECTION CAMPAIGN ACT

The Impact of Watergate

The 1972 campaigns, both for the presidency and for Congress, proved a high-water mark in campaign spending. Even though the reports of the Federal Communications Commission on spending in the presidential race indicate that the Republicans spent about one-third as much in 1972 for radio and television time as they spent in 1968 ($4.3 million compared with $12.6 million) and the Democrats spent about the same ($6.2 million compared with $6.1 million),[35] the 1972 race was still the most expensive in American history, estimates of the actual expenditures totalling as much as $100 million.[36] Add to this the expenditures for House and Senate seats and it becomes readily apparent that campaigning for a major office in the United States requires large expenditures and considerable financial support. Even in a state as politically safe for the Democrats as Mississippi, Senate incumbent James Eastland spent over $100,000 for television and radio in 1972.[37] In the more evenly contested and larger state of Illinois, in the same year, Senate incumbent Charles Percy spent over $275,000 on radio and television advertisements.[38] The fact that Eastland and Percy spent such large sums of money is indicative of the high cost of campaigning for state and national office.

It was not the high cost of campaigning, however, or even the general acknowledgement that existing campaign finance legislation was too loosely drawn to be effective, that provided the impetus for major reform, but rather Watergate and the domestic crisis it represented. From the time of the burglary in Democratic National Headquarters in June, 1972, to President Nixon's resignation in August, 1974, the domestic crisis deepened and with it came public outcries for meaningful campaign financial reforms. While it is unnecessary to go into the Watergate investigation in great detail, it is important to summarize the aspects of Watergate relating to campaign finance and the abuses of the 1971 legislation. Illegal contributions, deceptive reporting practices, and illegal expenditure of campaign funds were characteristic of the 1972 Nixon campaign. As the Senate Select Committee on Presidential Campaign Activities (hereafter referred to as the Watergate Committee) Final Report points out, the Nixon reelection campaign effort was actually split into two parts—before and after April 7, 1972, the starting date for the implementation of the 1971 Federal Election Campaign Act. In fact April 7 became important because of the disclosure requirement, which resulted in "large contributions . . . including many in cash" right before the deadline.[39] A review of Chapter 4 of the final Watergate Committee report on campaign financing provides a useful summary of abuses and statutory violations.[40] As a result of its investigation, the Watergate Committee recommended the following:

1. Establishing an independent and nonpartisan election commission to enforce federal elections laws;
2. Banning cash contributions and expenditures over $100 in all federal campaigns:
3. Requiring presidential and vice-presidential candidates to designate one committee as their central campaign committee, with one or more banks as their campaign depositories;
4. Setting presidential expenditure limits at twelve cents times the number in the voting-age population for the general election;
5. Setting individual contributions to presidential campaigns at $6,000, with that amount split equally between primary and general election campaigns;
6. Granting tax credits for individual contributions to political candidates;
7. Rejecting public financing of campaigns;
8. Excluding campaign contributions from foreign nationals;
9. Prohibiting presidential appointees and staff members from soliciting campaign funds while in governmental service or for a year after leaving;

10. Placing stringent limitations on organizations' contributions to presidential campaigns; and

11. Adopting felony statutes for any violation of the major provisions of the campaign legislation.[41]

Careful examination of these recommendations reveals the influence the allegations of secret slush funds, illegal attempts to disrupt opponents' campaigns, and extensive illegal contributions had on subsequent policy development. Perhaps the most important recommendations were those for limits on individual contributions, rejection of public financing, and establishment of an election commission. Debate and controversy characterized reaction to the recommendations. The stage was now set for the legislative interaction which was to produce the 1974 campaign reform legislation—legislation which would not only influence how candidates could raise and spend money, but which might even have far-reaching influence on the contenders' chances for nomination and election.

The Development of Legislation

As the preceding sections have indicated, the opportunity was now readily available for those wishing to bring about major campaign reform. Watergate coupled with the increasing costs associated with political campaigns made it clear that the 1971 legislation was not effective in preventing abuse. What happened in the ensuing months is useful to consider, not only in terms of campaign reform, but also in terms of American policy making.

To begin with, in order for legislation to be enacted, it must be passed by both the House and the Senate. Then a conference committee must resolve any differences between the two pieces of legislation. Once this is accomplished and the House and Senate both accept the conference committee report, the President must sign the legislation for it to become law or both the House and Senate must override his veto. *An often critical stage of legislative decision making is the preliminary stage in which the various committees and subcommittees develop and draft the legislation and then report it for action to the full House or Senate. It is towards the committees that lobbyists and others interested in bringing about change direct their major efforts to influence decisions on specific legislative provisions.* The campaign reform legislation of 1974 was no different.

Senate Action

In this case, the Senate and its Rules Committee, chaired by Senator Howard Cannon of Nevada, took the initiative. By late February, 1974, the committee had reported to the full Senate a comprehensive set of campaign reform amendments. Table 4.1 summarizes these.

As Table 4.1 indicates, the major changes in the 1974 Senate legislation (S3044). as compared with the 1971 legislation, were the requirements for an independent regulatory commission and the use of public financing for candidates for federal office. The discussion of an independent commission was not new. The general ineffectiveness of earlier attempts to enforce campaign finance laws suggested to

Table 4.1

Senate 1974 Campaign Reform Legislation (S3044)

Individual Limits:	$3,000 for each campaign
	$25,000 yearly total for all federal elections
	Candidate and family limits of $50,000 for presidency, $35,000 for Senate, $25,000 for House
	Cash contributions over $100 barred
	Bank loans to be viewed as contributions
Corporate Limits:	$6,000 per organization for each campaign
	$25,000 per organization for each year
Overall Expediture Limits:	House primaries—$90,000
	House general election—$90,000
	Senate primaries—$125,000 or 8¢ per each voting-age individual, whichever is higher
	Senate general election—$175,000 or 12¢ per each voting-age individual, whichever is higher
	Presidential primary—$11.4 million total or 8¢ per each voting-age individual in each primary state
	Presidential general election—$17 million or 12¢ per each voting-age individual
	Unsolicited expenditures on behalf of a candidate limited to $1,000
Expenditure Use:	Central campaign committees required
	1971 media spending limitations on radio and television broadcasting repealed
Regulations:	Seven-member independent regulatory commission to be established with the President appointing all members and the Senate ratifying
	Independent prosecution powers
	Quarterly financial disclosure requirements with specific regulations for period prior to elections
Public Finance:	Public funds to be provided for all candidates in presidential, House, and Senate contests
	Voluntary participation in public funding

SOURCE: *Congressional Record,* Vol. 120, No. 151 (October 7, 1974), pp. 10046–10068.

many the need for an independent regulatory body. As later discussion will indicate, this point has proven to be quite significant.

The public financing provision was new, but interestingly it was usually seen as a separate question from campaign finance reform. Congress had previously created an income tax check-off system by which taxpayers could have one dollar of their taxes earmarked to a fund to finance presidential elections. S3044 established how these funds were to be used. More important, however, was their source. The public financing provision was based on the contention that a combination of small private donations and public funds would increase the freedom a candidate would have from large vested interests and thus make the campaign process more democratic.

Perhaps one of the most thorough justifications of public financing was given by John Gardner in testimony to the House Committee on Administration's Subcommittee on Elections in November, 1973. Gardner, in explaining the Common Cause support of public financing, stated:

> Common Cause believes that the root evils of campaign financing can never be eliminated until candidates are assured of adequate funds to run a creditable campaign without having to rely on big-money contributors. This can never be accomplished until a comprehensive system of public financing is adopted. . . . Common Cause supports a mixed system of public financing combining public funds with small, private contributions. . . . It is vital that the amount be sufficient to allow nonincumbents to present their point of view as against better known opponents. . . . Public financing must be accompanied by an effective nonpartisan independent enforcement agency . . . we urge this Committee to act immediately to make . . . possible . . . the most important electoral reform of its kinds in our history—the public financing of federal elections.[42]

Despite Gardner's pleas, the House refused to take action on the Senate's 1973 legislation, forcing the Senate to initiate action again in 1974.

Senate deliberation on the proposed legislation was spirited and at times volatile. Conservatives, led by Alabama Senator James B. Allen, opposed the legislation and focused their opposition on the provisions providing public funding. Their opposition to the legislation was so intense that advocates of the legislation had to invoke cloture in order to shut off debate. (This parliamentary tactic for limiting Senate debate is difficult to achieve, not only because it requires a three-fifths vote, but also because many Senators, regardless of their position on a specific issue, will honor the Senate's tradition of unlimited debate.) Once cloture was achieved, numerous amendments were offered to the Rules Committee legislation; twenty-three of these were adopted and twenty-eight were rejected.[43]

During Senate debate, two types of opposition were most apparent. The first came largely from conservatives, who maintained that public financing was not in the best interests of the country and in fact was more a raid on the Treasury than a democratic safeguard. The contention here was that it was not up to the public to provide support for candidates to public office. The second type of opposition, a position represented by Senator Lowell P. Weicker of Connecticut, an individual who had gained considerable media exposure from his participation on the Watergate Committee, dealt with the failure of the legislation to adequately control campaign expenditures. As Table 4.1 indicates, the expenditure limits were higher than in past legislation and were such that a hotly contested set of presidential nominating battles could easily cost over $50 million. This figure is obtained by assuming that two or three candidates contest the nomination in each party, as happened in the 1976 primaries. After lengthy floor action, the Senate completed its work and sent to the House, in mid-April, its version of campaign reform. The ball was now in the House's court and specifically, in the corner of Representative Wayne L. Hays, Chairman of the House Administration Committee.

House Action

The House had refused to act on earlier proposals sent to it by the Senate. Representative Hays, who was to resign in 1976 after a major scandal over his personal involvement with a staff member, delayed consideration of campaign finance. The House's failure to act in 1973 and its delay in 1974 were both indicative of the power a committee chairman has. Hays steadfastly refused to be hurried and publicly clashed with advocates of campaign reform. The Democratic leadership in the House supported Hays and his committee despite objections from those such as John Gardner, who castigated the House in 1973 in these words:

> It is shocking that an entire year has passed now without the House of Representatives acting on any campaign finance legislation whatsoever. . . . Unfortunately, in a year which has seen almost unbelievable revelations of political financing corruption, the House Administration Committee has treated that issue as though it were the lowest of priorities. . . . 'The Nation deserves better treatment. The people of this country are entitled at a minimum to have critical issues decided by all of their elected representatives, and not tied up and burned by a few disapproving members not interested in providing remedies to the scandal of Watergate.[44]

Despite such broadsides, mounting public criticism, and the Senate's action in early 1974, the House did not begin considering campaign reform legislation until the early summer of 1974. By late July the House Administration Committee reported its version of the legislation to the full House. As Table 4.2 indicates, there were some major differences between the House and Senate versions of the campaign reform legislation. The House version lowered the amounts permitted for House and Senate elections and kept the presidential totals approximately the same. Even more significant were the provisions excluding House and Senate elections from public financing and the provisions establishing the regulatory agency. It was obvious that the House's version did not provide for as strong an independent regulatory agency as the Senate's. The House's version limited the powers of the regulatory commission; its role was seen as more of a "watchdog" than as an investigative and prosecuting agency as called for in the Senate version.

By historic coincidence, the House overwhelmingly passed the legislation on the same day that President Nixon resigned (August 8, 1974). Several key amendments were attempted, but all were defeated. The amendment to include public financing of House and Senate elections was defeated by forty-one votes. Thus the House had legislation which was also quite different from the existing legislation, but which was not popular with most of the campaign reform groups since it limited public financing and the role of the regulatory commission. In general, the House version seemed to contain too many provisions which could be abused or which were subject to differing interpretations. It was now left to the conference committee to decide the final content of the legislation.

Table 4.2

House 1974 Campaign Reform Legislation (H16090)

Individual Limits:	$1,000 for each campaign
	$25,000 yearly total for all federal elections
	Candidate and family limit of $25,000
	Cash contributions barred
	Bank loans to be viewed as contributions
Corporate Limits:	$5,000 per organization or political committee for each election
Overall Expenditure Limits:	House elections—$60,000 for each election
	Senate elections—$75,000 or 5¢ per each voting-age individual, whichever is higher
	Presidential primaries—$10 million for all primaries
	Presidential general election—$20 million
	Unsolicited expenditures on behalf of a candidate limited to $1,000
Expenditure Use:	Central campaign committee required
	25% of fund limitation permitted to be spent for fund raising—thus effectively increasing the ceilings
Regulations:	Supervisory Board of six controlled by four public members appointed by the Speaker of the House and the President of the Senate
	Prosecution powers retained by Justice Department
	Quarterly disclosure requirements with specific regulations for periods just prior to and after elections
Public Finance:	Full mandatory financing for presidential elections; national convention funding voluntary; House and Senate campaigns not funded

SOURCE: *Congressional Record,* Vol. 120, No. 151 (October 7, 1974), pp. 10046–10068.

The Conference Committee Report

By October 1 the conference committee members were able to reach final agreement on the campaign finance provisions. These are briefly summarized in Table 4.3. As the table indicates, compromise was possible on the contribution and expenditure-level questions. The two most important features of the final legislation were the establishment of public funding for presidential elections, with partial public funding for the primaries, and the establishment of an independent election commission to regulate campaign activities. The six-member commission was to have representatives appointed by the President, Speaker of the House and the Senate Vice President. The commission was not given full prosecuting authority,

Table 4.3

1974 Final Campaign Reform Legislation

Individual Limits:	$1,000 for each campaign
	$25,000 yearly total for all federal elections
	Candidate and family limits of $50,000 for presidency and vice-presidency, $35,000 for Senate, and $25,000 for House
	Cash contributions over $100 barred
	Foreign contributions barred
Corporate Limits:	$5,000 per organization for each election but no aggregate limit
Overall Expenditure Limits:	House elections—$70,000
	Senate primaries—$100,000 or 8¢ per each voting-age individual, whichever is higher
	Senate general election—$150,000 or 12¢ per each voting-age individual, whichever is higher
	Presidential primary—$10 million for all primaries; not allowed to spend more than two times amount permitted in Senate primary in individual state
	Presidential general election—$20 million
	Unsolicited expenditures on behalf of a candidate limited to $1,000
Expenditure Use:	1971 media spending limitations repealed
	20% of limits permitted to be used for fund raising
	Central campaign committees required
Regulations:	Quarterly filing reports and special provisions for election year
	Six-member full-time Federal Elections Commission to be established with the President, Speaker of the House, and President pro tem of the Senate appointing two members (one from each party) subject to Congressional confirmation
	Election Committee to have broad administrative and enforcement powers
Public Finance:	Matching funds for primaries of up to $4.5 million per candidate after $5,000 raised in 20 states with maximum contribution of $250; voluntary full public funding if desired in the general election

SOURCE: *Congressional Record,* Vol. 120, No. 151 (October 7, 1974), pp. 10034–10046.

but it was given the legal power to enter proceedings to gain injunctions against candidates or committees which were not obeying the law. The inclusion of this provision came only after a protracted discussion and the insistence of Senate members.

What were the major gains of the 1974 legislation? It is important to point out that the legislation did in fact incorporate some major new changes. Disclosure remained important, but public financing was seen as the major way to offset the dangers of large interests contributing significant amounts of money to individuals seeking election. The concept of public financing, long debated, was now an integral part of American campaign legislation, which would go into operation in the 1976 presidential campaign.

The creation of an independent regulatory commission was significant in that it marked the first time that Congress had been willing to relinquish its authority in this area. The passage of this provision was undoubtedly due to the insistence of numerous lobbying organizations and the wish of many in the electorate to bring more effective control to the administration and enforcement of campaign reform legislation.

This legislation illustrates the complexity involved in forging new policies in the United States. Policy making often takes considerable time, and offers multiple access points at which interest groups can exert pressure to slow or accelerate change. Policy change in the United States is often exciting, but it is rarely rapid. This has a variety of implications, but probably most important is the extensive advantage it gives to those supporting the status quo. If change in general is difficult to bring about, then it is unlikely that supporters for change will see their measures quickly adopted. *Thus groups which seek policy changes must have sufficient resources so that they can follow specific developments and make sure their point of view is heard when it is needed throughout the entire policy-making process and not just at one particular point in time.*

Finally, as in other cases of policy-making in the United States, the policy process didn't stop with the adoption of the legislation. The 1974 campaign reform legislation is an excellent example of this as its implementation resulted in a major Supreme Court case, presidential involvement, and subsequent congressional legislation.

THE AFTERMATH OF CAMPAIGN FINANCE REFORM

Just as the path towards legislative approval and President Ford's signature on Public Law 93-443 (The Federal Election Campaign Act of 1974) was laborious and complicated, so have been the administration of and subsequent debate over the major provisions of the legislation since its adoption. In fact campaign finance legislation, though it has not attracted extensive public interest, has been an important area of interaction between the legislative, judicial, and executive branches since it was adopted in October, 1974, and implemented on January 1, 1975. While it is too early to be sure of the effect the legislation will have on presidential elections, it is obvious that a great many people continue to be quite concerned over campaign finance and its regulation.

The activity focusing on campaign finance legislation is indicative of another central theme of American politics: if you lose in one arena of political conflict, try to shift the fight to another. This is exactly what happened in this case. Those who opposed the provisions of the 1974 legislation sought relief in the federal courts and when that relief was forthcoming, Congress and the President again became involved in the debate and decision making regarding the provisions of the final legislation. In order to illustrate these and related points, it is necessary to review the judicial action and subsequent executive-legislative decision making dealing with the campaign finance legislation between January, 1975, and June, 1976.

Judicial Action

The 1974 legislation went into effect January 1, 1975, and on January 2, 1975, a lawsuit was filed by a group of plaintiffs including the New York Civil Liberties Union, the magazine *Human Events,* Senator James L. Buckley of New York, and Eugene J. McCarthy, former Minnesota senator and presidential candidate.[45] Interestingly enough these diverse groups and individuals from both ends of the political spectrum were brought together in this cooperative venture because of their mutual opposition to the legislation.

The legal challenges to the legislation were complicated, but all centered on the constitutionality of the legislation. On the one hand, the argument was made that the provisions setting individual contribution and campaign expenditure limits were in fact a denial of personal freedoms of expression as guaranteed by the First Amendment of the Constitution. In addition, the argument was raised that public funding of presidential candidates violated the rights of minor parties and would make it more difficult, if not impossible, for them to develop. A third argument centered on the question of the constitutionality of the selection process for the Election Commission. Since both the President and Congress were to nominate members to the Federal Election Commission, it was alleged that the legislative provisions establishing the commission were unconstitutional because in the Constitution appointive powers are reserved to the President.

The legislation survived its first major judicial test on August 14, 1975, when the U.S. Court of Appeals in the District of Columbia ruled that the legislation's major points were constitutional.[46] The Appeals Court did not rule on the constitutionality of the provisions establishing the Federal Election Commission and justified its failure to do so on the grounds that the commission had not yet exercised the powers under challenge. In essence, the Court of Appeals' position was that while there were concerns over freedom of speech, the overriding need for major campaign finance reform justified bypassing their reservations in this area. The Court did declare a portion of the legislation unconstitutional, but the provision invalidated was not one of the major issues under debate.

The advocates of campaign finance reform had won a major test and it appeared that the legislation would not be struck down on constitutional questions. Opponents of the legislation had one final recourse. They appealed the case to the United States Supreme Court and received a faster than usual review process on the law's constitutionality because of its importance in the fast-approaching 1976 campaign year. Thus the stage was set for one of the most interesting and complicated decisions reached by the Supreme Court in recent years.

The Court announced its decision on January 30, 1976, and immediately the complexities and uncertainties surrounding campaign finance reform returned. The Supreme Court drew an important distinction between limiting campaign *contributions* and limiting campaign *expenditures.* Regarding the individual contribution limits, the Court justified its decision of holding them constitutional on the grounds that

> A contribution serves as a general expression of support for the candidate and his views, but does not communicate the underlying basis for the support. The quantity of communication by the contributor does not increase perceptibly with the size of his contribution, since the expression rests solely on the un-differentiated, symbolic act of contributing . . . A limitation on the amount of money a person may give to a candidate or a campaign organization thus involves little direct restraints on his political communication, for it permits the symbolic expression of support evidenced by a contribution but does not in any way infringe the contributor's freedom to discuss candidates and issues . . . We find that . . . the weighty interests served by restricting the size of financial contributions to political candidates are sufficient to justify the limited effect upon First Amendment freedoms. . . .[47]

However, the Court went on to rule unconstitutional the provisions limiting candidates' and their families' contributions to their own campaigns. The Court argued that the

> candidate, no less than any other person, has a First Amendment right to engage in the discussion of public issues and vigorously and tirelessly to advocate his own election . . . the First Amendment simply cannot tolerate restriction upon the freedom of a candidate to speak . . . on behalf of his own candidacy. We therefore hold section 608(a)'s restrictions on a candidate's personal expenditure unconstitutional.[48]

Despite this reasoning regarding contributions, the Court ruled expenditure limits for House, Senate, and presidential candidates unconstitutional on the grounds that such limitations violated First Amendment guarantees. The Court, maintaining that the evils of large expenditures could be stopped by limiting large individual contributions, ruled that all the expenditure limits were unconstitutional. The Court maintained nothing had been offered

> to justify the restriction on the quantity of political expression imposed by campaign expenditure limitations . . . the equalization of permissible campaign expenditures might serve not to equalize the opportunities of all candidate but to handicap a candidate who lacked substantial name recognition or exposure of his views before the start of a campaign. . . . The First Amendment denies government the power to determine that spending to promote one's political views is wasteful, excessive, or unwise.[49]

At the same time, however, the Court ruled that the legislation's provision for a ceiling of $20 million for presidential candidates receiving public funds was constitutional.

The Court also struck down the prohibitions on independent expenditures, which had been set at $1,000. It should be recalled that these types of expenditures had created problems under the 1925 legislation, so the Court's decision may have opened a major loophole in the campaign finance reform provisions. Under the Court's decision, any major contributor acting independently of the candidate can spend an unlimited amount of money to promote that individual's candidacy. Obviously, the potential for abuse is great.[50]

The Court also ruled that the disclosure and record-keeping provisions of the legislation were constitutional and added a unique interpretation of the constitutionality of the newly established Election Commission. The Court ruled that the commission's membership, because it was not entirely composed of presidential appointees, was unconstitutional and could not carry out the bulk of the duties assigned to it.[51] Despite this finding, the Court did decide that the administrative decisions and rulings reached by the Federal Election Commission prior to January 30 were valid and would remain in effect, and gave Congress thirty days to enact legislation establishing a new commission meeting the Court's constitutional requirements. Table 4.4 summarizes the key parts of the Court's decision.

It should be noted that a variety of dissenting and concurring opinions were filed, and it appears that subsequent legal decisions will be needed before the issues are finally decided. Note that, as Table 4.4 indicates, the Court chose to limit contributions, but not expenditures. This set of decisions may well have reflected the Court's response to the public concern over the contribution excesses exposed by the Watergate investigation.

Perhaps the most interesting provision of the legislation which the Court upheld was the public financing of presidential elections. Under this provision, major party candidates are to receive public funds at the start of the campaign and minor party candidates are to receive them after the campaign if they have received more than 5 percent of the general vote and if they are in debt. In the ensuing election, then, the minor party would receive its share of public funds on a proportional basis at the start of a campaign. Thus the minor party must first meet the task of getting 5 percent of the general vote before it receives any funds. The Court held that this provision was constitutional and that it would help prevent the proliferation of splinter parties.[52] Thus the stage was set for a debate about whether the legislation

Table 4.4
Summary of Supreme Court's Decision
Affecting the Federal Election Campaign Act of 1974

Individual Limits:	Upheld all individual limits
	Struck down limits on candidate and family contributions
Corporate Limits:	Upheld $5,000 per organization limit
Overall Expenditure Limits:	Struck down all expenditure limitations except $20 million limit for those accepting public financing
	Struck down independent expenditure restrictions
Expenditures Use:	Upheld committee structure
Regulations:	Upheld disclosure and reporting requirements
	Struck down Federal Election Commission, but gave Congress 30 days to reestablish it
Public Finance:	Upheld public financing provisions

SOURCE: *"Buckley v. Valeo," Supreme Court Reporter,* Vol. 96, No. 8 (February 15, 1976), pp. 612–796.

would help or hinder the formation and continuation of minor parties in the United States.[53]

The Supreme Court decision did not hand either side a decisive victory; both sides received some satisfaction. The reformers still had public financing and contribution limits, and their opponents had seen expenditure limits struck down and the regulatory process shaken by the decision affecting the Federal Election Commission. What the decision meant in practical terms was that the Congress and the President would again have to reach agreement on campaign reform after nearly two years of protracted and difficult interaction, and during a presidential political campaign. Thus the Court's decision settled little—in fact it may have increased the likelihood of specific suits aimed at other substantive constitutional questions which the Court had not considered. In addition, the Court's decision required additional congressional and executive interaction. Thus the Court acted as a catalyst for major policy decisions yet to come. These decisions centered on the subsequent structuring and powers of the Federal Election Commission and are discussed below.

The Federal Election Commission

Well before the Supreme Court's decision, the Federal Election Commission had already generated substantial controversy. Despite the demand for reform, it was difficult to break the long tradition of House and Senate internal regulatory procedures practiced under prior election legislation. Even before issuing its first directive, the commission became involved in a controversy over the individuals appointed to it.[54] On October 18, the two Senate choices were announced as being Republican Joan D. Aikens of Pennsylvania and Democrat Joseph F. Meglen of Montana. The choices were immediately criticized on the grounds that both nominees were party loyalists and veterans of the old-style campaigns. It was felt that their nomination signalled the intent of at least some to downgrade and discredit the commission before it even got underway.

To further complicate the matter, it appeared that the two nominees from the House side would be former members of the House, a decision which led some critics to contend that the Federal Election Commission was to be a retirement home for defeated politicians and not a major factor in bringing about meaningful enforcement of campaign legislation. President Ford, for his part, had still not named any members by late December, 1974, prompting critics to contend that the President was not seriously interested in major reform and was content to let the commission flounder. Naturally the White House denied these allegations and by early 1975 the commission had its full set of members and was in operation. Keep in mind that the commission was operating in heretofore unchartered waters and simply had to spend a great deal of time on initial internal organization and planning. In many respects, the Federal Election Commission was a small bureaucracy struggling to survive and strengthen its position. At the same time, diverse opposition to it had developed.[55]

Even after the commission got its members appointed and began to function, it ran into immediate difficulties. While the commission was independent of direct congressional control, it still required congressional approval of its operating funds. The record indicates that the House Administration Committee and its chairman,

Wayne L. Hays, wanted greater explanation and justification for the commission's first full budget than the commission's chairman, Thomas B. Curtis, was willing to provide.[56] In any case, the initial impasse over the budget occurred at about the same time that another major disagreement developed.

The Federal Election Commission's first major decision struck at a practice sacred to the members of Congress. Section 318 of the 1974 legislation read as follows:

> Any other amounts contributed to an individual for the purpose of supporting his activities as a holder of federal office, may be used by such candidate or individual, as the case may be, to defray any ordinary and necessary expenses incurred by him in connection with his duties . . . any such contribution . . . shall be fully disclosed in accordance with rules promulgated by the commission. . . .[57]

Using this authority the commission ruled that congressional office accounts were subject to the same set of contribution and expenditure limits as the other campaign accounts a senator or representative might have. This decision effectively closed a loophole in the 1974 law and made it more difficult for members of Congress to channel campaign funds through their office accounts and hence keep them from falling under the usual regulations. The impact of this decision was that large contributors could no longer evade the 1974 law by making contributions to an "office fund" rather than a campaign fund. Congressional reaction to this and other related decisions at about the same time (August and September, 1975) was so intense that the commission found itself under attack from both the House and the Senate, with the result that the commission had to modify its procedures for issuing decisions.[58] Some observers even contended that this initial run-in with Congress revived congressional distaste for an independent regulatory commission and therefore signified the beginning of the end of the commission's effectiveness.

Perhaps this clash of interests is best captured by several statements of involved observers. Representative William Frenzel felt "the commission has to be independent, but our relations should be better."[59] Robert N. Thompson, legal advisor to the Democratic Senatorial Campaign Committee put it a little more philosophically when he stated "this commission is entirely different from any other regulatory body. . . . Its clientele are the congressmen who also oversee its operation."[60]

Thus it should not be surprising that the Supreme Court's decision requesting new legislation to modify the composition of the Election Commission was viewed as a major opportunity for Congress to reconsider the specific powers and responsibilities of the commission. The subsequent congressional debate was tedious and often acrimonious as proponents and opponents stressed the need for their own specific blend of reform and control. Even more important in all of this was that the Federal Election Commission was to start distributing matching campaign funds to presidential candidates during the presidential primary season—the spring of 1976.

On May 11, 1976, President Ford signed the new legislation dealing with the powers of the Federal Election Commission, but only after the legislation had seen extensive congressional action and debate.[61] What happened in the interim was the result of numerous political forces at work. On the one hand, President Ford and his supporters in Congress advocated only legislation which would meet the Supreme Court's objections to the commission's composition. On the other hand, those who wanted more basic change saw this as an opportunity, and possibly the last one, to bring about such change. The legislation proved to be so controversial that Senator William Brock called it a "deceit, a sham, and a fraud on the American public."[62] Senator Edward Kennedy stated that "the integrity and independence of the commission have survived the unjustified assaults on it, and . . . the many other difficult issues have been resolved fairly and dispassionately."[63]

As finally approved by the President and Congress, PL94-283 released more than $2.2 million to presidential contenders and brought about several major changes for the 1976 campaign. Keep in mind that the new legislation was a result of the Supreme Court's request that Congress reconstitute the composition of the Federal Election Commission. Despite the narrowness of this specific request, Congress substantially altered the 1974 reform legislation. The new version did the following:

1. Determined that the President would appoint and the Senate confirm the members of the Federal Election Commission;[64]
2. Established specific procedural rules to be followed by the commission in reaching its rulings;[65]
3. Strengthened the commission's ability to initiate legal proceedings to enforce its decision;[66]
4. Gave Congress the power to disapprove individual sections of any regulation imposed by the commission;[67]
5. Imposed new regulations on political action committees of both corporations and labor unions;[68]
6. Set up provisions limiting the amount of funds a political action committee could contribute to any specific candidate;[69] and
7. Permitted individual contributions up to $5,000 per year to a political action committee and $20,000 per year to a national party committee.[70]

What is significant here is not the specifics of the legislation, but the fact that when Congress had another opportunity, given it by the Supreme Court's invalidation of the Federal Election commission under the 1974 legislation and the request that Congress reconstitute the commission, the reformist zeal of Watergate days had subsided to some extent and it now became obvious that Congress wanted again to increase its control over campaign regulation. The moral may well be that it may be naive and even dangerous to expect those being regulated to develop meaningful regulations!

Thus campaign reform legislation was completed for the time being. Certainly the demands of the 1976 campaign will provide some test of the legislation's adequacy and utility. By August, 1976, it appeared that the newly constituted Federal Election Commission was operating more smoothly and that both presidential candidates would accept public funding and the $20 million expenditure limit accompanying it. Thus an active five-year period in campaign reform history was concluded.

A noted expert on money and politics, Alexander Heard, has recently commented that "the truth is, of course, that for its own special setting our basic electoral system has embodied a large portion of rare political genius in pursuit of extraordinarily high aspirations . . . constant effort has been required to cope with corruption and political distortions produced by our representative processes. And steady changes in the social and economic context of American politics, in the many influences that shape political practices, mean that the tasks of reform and purification are perpetual ones."[71] Heard is undoubtedly correct—campaign reform will continue to be an issue, but to what extent this will be translated into policy decisions only history will determine. The implications of the campaign reform legislation may be more important than the legislation itself for an understanding of the American policy-making process. These implications are explored in the concluding section.

IMPLICATIONS FOR AMERICAN POLICY MAKING

A number of conclusions can be drawn from this case study about the general nature of public policy making in the United States. Each of these deserves a short description.

Certainly the incremental nature of policy development is well illustrated. Change was slow in coming and when it came, it tended to be additive to what had gone before rather than radically different. Nevertheless, through the incremental policy-making process, major changes did evolve. Thus the Federal Election Commission is a reality, and presidential candidates received public funding for the first time in 1976. So despite the predominance of incremental change, the end result can be major change.

Probably one of the more interesting aspects of American policy-making illustrated by this study of election reform is the large number of arenas in which policy decisions are made. Whether these included congressional committees, the full Congress, the Supreme Court, or presidential action, there was always more than one source of power capable of influencing outcomes. Obviously the American system of divided powers was at work; for instance, even the separate authority given the Federal Election Commission under the May, 1976, legislation still makes it dependent upon Congress for funds to operate.

The importance of this division of authority should not be overlooked. It clearly means that advocates of a particular legislative action or any other policy measure must be sure to follow the decision process at every stage. At the same time, the many arenas of policy making may make it easier for the opponents of a legislative action to block its passage, by enabling them to concentrate resources at one critical point (such as within a committee) and by giving them more than one chance to defeat the measure. Multiple arenas make it both more difficult and time-consuming to enact major policy changes.

The need for political resources is apparent if one wants to influence policy outcomes. In this case political resources mean more than just financial resources. Granted this case illustrates the importance of money, but in order to bring about major policy changes it is also important to be able to muster significant public and political support for the policy desired. Thus Common Cause and the proponents of electoral reform were successful both because they had sufficient funds to stay at the task and because they had strong public support, generated largely by Watergate, for some change in campaign finance legislation.

It should be kept in mind that financial resources are needed to provide the expertise and staff time required to stay with the decision-making process till it is completed. Without adequate financial resources, groups or individuals favoring change will find it difficult, if not impossible, to bring it about.

Finally, as this case study illustrates, policy making in the United States is characterized by a great deal of complexity—complexity not only in the decisions being considered, but also in the policy-making process itself. Coalitions are constantly shifting, and publicly recorded decisions may not accurately reflect the exchange and interaction responsible for them.

While campaign finance reform can be interpreted to mean many things, this case study has summarized the major legislative developments in this area and suggested their relationship to policy making in general in the United States. The concluding essay in this volume will place the points developed here in the broader context of American democracy.

5

The Politics of Housing and Community Development in America: The Housing and Community Development Act of 1974*

Richard L. Cole

On August 22, 1974, more than three years after its introduction, the Housing and Community Development Act of 1974 (Public Law 93-383) was signed into law by President Ford. In signing the bill, President Ford declared that this law represents "landmark" legislation, which can be expected to have "far-reaching and perhaps historic significance."[1] Likewise, Senator John Sparkman called this act "the most important legislation since the passage of the National Housing Act of 1934 . . . and the most important legislation on community development since the passage of the Housing Act of 1949."[2]

Presidential and senatorial declarations may at times be exaggerated; however, by almost any standard, the 1974 Housing and Community Development Act is a very important piece of legislation and its impact on urban America may be significant indeed. In terms of monetary outlay, the bill authorized the expenditure of over $11 billion for the fiscal years 1975 through 1977. By contrast, urban renewal, the single most costly federal program in the community development area prior to this act, received a total of only $3.2 billion for the three years prior to the passage of the Community Development Act.[3] Clearly, the 1974 act represents a large outlay of federal dollars in the areas of housing and community development.

However, the importance of this act goes beyond its financial impact. The 1974 Housing and Community Development Act represents an integral part of former President Nixon's program of "New Federalism"—a program intended to "streamline" the federal bureaucracy and to "start power and resources flowing back from

*I wish to express my appreciation to the George Washington University for providing research facilities and support and to David A. Caputo and Jeffrey Pressman for their insightful and helpful comments on this article.

Washington to the states and communities and, more important, to the people all across America."[4] President Nixon proposed to achieve his plan by (1) consolidating various cabinet positions, (2) creating common regional boundaries for all federal domestic programs, (3) securing the enactment of "general revenue sharing"—a program for dispersing over $30 billion to states and localities over its five-year life—and (4) inaugurating a series of "special revenue-sharing" programs in such areas as manpower, law enforcement, and community development. Unlike previous categorical grant programs in these areas, which largely reflected *nationally* defined goals and objectives, the general and special revenue-sharing programs were designed to leave expenditure decisions in the hands of state and local officials. Under this scheme, the federal government would provide most of the funds and local officials would decide how the funds should be spent on a community-by-community basis. As will be discussed later, this arrangement represents a significant change in the relationship between federal and local government.

Thus the Housing and Community Development Act of 1974, like the General Revenue-Sharing Act of 1972 and other programs of special revenue sharing which preceded it, represents more than simply another massive program of federal assistance to America's cities. It also represents major changes in decision-making procedures and political power within the American federal system, and has consequently been described by some as "revolutionary."

As such, the 1974 Housing and Community Development Act provides a rare opportunity for students of American politics to explore domestic decision making in a unique and exciting situation. Few theories of domestic policy making are more widely accepted than that which holds that major, innovative departure from the status quo is rarely possible. More typically, domestic decision making is claimed to represent only minor departures from previous policy. Consider for a moment the obstacles which must be overcome for a President advocating any degree of policy change.

OBSTACLES TO MAJOR POLICY CHANGE

Because of the separation of powers principle, the President must first convince a majority of the 535 members of the Congress (each of whom is responsible to a different voting constituency) to support his proposal. Note that the President must achieve a *positive* response from the Congress (in the way of legislation), not just passive acquiescence. Various groups become committed to existing programs and policies and, at each stage of the legislative process, all of these interested groups will have the opportunity during hearings and investigations to express their approval or disapproval of the various aspects of the new proposal.

If the legislation initiated by the President emerges successfully from the Congress (and if possible court challenges uphold the constitutionality of the law), the President must still obtain cooperation from the huge federal bureaucracy for the administration of the program. Often this is no easy task. The vast majority of the bureaucracy are independent of presidential control (in the sense that their jobs are not dependent on the current administration) and often bureaucrats are found to be more responsive to various group pressures than to the President. Here, too, the various bureaucratic agencies may hold investigations and hearings, at which time interested groups may receive special exemptions or considerations in the legislation.

Finally, the nature of federalism, itself, with its thousands of elected and appointed officials, all of whom are independent of presidential control but who may
be necessary for the successful implementation of the program, adds to the
President's problems in attempting to initiate and administer new and innovative
programs. *Thus in the American system of government there exist a multitude of
opportunities to block, modify, or delay policy alternatives.* At each stage of the
lengthy process, from program initiation to legislation to administration, the interests of all affected groups must be accommodated. It is no wonder, then, that
the normal decision-making process is almost always described as slow, conservative,
and "incremental." Compromises must continually be made; major change is
almost impossible.[5]

It is in this context that the consideration of the Housing and Community Development Act of 1974 becomes such a fascinating case study. While we shall defer
for a moment the question of whether this act was truly "revolutionary" (as
President Nixon called it), it undeniably does represent a major departure from
previous policy in this area. How did such major policy change take place in a
system normally described as incremental, and what were the unique events leading
to the act's passage? These are the questions which the reader should ask as we
examine the act from its inception to its eventual passage. The first section of this
chapter examines the events leading up to the passage of the 1974 act; the next
examines the provisions of the act itself; and the last section examines the fiscal and
political implications of the act.

HOUSING AND COMMUNITY DEVELOPMENT
IN AMERICA FROM 1934 TO 1974

The Housing and Community Development Act of 1974 can fully be understood
only in the matrix of historical events leading to its passage. This section presents
a brief chronology of the federal government's activities in the area of housing
and community development prior to 1974.

Federal Housing Authorities

The federal government became actively involved in the nation's housing market
for the first time with the passage of the Housing Act of 1934. Adopted during the
Great Depression, the act was designed both to assist the home buyer and to
stimulate the housing market by establishing a loan guarantee program. The 1934
act created the Federal Housing Authority, whose purpose is to determine the
conditions under which such loans will be federally guaranteed. Typical of FHA
loan requirements are those (1) requiring an independent appraisal of the home,
(2) limiting loans to the appraised value, (3) assigning the loan a maximum number
of years (typically thirty to thirty-five), and (4) establishing maximum allowable
loans ($45,000 in 1975). Since the lender is assured of payment (the federal govern-
ment pays the mortgage in case of buyer default), interest rates for FHA appraised
loans theoretically are lower than the current market rate. Presently FHA insured
mortgages represent about 15 percent of the mortgage market. While this legisla-

tion has succeeded very well in stimulating the purchase of homes by many Americans, some suggest that it has contributed to the decline of the central cities by encouraging and promoting the exodus of middle-class families from the central cities.[6]

The federal government's next major venture in the housing market came with the passage of the Housing Act of 1937. This act was designed "to remedy the unsafe and unsanitary housing conditions and acute shortage of decent, safe, and sanitary dwellings for families of low income. . . ." In so doing, the act established the United States Housing Authority, whose purpose is to administer funds for the construction of low-income housing. Over the years the Housing Authority has established many restrictions on the construction and rental of such units (such as maximum number of rooms, maximum cost of construction, income limitations, and so forth) and in many areas these "projects," as they became called, today are almost synonymous with the term "slum." Presently public housing financed under this program represents less than 1 percent of the total housing market.[7]

Urban Renewal

Except for a few programs designed to assist World War II veterans, the federal government's activities in housing lay dormant until 1949. With the passage of the Housing Act of 1949, the federal government became involved in the concept of "urban redevelopment." Under the provisions of this act, municipal governments were encouraged to acquire and clear slum property and then to sell the property to a private developer. The private developer was to use the land for a purpose determined by the municipality, and it was assumed that the land sold to the developer would be sold at a price less than the market value of the property. The difference between the municipality's purchase price and the price realized from sale to the developer was largely to be repaid to the municipality by the federal government. This was an immensely controversial piece of legislation and led to the charge by many of indiscriminate and impersonal removal of "undesirable" families solely for the purpose of inner city "beautification."[8]

Partly as a response to this "bulldozer" criticism, the Congress passed the Housing Act of 1954, whose purpose was to replace the concept of urban redevelopment with that of "urban renewal." In order to receive funds under this program, a municipality now would have to develop a "workable program," which had to receive federal approval. Among the important guidelines for developing a workable program were those requiring the city (1) to demonstrate that the project was based on a comprehensive plan, (2) to establish an ongoing building code enforcement program, (3) to demonstrate sufficient administrative skills to carry out the project as well as sufficient resources to pay its share of the costs, (4) to make provisions for the relocation of displaced persons, and (5) to incorporate a program of citizen involvement in the planning and execution of the project. This program, too, has not been without its critics, and many charge that the citizen participation committees formed in accordance with the requirements have been "blue-ribbon" panels appointed by the mayor or planning staff and largely ignoring input from residents of the project area. In response to this criticism, the Department of Housing and Urban Development (HUD) in 1969 began requiring the establishment of Project Area Committees composed of residents of the area in which rehabilitation activities are anticipated. To some, this new requirement promised a shift in emphasis toward more citizen input.[9]

The Model Cities Program

A series of less important housing acts were passed in 1956 (establishing the General Neighborhood Renewal Program)[10] and in 1959 (establishing the concept of community renewal);[11] however, the next significant federal involvement in housing and community relations came with the Demonstration Cities and Metropolitan Development Act of 1966, which established the program of "Model Cities." Unlike previous housing programs, which largely emphasized physical improvements, the Model Cities legislation was designed to incorporate all physical, social, and economic aspects of the community. In passing the act, the Congress declared that

> improving the quality of urban life is the most crucial domestic problem facing the United States. . . . The Congress further finds and declares that cities of all sizes do not have adequate resources to deal effectively with the critical problems facing them, and that Federal assistance in addition to that now authorized . . . is essential to enable cities to plan, develop, and conduct programs. . . .

The legislation, which provided federal grants covering up to 80 percent of the project costs, stipulated that activities should be designed to improve the general physical environment, housing conditions, transportation, education, employment, recreation and cultural facilities, and the quality of social services. Clearly, the Model Cities legislation represented a significant departure from earlier federal assistance programs in the area of housing and community development. It is distinguished largely by its comprehensive approach to the urban problem and by its focus on all physical, social, and economic aspects of the community. By 1974 the federal government had expended over $2 billion on the Model Cities program.[12]

The 1968 Housing and Urban Development Act

The next major federal effort in the area of housing and community affairs came with the passage of the Housing and Urban Development Act of 1968. The most significant provisions of this act were Sections 235, establishing a subsidized home ownership program, and 236, establishing a rental subsidy program. Section 235 was designed to assist low-income families in the purchase of homes by providing payments directly to lending institutions on behalf of the buyer. The act established a series of qualifications and regulations which had to be met, including the requirement of a minimum down payment ($200) made by the purchaser, established maximum mortgage amounts of $15,000 ($17,500 for buyers whose family size exceeded five members), and set income restrictions on eligibility. Payments, under this program, were to be in the amount necessary to make up the difference between 20 percent of the family's adjusted income and the required monthly mortgage payment (including principal, interest, taxes, and insurance). As the family's income increased, federal payments would be adjusted downward to the point of a $7,200 yearly income, after which subsidy payments would terminate.

Section 236 of the 1968 Housing Act was designed to provide rental assistance. Eligibility for this program was similar to that for 235 assistance, and, under these provisions, the renter was required to pay 25 percent of his income, after which subsidy would be provided. Tables 5.1 and 5.2 provide some basic data on the operations of sections 235 and 236. Table 5.1 shows that, through 1972, the median mortgage amount for 235 assisted loans was $18,500, that the median family income of participants was $6,500, and that almost two-thirds of program participants were white. Table 5.2 indicates that the median income of families assisted under the 236 rental subsidy program was $5,300 and that over three-fourths of these were white.

Of all the housing programs discussed to this point, perhaps none was more controversial than the 1968 act and especially Sections 235 and 236 of that act. In the first place, default rates on 235 loans were consistently on the rise, reaching a peak of over 6 percent by 1972. More important, extensive examples of abuses were uncovered as developers and realtors sought to maximize their profits by exploiting those inexperienced in home ownership. Studies by HUD, the General Accounting Office, and the House Banking and Currency Committee documented numerous cases of flagrant abuse. Among the examples cited in the House report was a home bought by a developer for $6,500 and sold, four months later, under the 235 program for $14,500. Also, it was found in the House study that many newly constructed homes (built especially for 235 ownership) were sold with holes in the walls, leaky roofs, obstructed plumbing, and defective equipment. The report concluded that "the construction of those homes is of the cheapest type of building materials; and, instead of buying a home, people purchasing these homes are buying a disaster."[13] The HUD survey found that 24 percent of the new homes and 39 percent of existing homes financed under 235 loans had significant defects. Partly in response to these abuses, and partly out of consideration of his own proposals, President Nixon in January, 1973, ordered the impoundment of 235 and 236 funds, calling the program "inequitable, wasteful, and ineffective."[14]

Table 5.1

Characteristics of the Section 235 Program, 1972

Units assisted through December 31, 1972	398,000
Total mortgage amounts through December 31, 1972	$7.0 billion
Maximum annual subsidies permitted by law through	
fiscal year 1973	$665 million
Median mortgage amount per unit	$18,500
Median buyer income	$6,500
Racial and ethnic composition of buyers:	
Nonminority white	66%
Black	22%
Spanish American	11%
Other	2%

SOURCE: U.S. Congress, Senate Committee on Banking, Housing, and Urban Affairs, *An Analysis of the Section 235 and 236 Programs* (Washington, D.C.: U.S. Government Printing Office, 93rd Congress, 1st Sess., 1973).

Table 5.2

Characteristics of the Section 236 Program, 1972

Units assisted through December 31, 1972*	142,000
Total mortgage amounts through December 31, 1972*	$2.2 billion
Maximum annual subsidies permitted by law through fiscal year 1973*	$700 million
Units in process and units finished processing at the end of fiscal year 1973*	451,000
Units completed by sponsor type	
Limited dividend	62%
Nonprofit	31%
Cooperative	7%
Median mortgage amount per unit	$16,700
Median income of new tenants	$5,300
Racial and ethnic composition of new tenants	
Nonminority white	76%
Black	20%
Spanish American	3%
Other	1%

*Excludes units financed through state and logcal programs and not insured by FHA.

SOURCE: U.S. Congress, Senate Committee on Banking, Housing, and Urban Affairs, *An Analysis of the Section 235 and 236 Programs* (Washington, D.C.: U.S. Government Printing Office, 93rd Congress, 1st Sess., 1973, p. 8).

An Overview of Federal Housing Policies up to 1974

Perhaps this discussion of federal housing programs can be placed in clearer focus by an examination of Table 5.3, which summarizes the important housing programs adopted since 1934. As Table 5.3 indicates, the several housing programs adopted since 1934 have embraced various purposes, various socioeconomic groups, and various financial commitments. The Federal Housing Authority established in 1934, in the midst of the Great Depression, was aimed primarily at the stimulation of home ownership by middle-class Americans. The 235 section of the 1968 act, adopted during a period of increased awareness of the problems of the disadvantaged, was aimed primarily at the stimulation of home ownership by less wealthy Americans. The Urban Renewal program of 1954 was designed to eliminate slums and blight in the central cities—often, it has been charged, to the neglect of the slum-dwellers themselves. The Model Cities program of 1966 was designed to improve all physical, social, and economic aspects of the community; however its funding was about half that of Urban Renewal.

Thus, even this brief review indicates the complexity involved in any discussion of housing in America. Programs have been adopted with little consideration of their ultimate impact on American society, and programs have been eliminated prior to a full evaluation of their merits. No consistent pattern of long-term policy goals and objectives of America's federally assisted housing program emerges from this historical consideration. Rather, programs appear to be initiated and terminated

Table 5.3

Summary of Federally Assisted Housing Programs, 1934–1968

PROGRAM	YEAR PASSED	PURPOSE	1974 EXPENDITURES
Federal Housing Authority	1934	Stimulation of middle-class home ownership through loan guarantees	$7,592,000,000*
Public Housing	1937	Provision of low-cost rental units	1,176,000,000
Urban Renewal	1954	Elimination of slums and blight	1,150,000,000
Model Cities	1966	Elimination of all physical, social, and economic problems of urban America	586,000,000
235 Home Ownership	1968	Stimulation of lower-income home ownership through loan guarantees	7,000,000,000**
236 Rental Assistance	1968	Stimulation of construction of low-cost rental units	2,200,000,000†

*Refers to gross amount of FHA insured mortgage loans in 1973.
**Refers to gross amount of 235 insured mortgage loans in 1972.
†Refers to gross amount of 236 insured mortgage loans in 1972.
SOURCE: *Statistical Abstract of the United States* (Washington, D.C.: Government Printing Office, 1974), pp. 249 and 707.

basically in response to short-term political and social forces. It is no wonder that the National Commission on Urban Problems established by President Johnson in 1967 stated in its 1968 report to the Congress and the President that

> The past has been characterized by inadequate programs with low priorities, with widely vacillating support from the Congress, carried out by a fractionalized industry in the sufferance of a largely indifferent or, on occasion, hostile, bureaucracy. Neither public programs nor private endeavors can function in this roller coaster atmosphere. . . .[15]

Several themes which are important to our understanding of domestic policy making have been touched upon in this brief history of federal involvement in housing and community development. It should be obvious, in the first place, that the commitment of the federal government to this area of domestic policy has risen substantially in the time period covered by this analysis. Beginning from almost nothing in the early 1930s, the federal government expended almost $4 billion in the area of housing and urban development in 1974. This compares with almost $1.4 billion spent in that same year on agricultural development and research, $2.7 billion spent on natural resources, $6 billion spent on transportation, $6.7 billion spent on education, and $7.5 billion spent on health.[16] Clearly, housing and community development is now considered an important area of federal concern. Of course this increased interest of the national government in domestic activity has occurred in many other areas, as well. It is only since the 1930s that the national government has become a major actor in such fields as health, education, transportation, and social services as well as housing. Previously these were areas left almost exclusively to state and local control or to the the private sector.

With increased federal spending has come an increased federal role in decision making. By the late 1960s, it was sometimes argued, the federal government was using these programs to carry out *nationally* defined objectives. State and local decision makers were largely left with only the question of whether or not to apply for a particular program. Once an application had been approved, federal requirements were so rigidly structured that little local deviation was possible. In fact the 235 and 236 Sections of the 1968 Housing Act represented contracts made directly between lending institutions, the federal government, and individual home buyers. The local government's role was almost completely eliminated in these transactions.

Thirdly, it should be clear that domestic policy making is extremely controversial. Few people are left untouched by decisions made in the areas of health, welfare, education, transportation, and housing. Passions are easily aroused, and the federal government is today at the center of many of these controversies. In the area of housing, the principal actors (in addition to the federal government) include mortgage lenders (private banks and savings and loan institutions), home and construction builders, insurance companies, realtors, people in need of housing and community services, and state and local officials. The Congress and the various administrations have continued to struggle with the questions of which groups should be served by the programs, which should receive direct grants of money, and which should share in the major decisions. As our discussion indicates, these questions have been answered differently by the different programs.

It is against this background that President Nixon proposed in 1971 a new housing act. The following sections examine in detail the legislative history and provisions of that act as finally passed in 1974.

THE HOUSING AND COMMUNITY DEVELOPMENT ACT OF 1974: PHILOSOPHICAL AND LEGISLATIVE BACKGROUND

The discussion of housing legislation prior to 1974 has indicated that decisions in the housing and community development sector often are highly politicized and that the stakes, in terms of monetary outlay and decision-making authority, are large, indeed. It should not be surprising, then, that a new Republican administration would develop its own approach to housing policy.

As mentioned at the outset of this essay, President Nixon's housing and community development proposal represented more than simply an incremental addition to existing legislation. His community development program was, in fact, a key element of his overall domestic program of "New Federalism." New Federalism was viewed by Republican officials as a complete break from the way in which domestic programs of the past forty years had been conceived, financed, and administered. Edwin Harper, assistant to President Nixon's domestic adviser, John Ehrlichman, is quoted as saying:

> New Federalism is a positive Republican alternative to running things out of Washington through the categorical grant-in-aid system. It's something to be positive about. Our party has been in a negative position—we've been against things—for forty years. Now we have something to be for.[17]

New Federalism, then, became the slogan of the Nixon administration's domestic policy, following in the tradition of Lyndon Johnson's "Great Society," John Kennedy's "New Frontier," and Franklin Roosevelt's "New Deal."

Although Nixon's forced resignation possibly prevented a full fruition of his New Federalism proposals, the President's intentions were made relatively clear in numerous public statements. Essentially, New Federalism meant a streamlining of the federal bureaucracy; a consolidation of what the President considered to be a fragmented and ineffective grant-in-aid system; and a returning of decision-making authority to state and local units of government. In order to carry out these plans, President Nixon established common regional boundaries for all major domestic departments and agencies, requested that the Congress drastically reorganize the Cabinet and the federal bureaucracy, and proposed a series of "general" and "special" revenue-sharing programs—one of which was in the area of housing and community development. Operationally, President Nixon's revenue-sharing programs would differ from the so-called "categorical" grant programs of the past in that under Nixon's proposals the many grant programs would be consolidated into a very few and decision-making authority—that is, questions of where, how, and when to spend the money—would be left with the recipient units of government, not with Washington.[18]

Perhaps no one has more eloquently summarized the New Federalism philosophy or more vividly portrayed its potential impact than did President Nixon himself in his 1971 State of the Union address, in which he presented many of his new proposals. In that speech the President stated that he would be asking the Congress for more than simply new programs within the established federal framework. Rather, the President stated, "I shall ask [Congress] to change the framework of government itself—to reform the entire structure of American government. . . ."[19] Further in that address the President stated:

> The time has now come for a new partnership between the federal government and the states and localities . . . a partnership in which we entrust the states and localities with a larger share of the nation's responsibilities, and in which we share our federal revenues with them so that they can meet those responsibilities.[20]

In subsequent addresses President Nixon submitted to the Congress his requests for a general revenue-sharing plan and for special revenue-sharing measures in the areas of law enforcement, manpower, community development, education, transportation, and rural development. Eventually all of these proposals passed in one form or another, with the exception of special revenue-sharing proposals in the areas of education, transportation, and rural development.

President Nixon's community development legislation, then, must be understood not only as an outgrowth of historical developments, but also as an integral part of a new philosophical approach to government—one stressing consolidation of programs and decentralization of decision-making authority. Obviously, such a major departure from the previous way of doing things would arouse considerable criticism and opposition. This opposition, in fact, explains the four-and-a-half year delay between the introduction and passage of the act.

In introducing his bill to the Congress on March 5, 1971, President Nixon focused on the failure of previous efforts in the housing and community development area. "On every hand," he stated, "we see the results of this failure: a sorely inadequate supply of housing and community facilities, vast wastelands of vacant and decaying buildings, acre upon acre of valuable urban renewal land laying empty and fallow, and an estimated 24 million Americans living in substandard housing."[21] The basic problems, the President stated, were that existing programs in the community development area were too fragmented and that the programs were controlled to too great an extent at the federal level. "There is simply no good reason," Nixon declared, "why a Federal official should have to approve in advance a local community's decision about the shape a new building will have or where a new street will run or on what corner it will put a new gas station. Yet that is precisely the kind of matters that now must be reviewed at the Federal level."[22]

As initially proposed, the President's community development legislation would have consolidated the programs of urban renewal, Model Cities, water and sewer grants, and loan rehabilitation into a single program expending about $2 billion a year. At a later date, the President would have added the functions carried out by the Office of Economic Opportunity to this package. The President's program would have assigned 80 percent of the money to be spent for use in the nation's 247 Standard Metropolitan Statistical Areas (SMSAs).[23] The money would be allocated to the SMSAs according to a formula weighting heavily the factors of population and need (defined as percentage of population below a nationally defined "poverty line"). President Nixon's proposal also included a "hold harmless" provision which would have ensured that for the first several years of the program's operation no major city would receive less in federal funds from the new program than it had from the old categorical grant programs. The remaining 20 percent of the money would be used to assist smaller communities, encourage state involvement in urban community development, and conduct research.

Characteristic of the President's philosophy of New Federalism, very few spending restrictions were to be placed on cities receiving the money. The wide range of permissible expenditures was illustrated by the President's statement that "cities could use their allocations to acquire, clear, and renew blighted areas, to construct public works such as water and sewer facilities, to build streets and malls, to enforce housing codes in deteriorating areas, to rehabilitate residential properties, to fund demolition projects, and to fund a wide range of human resource activities including those now funded by Model Cities and Community Action programs."[24] In deciding which of these areas to spend its money on, a city would need "no federal approval," declared the President.

From the outset Nixon's proposal faced stiff opposition both within and outside of Congress. Major opponents included the housing industry, which felt that the bill did not do enough to stimulate the purchase of new housing, urban poverty groups, who were disappointed with the phasing out of Model Cities and the possible elimination of OEO grants, and officials of smaller cities and counties, who felt largely ignored by the bill. As was true for the President's other revenue-sharing proposals, many members of Congress opposed such a complete separation of responsibilities of raising and spending federal money, and some feared the loss of control which the Congress wielded over the numerous categorical programs. As a result, President Nixon's original proposal died in the House of Representatives in 1972.

Congressional action on the community development measure in 1973 and 1974 was stimulated by increased administrative pressures following President Nixon's massive 1972 election victory and by President Nixon's termination of Sections 235 and 236 of the 1968 Housing Act. Ironically, in the later months it was also spurred by fears that lengthy impeachment hearings would soon be tying up much congressional time and energy. Accordingly, the Senate, in June of 1973, and the House, in October of 1973, began holding extensive hearings on what the administration was now calling the "Better Communities Act."

During those hearings the opposition to the new program was clearly revealed. Senator Robert Taft (Rep., Ohio) was particularly concerned with the act's lack of federal guidelines. During one exchange, Senator Taft stated:

> Many observers—I'd say perhaps even an increasing number—feel that the experience of general revenue sharing thus far indicates that the money isn't going to be used to address the needs of the citizens who most need help. . . . We have seen golf courses built with general revenue-sharing funds and similar horror stories in various parts of the country.[25]

Detroit Mayor Roman Gribbs, representing the National League of Cities and the U.S. Conference of mayors, favored some new community development bill but strongly opposed several aspects of the President's proposal. According to Mayor Gribbs, "The bill proposes to assign to the states the responsibility of making the funding decisions for the smaller . . . towns of this nation. The League of Cities and the Conference of Mayors strenuously oppose this suggestion." Further, Gribbs stated, "Another point of concern for the cities about the administration's bill is that it would eliminate the all-important minimum funding guarantee—the so-called hold harmless commitment—after a short period of four years. . . ."[26] Testifying before the House Subcommittee on Housing, William Morris, Director of Housing Programs for the National Association for the Advancement of Colored People, stated:

> This is not the time for our national government to withdraw or lessen its commitment to assure all Americans of decent housing in suitable environments. Nor is it a time for retrenchment in the pursuit of the goals established in the Housing and Urban Development Act of 1968.[27]

Finally, speaking for the American Association of Retired Persons, Cyril Brickfield stated that:

> The allocation and distribution of funds formula suggested in [the Better Communities Act] appears to be both unjust in its immediate consequences and shortsighted in the long-range effects. There is no provision in the bill that would allocate monies in relation to need. . . . It grants too great a

decision to local authorities without insuring national priorities, and we view the measure as a systematic retreat by the federal government from its commitment to confront pressing urban problems. Therefore, our associations are pressed to oppose this legislation.[28]

In spite of these objections, the Senate and House, early in 1974, passed versions of the Housing and Community Development Act. The Senate version deviated significantly from that proposed by President Nixon. The Senate bill set a higher level of funding than requested by the President, retained more strict federal control over use of the funds, and based allocations on previous use of categorical grants, rather than on President Nixon's population/needs formula. In addition, the Senate bill would have renewed Sections 235 and 236 of the 1968 Housing Act.

The House bill very closely resembled the administration's original request. Both because of pressure from HUD and the impending impeachment hearings, the House-Senate compromise committee acted quickly to adopt the House version of the bill on most key issues. The bill which emerged from the compromise committee in August 1974 did reauthorize funds for Sections 235 and 236 programs, however HUD officials declared that those funds would not be spent.[29] On August 22, Gerald Ford, having been President for only fourteen days, signed the new bill into law.

THE HOUSING AND COMMUNITY DEVELOPMENT ACT OF 1974: PROVISIONS

As passed by the Congress and approved by the President, the 1974 Housing and Community Development Act authorized the expenditure over a three-year period (fiscal 1975 through 1977) of over $11 billion. Table 5.4 indicates the precise breakdown of these funding allocations.

As the funding distribution makes clear, the two important sections of the special revenue-sharing bill are those concerned with community development and housing authorizations. Each of these is discussed in turn.

Community Development

The community development section of the bill merged ten previous categorical grant programs. These included the programs of Model Cities, urban renewal, neighborhood development, rehabilitation loans, water and sewer grants, public and neighborhood facility loans, and grants for open space, urban beautification, and historic preservation. The formula for fund distribution is based on three factors: population, overcrowded housing, and poverty. In applying for funds, a city need only submit one application which: (1) identifies community development needs, (2) formulates a program to meet those needs, (3) outlines a housing assistance plan, (4) shows conformance with civil rights acts, and (5) includes assurances that citizens have an opportunity to participate in the formulation of the application. The act provides that 80 percent of the funds are to go to SMSA areas and 20 percent to non-SMSA areas. In addition, the act earmarks 2 percent of apportioned funds to a discretionary fund for use by the HUD Secretary.

Table 5.4

Total Authorizations of the
Housing and Community Development Act, 1974–1977

PROGRAM	TOTAL AUTHORIZATIONS*
Community development	$ 8,600,000,000
Housing assistance	1,225,000,000
Section 236 rental assistance	75,000,000**
Housing for the elderly	800,000,000
Rural housing	112,250,000
Comprehensive planning	287,000,000
Urban homesteading	10,000,000
National Institute of Building Sciences	10,000,000
Total	$11,119,250,000

*Total authorizations are used because not all individual authorizations are designated by specific fiscal year. Generally, authorized sums do not run beyond fiscal year 1977.

**Treasury borrowing authority.

SOURCE: S3066 authorization provisions.

In order to avoid sudden loss of funds (which might occur in those cities receiving more money from the consolidated grant programs than from the new act), the act includes a "hold harmless" provision which ensures that for the first three years of the program all cities will receive an amount equal at least to that which they received before the law. During the next three years, cities are assured of receiving at least two-thirds of that which they received under the old programs; and by the sixth year all cities are to receive funds according to the formula.

Because of the special dependency of some community organizations on Model Cities funds, this program was handled somewhat differently. During the first five years of the act, a city receiving Model Cities money will continue to receive the full amount of those funds. During the next three years, Model Cities funds are phased out by fifths. By the act's ninth year (1983) Model Cities will have been completely phased out.

Cities over 50,000 are affected by the formula discussed above. Cities under 50,000 within an SMSA that have previously received merged categorical grant funds are placed on a hold harmless status for three years. In the fourth year, these cities receive two-thirds their hold harmless amount, and one-third the following year. In the act's sixth year, these smaller cities must apply for money from the discretionary portion of the act's funding. Cities under 50,000 which have not previously participated in categorical funding must apply for discretionary funds from the outset.

Of course the act retains, at least in modified form, the revenue-sharing feature sought by President Nixon, meaning that cities are free to spend their money in the area of community development as they see fit. This feature is modified only to the extent that, as indicated above, applicants for funds must identify specific needs and HUD officials are directed to periodically review spending procedures.

Housing Assistance

The housing section of the bill authorized the expenditure of $1.225 billion in fiscal 1974–75 for public housing, which is expected to result in the construction of 40,000 to 50,000 new units annually. The act also authorized $800 million for loans to developers of housing for the elderly, $15 million in fiscal 1975 and 1976 for public housing for Indians, and $75 million for an extended rental assistance program. As mentioned above, one of the most controversial aspects of the House-Senate debates on the new act was the issue of Sections 235 and 236 (subsidized home ownership and rental) of the 1968 Housing Act. It was also reported that the Senate version prevailed and these sections were included in the 1974 act as well. However, the sections were substantially altered so as to be much less appealing to low income groups. The final bill extended Section 236 for only two years (at $75 million in 1975), and Section 235 for only one year. Reflecting the pressure from the administration and the House, the bill contained no mandatory spending provisions for either section. In addition the new 235 section raises the income eligibility to 80 percent of an area's median income and boosts the down payment required to 3 percent of purchase price (rather than $200 as previously required).

Section 8 of the new law focused on leased housing. Under existing procedures, local housing authorities had been permitted to lease units in existing and new private units to low-income families. Furthermore, existing procedures had guaranteed developers of such rental units 100 percent of the rent for the housing complex, regardless of vacancy rates. Section 8 of the new law gives local housing authorities only a small role in acquiring and operating leased housing units. Previously, the housing authority selected the developer. The new law places greater responsibility on the tenant by allowing him to enter into his own lease arrangement. Under Section 8, those whose income is no higher than 80 percent of an area's median income are eligible for assistance, but at least 30 percent of the tenants in an area's leased units must have incomes lower than 50 percent of the area's median income. This section, it is expected, will yield almost 400,000 new rental units. It explains why many criticize the 1974 act for stressing rental arrangements to the neglect of home ownership.

Miscellaneous Provisions

While the major sections of the 1974 act dealt with those community development and housing programs discussed above, a number of miscellaneous provisions of the act are important and are worthy of at least brief mention. For the first time in six years, the act increased FHA mortgage limits (from $33,000 to $45,000), and increased the maximum FHA home improvement loan from $5,000 to $10,000. In terms of rural housing, the act increased the maximum Farmers Home Administration rehabilitation loan from $3,500 to $5,000. The act also authorized $1 million in each of the years 1975, 1976, and 1977 for research in the area of rural housing problems.

In terms of housing for the elderly, the act authorized the expenditure of almost $900 million on direct loans to sponsors of such housing. These loans are expected to produce about 45,000 units. In addition, the act required HUD to establish mobile home safety standards and authorized HUD to make grants to states available for the purpose of identifying needs in the area of mobile home construction.[30]

Thus, over four years after its initial introduction, the Housing and Community Development Act finally became law. As passed, the act represents the first major alteration in the nation's housing policy since the passage of the 1968 Housing Act. It should be stressed, once again, that the 1974 act is more than just an incremental addition to existing legislation. Rather, it is an important element in a new philosophy of government, one which the Nixon-Ford Administrations have labeled New Federalism. Such a philosophy stresses the decentralization of power and resources and places the burden of decision making on local units of government. Truly, this marks a significant departure in the nation's response to community problems. While the act itself is not an admission that older programs, such as urban renewal and Model Cities, have failed, it does, in effect, embrace the perspective that local decision makers—not the national government—should have the right and the responsibility to establish community priorities. It is in this context that President Ford's comments on signing the bill can best be understood. On that occasion, President Ford stated:

> In a very real sense, this bill will help to return power from the banks of the Potomac to people in their own communities. Decisions will be made at the local level. Action will come at the local level. And responsibility for results will be placed squarely where it belongs—at the local level.[31]

At this point, then, the questions of allocation and program impact arise. How much money have cities received? How do these allocations compare with previous receipts? How is the money being spent? What community groups are benefiting from the program? How do local officials evaluate the program? And how do all of these relationships vary by important demographic and political characteristics? These questions are addressed in the following section.

PROGRAM ALLOCATIONS AND ASSESSMENT

At this writing, the Housing and Community Development Act of 1974 has been in effect for only a little over two years and, of course, this is hardly enough time to allow for an evaluation of the total fiscal and political impacts of such comprehensive and far-reaching legislation. However, some data are available, and this section presents a preliminary assessment of the 1974 act.

Distribution of Funds

First, it is appropriate to consider how much money has been allocated to various communities. Table 5.5 presents a summary analysis of fiscal 1975 community development allocations.

As is indicated in Table 5.5, the bulk of the community development funds allocated under the 1974 act went to the larger cities in the nation's SMSAs. Of the $2.5 billion authorized in fiscal 1975, approximately $2 billion (80 percent) was allocated for use in SMSA areas and about one-half billion (20 percent) was allocated to nonmetropolitan areas.

Table 5.6 presents a more detailed breakdown of 1975 community development entitlement allocations. Table 5.6, it can be seen, examines these allocations for the fifty largest American cities and their SMSAs. It will be recalled that the formula

Table 5.5

*National Breakdown of Allocated Community
Development Funds for Fiscal Year 1975*

ALLOCATION CATEGORY	NUMBER OF UNITS TO WHICH ALLOCATION WAS MADE	DOLLAR AMOUNT ALLOCATED
Metropolitan areas (SMSAs)	312	$2,003,572,000
Metro cities	521	1,657,189,000
Urban counties	73	119,176,000
Small hold harmless units	299	172,565,000
Discretionary balance funds	302 (SMSAs)	54,642,000
Nonmetropolitan areas	51	469,493,000
Small hold harmless units	449	269,799,000
Discretionary balance funds	51 (states)	199,694,000
Secretary's discretionary fund		26,935,000
Total allocation		$2,500,000,000

SOURCE: U.S. Department of Housing and Urban Development, Community Development Block Grant Program, *Directory of Allocations for Fiscal Year 1975* (Washington, D.C.: U.S. Government Printing Office, 1975), p. iii.

Table 5.6

*Community Development Entitlement Amounts
for 50 Largest Cities in 1975 (thousands of dollars)*

CITY	CENTRAL CITY ENTITLEMENTS	SMSA ENTITLEMENTS	PREVIOUS SMSA RECEIPTS*	PERCENTAGE DIFFERENCE
New York	$102,244	$122,042	$121,213	.68%
Chicago	43,201	51,686	45,005	14.84
Los Angeles	38,595	71,592	67,617	5.87
Philadelphia	60,829	71,238	68,425	4.11
Detroit	34,187	58,536	54,390	7.62
Houston	13,257	15,218	13,523	12.53
Baltimore	32,749	35,302	33,917	4.08
Dallas	3,998	13,191	9,149	44.18
Washington, D.C.	42,748	42,748	42,748	0.00
Cleveland	16,092	20,733	18,981	9.23
Indianapolis	13,929	14,466	13,929	3.86
Milwaukee	13,383	14,224	13,486	5.48
San Francisco	28,798	58,839	55,375	6.26
San Diego	9,148	12,200	10,491	16.29
San Antonio	17,904	18,466	18,171	1.62
Boston	32,108	52,541	50,787	3.45
Memphis	6,043	6,344	6,043	4.98
St. Louis	15,194	20,015	17,908	11.77
New Orleans	14,808	16,493	14,930	10.47
Phoenix	2,570	5,493	4,018	47.96
Columbus	9,194	10,178	9,194	10.70
Seattle	11,641	14,303	13,265	7.83
Jacksonville	5,193	5,400	5,193	3.99
Pittsburgh	16,429	36,282	33,466	8.41
Denver	15,805	18,291	17,293	5.77
Kansas City, Mo.	17,859	20,074	19,799	1.39
Atlanta	18,780	22,228	20,670	7.53

for fund allocation includes the three criteria of population, overcrowded housing (units with more than 1.01 persons per room), and poverty (weighted double). The data used by HUD in allocating 1975 funds were compiled from the 1970 Census of Population and Housing with updated information reflecting boundary, annexation, and consolidation changes through 1972.[32] In considering Table 5.6, it must be remembered that the dollar amounts indicated are *entitlement* allocations, only. Although these figures represent the total community development funds which various communities are entitled to under the 1974 act, all communities must apply for funds and must have their applications approved before money is appropriated. Thus some communities and some SMSAs may not receive the full amounts to which the allocation formula would indicate they are entitled.

The data in Table 5.6 indicate the amount of community development funds authorized for each of the nation's fifty largest cities in 1975, the amount authorized for each of these cities' SMSA, the amount of funds previously received by each SMSA from the consolidated categorical grant programs, and the extent to which funds received under the 1974 act exceed those received under the consolidated categorical grant programs (expressed in percentages). A number of interesting facets of the community development act's allocations are revealed in Table 5.6.

In the first place, it can be seen—as also was shown in Table 5.5—that the large central cities receive the bulk of the community development funds allocated under the act. Thus New York and Chicago are entitled to about 84 percent of the total amount of funds allocated to their SMSAs; Philadelphia is entitled to 85 percent;

Table 5.6 (*Continued*)

CITY	CENTRAL CITY ENTITLEMENTS	SMSA ENTITLEMENTS	PREVIOUS SMSA RECEIPTS*	PERCENTAGE DIFFERENCE
Buffalo	11,685	17,209	15,857	8.53
Cincinnati	18,828	21,918	20,964	4.55
Nashville-Davidson	9,609	11,899	11,507	3.41
San Jose	6,554	8,505	7,089	19.97
Minneapolis	16,793	39,622	38,147	3.87
Fort Worth	1,879	13,191	9,149	44.18
Toledo	11,831	12,123	11,831	2.47
Newark	20,513	27,288	26,217	4.09
Portland	8,760	9,310	8,760	6.28
Oklahoma City	8,183	10,459	9,937	5.25
Louisville	8,639	11,648	11,496	1.32
Oakland	12,738	58,839	55,375	6.26
Long Beach	1,514	51,686	45,005	5.87
Omaha	1,390	1,496	794	88.41
Miami	3,165	25,851	24,983	3.47
Tulsa	9,312	10,219	9,805	4.22
Honolulu	13,099	13,099	13,099	0.00
El Paso	2,195	2,295	854	168.74
St. Paul	18,835	39,622	38,147	3.87
Norfolk	17,766	23,705	22,993	3.10
Birmingham	5,040	7,980	6,326	26.14
Rochester	14,684	17,911	17,304	3.51
Tampa	8,577	11,747	9,410	24.84

*Includes all money received from the consolidated categorical grant programs.

SOURCE: U.S. Department of Housing and Urban Development, Community Development Block Grant Program, *Directory of Allocations for Fiscal Year 1975* (Washington, D.C.: U.S. Government Printing Office, 1975), p. 28.

Baltimore 93 percent; Houston 87 percent; and so forth. Of course this is not surprising given the purpose of the act and the elements comprising the distribution formula. Some critics have contended that the act would distribute a disproportionate amount of funds to suburbs and rural areas.[33] While it might be argued that central cities should be entitled to an even larger proportion of the funds, the data indicate that, in general, the bulk of the money is being allocated to large central cities.

Table 5.6 also compares the amount of community development funds received by each SMSA with the total amount previously received by these same SMSAs from the consolidated categorical grant programs. With the exceptions of Washington, D.C. and Honolulu, whose central cities comprise the entire SMSA, it can be seen that every SMSA considered in Table 5.6 is entitled to an increase over previous funding levels. Most interesting, however, is an examination of the percentage increase in funding levels. Here it can be seen that, in general, smaller western SMSAs are receiving far greater increases than some of the larger eastern SMSAs. The Dallas-Fort Worth SMSA, for example, is entitled to an amount which is about 44 percent greater than it received under the categorical grant programs. The Phoenix SMSA is entitled to almost 48 percent more, Omaha is entitled to 88 percent more, and the El Paso SMSA is entitled to an amount which is more than 100 percent greater than it received under the categorical grant programs. In contrast, the large eastern SMSAs of New York, Philadelphia, Baltimore, Boston, Pittsburgh, Buffalo, and Newark all are entitled to amounts which are less than 10 percent greater than they received under the consolidated categorical programs. Thus, while the "hold harmless" provisions of the act have ensured that no city or SMSA initially will receive less than that received under the categorical grant programs, it is clear that some cities and SMSAs (notably those which are smaller and in the western portions of the nation) are receiving increases which far exceed other areas'. It might be expected, therefore, that support for the program will vary among community leaders and that those of the larger eastern cities will be less favorable toward the 1974 act. This assumption is to be examined in a later section of this essay.

Use of Funds

Of primary interest, of course, is the manner in which the recipient communities have allocated their community development funds. The act urged the expenditure of the money in seven areas identified as "national objectives"—(1) the elimination of slums and blight, (2) the elimination of conditions which are detrimental to health, safety, and public welfare, (3) the conservation or expansion of the nation's housing stock, (4) the expansion and improvement of the quantity and quality of community services, (5) the more rational utilization of land and community resources, (6) the reduction of the isolation of income groups and the promotion of neighborhood diversity, and (7) the restoration and preservation of properties for historic, architectural, and aesthetic reasons. In May of 1975, HUD issued a report analyzing the applications of twenty-five cities for their proposed use of community development funds.[34] Table 5.7 describes the cities' priorities, in terms of the seven priority areas identified by the act.

As can be seen in Table 5.7, most of the reported use of community development funds by these twenty-five cities is heavily skewed in favor of physical development

Table 5.7

Reported Use of Community Development Funds: 25 Cities

OBJECTIVE	AMOUNT	PERCENTAGE
Elimination of slums and blight	$36,789,000	35%
Elimination of detrimental conditions	10,194,000	10
Conservation or expansion of the nation's housing stock	16,913,000	16
Expansion and improvement of the quantity or quality of community services	18,437,000	17
More rational utilization of land or resources	21,462,000	20
Reduction of isolation of income groups	341,000	00
Restoration and preservation of properties for historic, architectural, or aesthetic reasons	1,935,000	2

SOURCE: U.S. Department of Housing and Urban Development, *Community Development Block Grant Program, A Provisional Report* (Washington, D.C.: U.S. Government Printing Office, May, 1975), p. 28.

activities. Elimination of slums and blighted areas, elimination of detrimental conditions, housing conservation, and land use received over 80 percent of the funds expended by this sample of cities. More specific examples of the use of the funds in each of these areas are as follows. Activities in the area of elimination of slums and blight included street improvement, water and sewer construction, downtown beautification, and renovation of community centers. Activities in the area of the elimination of detrimental conditions included housing and building code enforcement, demolition, control of rodents, and flood control. Examples of use of the funds in the area of housing conservation included rehabilitation, acquisition, site selection, and assistance to private developers. Activities in the area of rational land use included development of parks, improvement of recreational facilities, streets, and parks, and flood control.

By contrast, the area of expansion and improvement of social services received only about 17 percent of the funds expended by these cities. Specific examples of activities in the human services area included housing counseling, continuation of Model Cities services, health services, elderly services, day care and child services, drug programs, summer youth programs, and cultural heritage services for minority groups. While it should be remembered that this analysis is based on the applications of only twenty-five cities, if these cities are in any sense representative of all recipient communities it is clear that the human and social service areas are receiving a very small proportion of the total community development funds and that the areas of physical development are emphasized.[35]

Another interesting aspect of the HUD report is its indication of the distribution of community development funds by income sectors of the twenty-five communities. The act requires that communities give priority to activities which will benefit low- or moderate-income families or are designed to meet community development needs having a particular urgency. Table 5.8 examines the distribution of community development funds by income sectors.

Table 5.8

Distribution of Community Development Funds by Income Sectors: 25 Cities

TYPE OF AREA	LESS THAN 80% OF MEDIAN INCOME	81–99% OF MEDIAN INCOME	ABOVE MEDIAN INCOME	CITYWIDE/VARIOUS UNSPECIFIED AREAS	TOTAL	%
Urban renewal/neighborhood development programs	$26,612,000	$ 5,943,000	$ 4,370,000		$ 36,925,000	35%
Other blighted areas	8,807,000	7,147,000	3,114,000		19,068,000	18
Other areas	7,424,000	4,304,000	3,858,000		15,586,000	15
Model neighborhoods	13,925,000				13,925,000	13
City-wide/Various unspecified areas				$18,675,000	18,675,000	18
Total	$56,768,000	$17,394,000	$11,342,000	$18,675,000	$104,179,000	99
Percentage	54	17	11	18	100	

SOURCE: U.S. Department of Housing and Urban Development, *Community Development Block Grant Program, A Provisional Report* (Washington, D.C.: U.S. Government Printing Office, May, 1975), p. 56.

As Table 5.8 indicates, those areas designated as urban renewal, neighborhood development, model neighborhood areas, and other "blighted" areas received about 66 percent of the total community development funds expended by these twenty-five cities. Table 5.8 also indicates that 54 percent of the money spent by these cities was appropriated in sections of the communities having less than 80 percent of the community's median income, 17 percent spent in sections having a median income of from 81 to 99 percent of that for the community as a whole, and 11 percent expended in sections having a median income above that of the community as a whole.

One final aspect of the HUD study of interest here concerns the breakdown of community development expenditures by neighborhood income level. Table 5.9 presents this information.

As Table 5.9 indicates, considerable variation in the expenditure of community development funds by neighborhood income level was reported. It can be seen that the bulk of the funds allocated in low-income neighborhoods was spent in the areas of renewal, housing, and public works, whereas the bulk of the money spent in neighborhoods having a median income greater than that of the community as a whole was spent in the areas of water and sewer construction, open-space and neighborhood facilities, and public works. It is also seen that neighborhoods having a median income less than that of the community as a whole received far greater proportions of community development funds earmarked for social service programs than did those neighborhoods having median incomes greater than the community average (although the proportion spent on social services still was relatively small even in low-income neighborhoods).

While it must be stressed again that these data are derived from the reports of only twenty-five cities, to the extent that these cities are representative several conclusions concerning the expenditure of community development funds at this early stage of the program's life are possible. It is apparent, in the first place, that most of the funds are being spent in low-income areas of the recipient communities. As reported above, the proportion of community development money received by low-income neighborhoods is at least 71 percent of the total and may be as high as 89 percent (when considering unspecified area expenditures). Also it is clear that the use of the community development funds varies by type of neighborhood. Communities are spending their community development money in low-income neighborhoods primarily for renewal and housing activities. Also, low-income areas are receiving a disproportionately large share of the community development funds being expended for social service programs. Communities are spending their community development money in higher-income areas primarily for programs of open space, water and sewer construction, and public works. Finally, it can be concluded that, overall, the greatest proportion of community development funds is being allocated in the area of physical development (including housing, building, and land acquisition), and that much smaller proportions are being spent in the area of social services. It will be especially interesting to discover if future and more complete studies confirm these initial findings.

Local Assessments

A final area of interest is the response of local officials to the community development program. How does their experience with the new program compare with

Table 5.9

Distribution of Community Development Funds by Activity and Income Sectors: 25 Cities

ACTIVITY	LESS THAN 80% OF MEDIAN INCOME	%	81-99% OF MEDIAN INCOME	%	ABOVE MEDIAN INCOME	%	CITYWIDE/VARIOUS UNSPECIFIED AREAS	%
Renewal	$15,716,000	34%	$ 3,883,000	22%	$ 919,000	8%	$ 6,671,000	36%
Code enforcement	2,168,000	5	623,000	4	126,000	1	2,772,000	15
Other public works	7,837,000	17	2,782,000	16	4,165,000	37	2,917,000	16
Water and sewer construction	1,229,000	3	1,928,000	11	3,279,000	29	830,000	4
Open-space neighborhood facilities	3,532,000	8	1,464,000	8	1,750,000	15	1,153,000	6
Housing	11,323,000	24	3,190,000	18	539,000	5	1,412,000	8
Service-related facilities	2,253,000	5	897,000	5	402,000	4	655,000	4
Public Services	2,755,000	6	2,628,000	15	162,000	1	2,265,000	12
Total	$46,813,000	102%	$17,395,000	99%	$11,342,000	100%	$18,675,000	101%

SOURCE: U.S. Department of Housing and Urban Development, *Community Development Block Grant Program, A Provisional Report* (Washington, D.C.: U.S. Government Printing Office, May, 1975), p. 60.

their experience with previous categorical grant procedures? How satisfied are community leaders with the community development program? And how do their concerns vary by type of city? Here another HUD survey is of interest. Analyzing questionnaire returns from 128 cities, HUD compared various practices under the old and new programs. The results are shown in Table 5.10.

Comparing the community development program with previous categorical grant programs, 63 percent of these cities indicated that the new program had resulted in an increase in coordination between local agencies, and 69 percent reported a decrease in federal intervention in local decision making. Interestingly, 53 percent indicated an *increase* in book and paper work required for the receipt of funds, and 10 percent reported an increase in federal "red tape." Of course simplified administration procedures at the local level have from the outset been cited as a major argument in favor of the community development, special revenue-sharing approach. It is intriguing to discover now that a considerable number of cities find certain aspects of the new approach to be even more burdensome than before.[36]

Although not shown in Table 5.10, it also was found in this survey that about 77 percent of these cities reported an increase in the participation of citizens in preparing grant applications, and 79 percent indicated the community development program had increased their ability to respond to local needs.

An independent study conducted by this author and David A. Caputo[37] of chief executive officers in all American cities with populations over 50,000 yielded some interesting differences in responses to the new program. In that study city officials were asked to indicate (1) the extent to which they anticipated using community

Table 5.10

*Comparison of Community Development
and Categorical Grant Experiences*

FACTOR COMPARED WITH CATEGORICAL GRANT EXPERIENCE	CITIES INDICATING INCREASE	CITIES INDICATING DECREASE	CITIES INDICATING NO CHANGE
Coordination between local agencies	63%	1%	36%
Competition between local groups wanting projects funded	56%	6%	37%
Bookkeeping and paperwork requirements for the city	53%	19%	28%
Federal "red tape"	18%	46%	36%
Federal intervention in local decisions	10%	69%	21%
Federal technical assistance to the city	18%	25%	57%

SOURCE: U.S. Department of Housing and Urban Development, *Community Development Block Grant Program, A Provisional Report* (Washington, D.C.: U.S. Government Printing Office, May 1975), p. 22.

development funds to support social service programs, (2) the impact of the community development legislation on the total amount of federal funds received by the cities, and (3) the extent to which they were satisfied with the community development legislation. This study is of particular interest since it allows for the comparison of responses by various demographic and political characteristics of the cities. Tables 5.11, 5.12, and 5.13 present these findings.

In Table 5.11 it can be seen that most officials in this sample believed that the community development and general revenue-sharing programs would result in their cities receiving greater amounts of federal funds. Over 60 percent of the officials believed that the programs would result in greater funds, whereas only about 20 percent believed the programs would result in a net decline. Most interesting, however, is a comparison by the various demographic characteristics presented in Table 5.11. Officials of smaller cities and those in the South and West were much more likely to believe that the revenue-sharing program would result in a net increase of funds. Likewise, it was found that a significantly greater proportion of the officials of very large cities (those over 500,000) believed the programs would result in a net loss of funds. These attitudinal data parallel very closely the allocation figures discussed earlier (see especially Table 5.6 and accompanying discussion). The HUD data indicate that smaller western communities are receiving increases far in excess of those received by the larger northern communities and these attitudinal data certainly confirm the fact that local officials are aware of these differences. It should be noted, as well, that officials of suburban communities were much more likely to believe that the revenue-sharing programs would result in a net increase of funds than were officials of central cities (by a margin of 83 to 54 percent).

Table 5.12 presents additional data concerning the use of community development funds for social service programs. It has already been noted (see Table 5.7) that only a very small proportion of the total community development funds has been spent in the area of human and social services. Data presented in Table 5.12, however, indicate that over half the cities are using their community development funds to support such programs at higher levels than in the past. Again, interesting regional and size differences are apparent. Smaller cities and those in the South and West (and, to some extent, suburban communities) are more likely to earmark community development funds for use in social service areas than are other cities.

Finally, in terms of program satisfaction, Table 5.13 indicates that officials of most smaller cities are satisfied with the community development legislation. Only 8 percent, in fact, expressed any degree of dissatisfaction (and only 1.5 percent were *very* dissatisfied). Once again, interesting variance can be seen in these responses. As would be expected given the above data, smaller cities in the South and West are somewhat more likely to be satisfied with the community development program than other cities.

The Impact of Community Development Legislation

In summarizing the impact of the community development legislation, it needs to be stressed once again that it is still much too early in the life of the program for any sort of definitive evaluation. By contrast, over two decades after its inception, analysts still are examining and debating the full impact of the urban renewal

Table 5.11

*Comparison of Total Funds Received from Revenue-Sharing Programs
Versus Categorical Grant Programs*

	SIGNIFICANTLY GREATER	SOMEWHAT GREATER	ABOUT THE SAME	SOMEWHAT LESS	SIGNIFICANTLY LESS
All Cities	63 (32.1%)	59 (30.1%)	33 (16.8%)	26 (13.3%)	15 (7.7%)
Region					
Northeast	8 (27.6)	5 (17.2)	6 (20.7)	7 (24.1)	3 (10.3)
North-central	10 (18.9)	18 (34.0)	14 (26.4)	6 (11.3)	5 (9.4)
South	17 (30.4)	18 (32.1)	10 (17.9)	8 (14.3)	3 (5.4)
West	27 (52.9)	16 (31.4)	2 (3.9)	4 (7.8)	2 (3.9)
Population					
50,000–100,000	52 (45.6)	37 (32.5)	12 (10.5)	9 (7.9)	4 (3.5)
100,000–250,000	8 (16.3)	14 (28.6)	13 (26.5)	9 (18.4)	5 (10.2)
250,000–500,000	2 (10.0)	4 (20.0)	5 (25.0)	5 (25.0)	4 (20.0)
Over 500,000	1 (7.7)	4 (30.8)	3 (23.1)	4 (23.1)	2 (15.4)
City Type					
Central city	29 (22.3)	41 (31.5)	28 (21.5)	21 (16.2)	11 (8.5)
Suburb	32 (55.2)	16 (27.6)	4 (6.9)	4 (6.9)	2 (3.4)
Form of Government					
Mayor	14 (24.6)	16 (28.1)	12 (21.1)	11 (19.3)	4 (7.0)
Manager	44 (37.3)	37 (31.4)	12 (12.7)	14 (11.9)	8 (6.8)

SOURCE: Unpublished report prepared by David A. Caputo, Purdue University, and Richard L. Cole, the George Washington University, 1976.

Table 5.12

Comparison of Use of Community Development Funds Versus Previous Funds For Social Service Programs

	SIGNIFICANTLY HIGHER	SOMEWHAT HIGHER	ABOUT THE SAME	SOMEWHAT LOWER	SIGNIFICANTLY LOWER
All Cities	38 (23.7%)	60 (37.5%)	41 (25.6%)	18 (11.2%)	3 (1.9%)
Region					
Northeast	3 (13.0)	7 (30.4)	8 (34.8)	5 (21.7)	
North-central	7 (17.9)	13 (33.3)	12 (30.8)	6 (15.4)	1 (2.6)
South	12 (24.5)	16 (32.7)	13 (26.5)	6 (12.2)	2 (4.1)
West	13 (31.0)	21 (50.0)	7 (16.7)	1 (2.4)	
Population					
50,000–100,000	27 (30.7)	35 (39.8)	20 (22.7)	6 (6.8)	
100,000–250,000	8 (17.8)	14 (31.1)	15 (33.3)	7 (15.6)	1 (2.2)
250,000–500,000	1 (7.1)	7 (50.0)	2 (14.3)	3 (21.4)	1 (7.1)
Over 500,000	2 (15.4)	4 (30.8)	4 (30.8)	2 (15.4)	1 (7.7)
City Type					
Central city	25 (22.7)	37 (33.6)	30 (27.3)	15 (13.6)	3 (2.7)
Suburb	10 (23.3)	20 (46.5)	10 (23.3)	3 (7.0)	
Form of Government					
Mayor	10 (20.4)	12 (24.5)	20 (40.8)	6 (12.2)	1 (2.0)
Manager	24 (24.7)	39 (40.2)	20 (20.6)	12 (12.4)	2 (2.1)

SOURCE: Unpublished report prepared by David A. Caputo, Purdue University, and Richard L. Cole, the George Washington University, 1976.

Table 5.13

Official Satisfaction with the Community Development Act

	VERY SATISFIED	SOMEWHAT SATISFIED	UNCERTAIN	SOMEWHAT DISSATISFIED	VERY DISSATISFIED
All Cities	42 (21.1%)	74 (37.2%)	67 (33.7%)	13 (6.5%)	3 (1.5%)
Region					
Northeast	4 (13.8)	7 (24.1)	13 (44.8)	3 (10.3)	2 (6.9)
North-central	13 (24.1)	22 (40.7)	14 (25.9)	4 (7.4)	1 (1.9)
South	9 (16.1)	25 (44.6)	20 (35.7)	2 (3.6)	
West	16 (30.2)	19 (35.8)	15 (28.3)	3 (5.7)	
Population					
50,000–100,000	25 (21.6)	47 (40.5)	36 (31.0)	5 (4.3)	3 (2.6)
100,000–250,000	12 (24.0)	17 (34.0)	16 (32.0)	5 (10.0)	
250,000–500,000	1 (5.3)	5 (26.3)	10 (52.6)	3 (15.8)	
Over 500,000	4 (28.6)	5 (35.7)	5 (35.7)		
City Type					
Central city	32 (24.4)	51 (38.9)	39 (29.8)	9 (6.9)	3 (5.0)
Suburb	10 (16.7)	22 (36.7)	22 (36.7)	3 (5.0)	
Form of Government					
Mayor	13 (22.4)	22 (37.9)	20 (34.5)	2 (3.4)	1 (1.7)
Manager	25 (20.8)	48 (40.0)	36 (30.0)	9 (7.5)	2 (1.7)

SOURCE: Unpublished report prepared by David A. Caputo, Purdue University, and Richard L. Cole, the George Washington University, 1976.

legislation. At this writing the community development program is barely two years old. Data for only a few cities have been collected, and much of the available information is subjective and impressionistic in nature. Still the available data do permit some tentative speculation.

In terms of fund distribution, the hold harmless provisions of the act have ensured that no large communities initially are receiving less money than they received under the merged categorical grant programs. It is obvious, however, that some cities—notably smaller communities and those in the southern and western portions of the nation—are receiving increases which proportionally are much greater than those received by larger northern cities. This conclusion is supported not only by objective data released by HUD but by subjective impressions of city officials themselves. At a time when these larger American cities are facing financial strains of a most severe nature, it seems appropriate to at least raise the question of whether or not the distribution formula should be altered so as to provide even more funds for the larger and older cities.

In terms of the actual expenditure of community development funds, it is found that cities are spending most of their funds in low-income areas, that the use of community development funds varies somewhat by income area, that cities are allocating their funds largely in the areas of physical improvement, and that social service programs are receiving only very small proportions of the distributed funds. It was shown, as well, that larger central cities—those facing the most severe financial problems—report spending even smaller proportions of community development funds for social service programs than do other cities. Again, it might be expected that a formula alteration favoring larger cities would result in these cities spending greater proportions in the area of social needs.

Finally, it was found that, on the whole, most cities are satisfied with the community development program, although a third still are reporting a "wait and see" (uncertain) attitude. It is clear, as well, that smaller southern and western cities are more satisfied with the program, and that larger northern cities are more uncertain. It will be especially interesting to see if these city differences persist in future years and if coalition realignments will result in the renewal debates.

IMPLICATIONS FOR AMERICAN POLICY MAKING

Earlier it was noted that domestic policy making in the United States is almost always described as slow, marginal, and conservative. Major policy change rarely is possible. If there are policy changes from one period to the next, these are almost always incremental and marginal in impact. The forces of the American political system, which stress bargaining, negotiating, and compromise, are overwhelmingly opposed to major change.

Yet the Housing and Community Development Act of 1974 does represent a significant departure from previous policy in this area. While it is an exaggeration to label the change "revolutionary," this act did significantly alter the direction of federal policy in the area of housing and community development. It is for this reason, as mentioned at the outset, that this measure provides such an intriguing case study for the student of American politics. How did such major change take place? Were the forces involved truly unique? Will these conditions be present again in the near future?

By now the reader should have begun to frame his or her own conclusions to these questions. It should be apparent, as well, that no single reason provides a complete explanation. Rather, it appears most likely that a number of factors contributed to the passage of this legislation.

In the first place, it must be remembered that although this act may have represented major policy *change* it certainly was not *immediate*. President Nixon first introduced his housing program to the Congress in 1971. More than three years later, after intensive and prolonged executive pressure, the act was passed. One lesson to be learned, then, is that, even on those rare occasions when comprehensive change is possible, it still can be very slow.

Another factor to be recalled from this discussion is that the history of housing legislation in this country is not one of consistency and uniformity in terms of objectives or purpose. Rather, housing legislation has been compared to a roller coaster—policy goals which seemed important in one era may be altered or abandoned in a few short years. An examination of the history of housing legislation in this country reveals almost an expectation on the part of the principal actors that change will be frequent and sometimes significant.

Related to this point is the fact that the housing issue is extremely complex and different people may have honest and legitimate differences of opinion as to the best course of action. In the area of housing no ultimate standards have emerged which would allow for universal judgment of policy alternatives. Compare, for a moment, the area of housing with that of voting rights. In the latter case, most Americans agree with the principle of universal suffrage and with the elimination of whatever social and legal barriers may impede the attainment of universal voting rights. The ultimate standard in this area is democracy itself—most Americans believe that every adult American should have the right to participate in the political arena. While progress even in this area has at times been excruciatingly slow, and while occasional reversals have occurred, the long-term trend has been for the expansion of voting rights based on the ultimate principle that everyone has a right to participate in a democratic government. Policy proposals in this area can be evaluated in terms of a standard almost universally agreed upon. Imagine what the reception would be to a proposal suggesting the elimination of female suffrage, or a return to the white primary, or the imposition of religious requirements for voting. Each of these is in violation of the principle of universal suffrage and would certainly be rapidly discarded as a serious policy alternative.

The important point which is being made here is that in the area of housing no comparable standard of judgment has emerged which automatically determines which proposals will and which will not be given serious consideration. Some believe that our national housing policy should be designed to provide low-cost homes which can be purchased by the economically disadvantaged. Others argue that these groups are not prepared for home ownership and that emphasis should be placed on rental units. Some believe our national policy should be directed at providing tax relief and other financial incentives to stimulate the housing and building industries. Others feel we should direct our energies toward eliminating the slums and blight of inner cities. Still others believe we should stimulate the purchase of homes by the upper and middle classes and allow these homes to "filter down" to the poor and needy.

Superimposed on these issues is the question of just which level of government should be responsible for financing and administering this area of domestic policy. Should this be a national concern, or should it be left to state and local governments? Or should it be left to the private sector? In a situation where no one can conclusively demonstrate that one policy alternative is superior to all others and the various affected groups are divided among themselves, significant and frequent policy deviations are possible.

Other factors contributing to the passage of the 1974 housing act center on the presidency. Recall that an earlier proposal by President Nixon had died in the Congress. It was only after winning a massive electoral victory in 1972 that his proposal was seriously considered and ultimately passed. Thus the appearance of having an overwhelming mandate from the American public serves as a tremendous boost to a President's ability to influence the forces of Congress. Also, we should not forget the extraordinary efforts applied by President Nixon and his administration on behalf of his program. A year and a half earlier, the President had effectively terminated the nation's housing program by impounding (that is, refusing to spend) money authorized under sections 235 and 236 of the 1968 housing act. Pressures were building on the Congress from all affected groups for relief. As often is the case, the Congress had neither the time nor the resources to draft a meaningful alternative to the President's proposal. Through his administrative tactics, President Nixon had maneuvered Congress into a position in which the choice was largely between the President's program, in modified form, and no housing program at all. In addition to all of these factors, the impending impeachment hearings denied the Congress time which it might have used to formulate viable alternatives.

Other factors contributing to the success of the President's proposal could be mentioned (such as the discontent of the nation's state and local officials with the previous approaches and the relatively unorganized situation of America's poor); however, the point should now be quite clear. Major policy change in the American system, when it occurs at all, is the product of many varied and unique forces. No single factor dominates. Given the right circumstances, a determined President can effect major change; however, these occurrences remain the exception, not the rule, in domestic policy making in the United States.

Thus, after a four-and-a-half year period of gestation, and forty years after the first significant federal housing assistance act, the Housing and Community Development Act of 1974 is now law. The location, quality, and availability of housing are such important features of our social milieu that any legislation which affects public housing is important. Adequate shelter from environmental forces is, of course, important to an individual's and a family's well-being. However, the location of housing also has a tremendous impact on one's social development and opportunities. To a considerable degree the location of housing determines one's educational opportunities, job opportunities, social acquaintances, and access to community services, such as parks and hospitals. With the exception of the family, perhaps no single factor is as important to the development of the individual as is the opportunity for decent housing. In recognition of this, the Kerner Commission, in its analysis of the urban disorders of the 1960s, recommended that six million new homes be constructed for low- and moderate-income families within a period of five years and further recommended that many of these homes be constructed in the suburbs, to provide the opportunity for inner-city residents to escape ghetto living conditions.[38] Of course no housing act, including the 1974 act, has yet to achieve the ambitious goals suggested by the Kerner Commission Report; however the report does represent recognition of the importance of available high-quality housing for a well-integrated society.

A major theme of this essay, moreover, is that the Housing and Community Development Act of 1974 is important for reasons which go beyond those generally associated with any housing act. The 1974 act must be understood as part of a "package" of proposals designed by the Nixon administration and to redirect America's federal system of government. Previous programs, such as urban renewal and Model Cities, were characterized by the Nixon administration (as well as others) as programs channeling the flow of federal power and influence to the national government. The general and special revenue-sharing measures (including the Community Development Act) would reverse this flow of power, according to New Federalism advocates, and would redirect decision-making authority to states, cities, and communities. Under such a philosophy, the national government would provide much of the funds and the local units of government, through their elected officials, make most of the decisions as to how those funds should be spent. To the extent that this "flow of power" has been reversed, these programs do represent changes of a very significant nature in the American federal system.

As power changes, moreover, so do the costs and benefits of decision making. One of the oldest axioms in American politics is that national decision making tends to be more redistributive and localized decision making tends to be more conservative.[39] National leaders, so the assumption goes, because of their political dependence on large urban centers tend to respond more favorably to inner-city, poverty demands; local leaders, especially those in areas where the disadvantaged are small in number or lack effective organization, tend to be more conservative in their decision making. Thus a shift in political power may mean more than simply granting authority to different people: it may dramatically affect the outcome of those decisions.

It is in this context that the Housing and Community Development Act of 1974 (and, indeed, all the revenue-sharing programs) must finally be evaluated. The political question which is paramount is whether community leaders are spending these funds in a manner which bypasses the needs of the socially and politically disadvantaged or whether these groups are now strong enough to significantly affect community decision making in the absence of national requirements. At this point no definitive answers are possible. It has been observed that most of the funds are being spent in impoverished areas; however, only a very small proportion of these funds are being used to support programs of social and human services. In order to influence the distribution of these funds it would seem that interested groups must organize and must compete in the community power struggle. The question of whether or not such organization and such efforts can meaningfully affect the expenditure of these funds must await future and more extensive analysis.

Multilateral Foreign Policy Making: The Conference on Security and Cooperation in Europe

William I. Bacchus

On July 30, 1975, heads of government or their representatives from thirty-three European nations and the United States and Canada gathered at Helsinki for the largest European summit meeting since 1815. Their purpose was to sign the Final Act of the Conference on Security and Cooperation in Europe (CSCE), more than two decades after such a conference was first proposed, and almost three years after the preliminary stage of the conference was begun. The results are subject to widely varying interpretations, their ambiguity reflecting the sometimes fundamentally opposed perspectives of the participating states and the sheer complexity of the many issues discussed. Except for the publicity surrounding its conclusion, the conference itself gained little public attention. Still, it was of considerable consequence, both as one element of the larger process of accommodation, or détente, in Europe and as a portent of future patterns of international relations. The problems of political and military security, of cooperation in a range of economic and technical fields, of the exchange of information, and of contacts between individuals, which the conference addressed, are fundamental questions for the future of Europe. The ultimate value of CSCE will not be known for some time, but certainly future intra-European relationships will be influenced considerably by this episode.

This case is the story of American participation in that conference, and more particularly, the story of how American policy was developed and carried out. It shows how foreign policy making differs from domestic policy making, and also how CSCE strategy and tactics differed from traditional views of how foreign policy is made. Before turning to the case itself, it is useful to consider the larger foreign policy process of which it was a part.

THE PROBLEM OF CONCEPTUALIZING
THE FOREIGN POLICY PROCESS

In recent years analyses of foreign policy have focused as much on the complex process by which modern governments decide upon and conduct their policies as on the substance of the policies themselves. This new concern with the policy process has raised questions about how we should view that process—that is, what general model or models are most likely to provide us with the most help in understanding how the foreign policy process works? A number of such models, or conceptual frameworks, have been suggested. For example, Allison has codified three alternative frameworks, which show policy respectively as (1) the outcome of rational choice among alternatives by nations as actors, (2) the product of large organizations functioning through regular patterns of behavior, and (3) the result of bargaining between critical individual actors or "players" in the game of bureaucratic politics.[1] In a later treatment, Allison and Halperin present a framework combining the second and third of these,[2] which Halperin has elaborated.[3] Most recently, Steinbruner has developed a largely compatible approach, derived from cybernetic theory, which maintains that policy is heavily determined by the cognitive capabilities of the individual mind working in interaction with the organizational structure of the government.[4] Davis has argued that foreign policy formulation can be viewed in terms of exchange theories derived from microeconomic analysis.[5] Earlier approaches of Lindblom, March and Simon, Deutsch, Wilensky, and Downs, among others, have also been applied to the foreign policy process, although they were not specifically designed for that purpose.[6] Recent studies also draw upon related work of Huntington, Neustadt, Schelling, Hilsman, and Snyder and his associates.[7]

Given these many contending approaches, it is important, as Allison has argued in his works cited, to be explicit about the assumptions made in analyzing the process leading to any given decision, since they affect the way we see the result; they provide the conceptual lenses which deepen some colors and filter out others.

A good starting point is the systems approach presented in the introduction to this volume. *In applying the systems model to foreign policy, which involves interactions between two or more governments, it is helpful to think of more than one system: while the environment may be shared, the outputs of one system or government constitute a part of the inputs of the other, and vice versa.* When many states are involved, as with CSCE, and when another group of "systems" is also important—in this case the two major alliances, the North Atlantic Treaty Organization (NATO) and the Warsaw Treaty Organization (WTO), as well as the European Community and more informal groupings of states—the pattern indeed becomes complex. Our chief concern here is with the "black box," or decision-making process, within the United States, but references will be made as appropriate to other parts of the American system and to the larger constellation of systems involved in the whole CSCE process.

Characteristics of the American Foreign Policy Process

While it will be clear by the end of this case that CSCE policy making differed in some respects from the normal foreign policy process, it may be useful as a base line from which to begin a consideration of this specific case.[8]

As a rule, the foreign policy process is a *collective* one, involving officials in many agencies and departments, increasingly the Congress, and more often than not, private groups and individuals. Each participant will have a different perspective and different *goals,* and the policy *process* provides a means of accommodation among them. Very seldom can any actor or group, however powerful, dictate policy which has no support among others involved. Effective policy is likely to be consensus policy, not dictated policy.

Second, the process is *continuous.* Each episode like CSCE is linked both sequentially and temporally with other episodes. It is structured in large measure by prior occurrences, and in turn sets the stage for subsequent ones, and it takes place simultaneously with a number of related events and policies which may have an impact upon it.

A third feature of the process is its *"open-system"* character. Information is often ambiguous, motivations of other parties are unclear, and the nature of the relevant environment is indeterminate. All this leads to the inability to foresee all alternative solutions to a problem, or many of the possible consequences of any visible potential solution.[9]

The fourth feature, *dissatisfaction* with what is currently being done, due either to new circumstances or reanalysis, is the precipitator of action. The incitement to change may come from within government, or it may take the form of new inputs such as activities of other governments or domestic actors. As a result, one or more of those involved decide that goals will better be served by a different policy; their efforts to devise and carry out these new policies constitute the policy-making process.

Fifth, there is an almost constant *interplay between organization and individual,* or bureaucratic and personal factors. Sometimes rank in the hierarchy (or power internationally) largely determines which position carries the day, while at other times personal relationships and individual skills and power predominate. What can be called "institutionalized personal power," which accrues to an individual because of his relationship to other individuals but which must be used in "legitimate" ways, is often a major factor.

Sixth, as is evident from the other features, the nature of the problems faced and the multiplicity of them often result in great *complexity.* This often forces problems upward for final decisions, but at the same time results in reliance upon experts, and cooperation among many experts.

Seventh, the process is often *reactive.* It is set in motion by perception of problems, rather than by a desire to meet abstract goals. It is attuned to what is or is perceived to be happening, rather than to what ought to be.

A final important feature is *the ambiguity of outcomes.* Their meaning is usually uncertain, and they only partially reflect fulfillment of desired goals. They tend to be disjointed and incremental, rather than comprehensive and final, meaning that major problems must generally be approached through a number of small steps, rather than a single large one. Participants in the process do not inhabit a neatly defined and regular world.

Traditionally, foreign policy, unlike domestic policy, has tended to be seen as the prerogative of the executive branch of government, rather than of Congress or parliament. When, as increasingly seems likely, the dividing line between domestic and foreign policy becomes blurred, the Congress will become more involved.

Reaction to Vietnam, and to secret executive actions, and the increasing prominence of economic issues with domestic ramifications make congressional participation all the more likely in the future.[10] Such involvement does not change the basic features of the process, but intensifies them. More actors, more uncertainty, and more complexity result.

Much the same is true when the policy in question involves many countries, rather than just two or three. CSCE, a multilateral conference involving thirty-five states, featured complex relationships not only within the U.S. government, but also between the members of the participating blocs (NATO, WTO, neutrals), and between the various groupings.

In short, the model sketched here is broadly applicable, but the dynamics involved and the relative weight of the factors will differ in "CSCE-type" situations from more traditional foreign policy episodes. With this in mind, we are ready to turn our attention to CSCE itself.

THE BACKGROUND OF CSCE:
"A DIALOGUE OF COMMUNIQUES"[11]

Although the origins of CSCE can be traced as far back as a 1954 Soviet proposal for an "All-European treaty of collective security," and the 1957 Polish "Rapacki Plan" for a nuclear free zone in Central Europe, it was not until the mid-1960s that such a conference became even a remote possibility. Only with the beginnings of détente (the limited relaxation of tension between the two blocs due to gradual recognition of some shared interests), and the partial dissipation of the heavy cold-war atmosphere of the 1950s and early 1960s, were the key actors of both the East and West willing even to consider the concessions necessary to reaching an agreement about such a conference.[12] Even so, final arrangements were not completed until the fall of 1972, owing primarily to caution exercised by Western nations, particularly the United States.

Major events of the latter 1960s with a direct bearing on CSCE included the following:

March 25, 1966	Beginnings of West Germany's *"Ostpolitik"*; Bonn offers to negotiate bilateral nonaggression treaties with U.S.S.R. and other East European States; proposes nuclear arms reduction and safeguard agreements. Détente receives major impetus.
1965–1968	*Group of Nine* (later Ten) smaller NATO and WTO states meet periodically to consider collective security proposals.
July 9, 1966	Warsaw Pact issues Bucharest *"Declaration on Strengthening Peace and Cooperation in Europe."* European Security Conference (ESC) proposed, with objectives of dissolution of blocs, removal of foreign bases, establishment of an all-European collective security system, furthering of economic, technical, and scientific cooperation. Status of proposed U.S. participation ambiguous. Proposal reiterated

in various contexts over next few years. Beginning of a *"Dialogue of Communiqués"* between the two blocs.

December 14, 1967   NATO ministers endorse *Harmel Report*, a NATO Council study on the future tasks of the alliance, which included indirect acknowledgement NATO was studying WTO proposals. Origin of Mutual and Balanced Force Reduction Negotiations (MBFR) idea.

June 25, 1968   NATO Ministers at Reykjavik propose force reduction talks (MBFR). No mention of WTO proposal for an ESC.

August, 1968   *Invasion of Czechoslovakia* by WTO states brings temporary halt to ESC consideration.

1969   Active interchange of communiqués, refining terms of each side, and bilateral private discussions take place. October 29, West Germany acknowledges existence of "two Germanys."

October 31, 1969   WTO ministers propose an ESC agenda: ensuring European security and renunciation of force among European states; expanding commercial, economic, technical, and scientific cooperative relationships.

The conference outlines which emerged by the end of 1969 from the "dialogue of communiqués," to quote a State Department release, were considerably more modest than those the East had proposed in 1966. However, a number of difficulties had to be overcome before the conference could be convened.

The West would not agree to begin until a number of political preconditions had been met, and at the insistence of the United States in particular, until provisions for separate negotiations on force reductions (MBFR) had been accepted. Western demands that the agenda explicitly include two very sensitive topics, the freer movement of individuals and noninterference by any European state in the internal affairs of any other,[13] also led to delays. Ultimately the Soviets grudgingly chose to allow discussion of them, in order to have the talks take place and to gain their primary goal of ratifying the political status quo in Europe.

Some idea of the complications involved can be seen from the following chronology of events leading ultimately to the Security Conference:

May 27, 1970   *NATO foreign ministers (Rome)* set "prerequisites" for ESC, specifically progress in Strategic Arms Limitation (SALT), Berlin, Intra-German, Bonn-Warsaw, and Bonn-Moscow negotiations; separate MBFR declaration gives principles to guide exploratory discussions.

June 22, 1970   WTO ministers expand proposed ESC agenda to include a "permanent organ" of European Security, and add cultural and environmental issues to topics for "cooperation." For the first time, U.S. and Canadian participation are explicitly accepted.

August 12, 1970   *West German–U.S.S.R. Nonaggression Treaty* signed (similar treaty with Poland follows on December 7, 1970).

December 1970   At respective ministerial meetings, WTO expresses disappointment at delay, NATO adds successful completion of Four-Power Berlin Agreement to other conditions for ESC listed in May. In February 1971, WTO again expresses impatience at "artificial obstacles" being placed in way of preparatory ESC talks.

June 11, 1971   Soviets accept in principle the condition that MBFR should be separate from ESC.

Summer 1971   Soviets attempt to further ESC through bilateral talks with Western states.

September 3, 1971   *Four-Power Berlin Agreement initialed;* a major obstacle to ESC removed.

Fall 1971   U.S. government establishes Security Conference Task Force under Assistant Secretary of State for European Affairs.

December 10, 1971   NATO reaffirms willingness to begin ESC preparatory talks when Berlin agreement signed, and lists four possible agenda items: security, including relations between states and some military issues; freer movement of people, information, and ideas; cooperation in economics and science and related areas; cooperation to improve the human environment. East told by NATO Secretary General Luns that without MBFR, ESC can have little significance.

January 6, 1972   WTO indicates willingness to add national as well as foreign armies to topics for force reduction talks; lists seven principles of European Security as basis for ESC.

February 1972   Nixon China visit heightens Soviet concern and willingness to compromise to begin ESC.

May 19, 1972   West Germany ratifies treaties with Poland and U.S.S.R.

May 29, 1972   *Moscow Summit.* U.S. agrees to multilateral preparatory talks for security conference "without undue delay," and to separation of MBFR from security conference. Soviets accept U.S. position that "the conference should be carefully prepared" before formally beginning, and new title, a "Conference on Security and Cooperation in Europe" (CSCE), to make it clear it was not limited to European states.

June 1, 1972   NATO endorses Moscow Summit formula for CSCE, with addition of discussion of freer movement of people, ideas, and information; expresses hope MBFR preparatory

talks can begin concurrently with or before CSCE preparatory talks.

September 10, 1972   During Kissinger visit to Moscow, November, 1972, dates
                       proposed by Finland for beginning of CSCE; MBFR
                       preparatory talks tentatively accepted.

By September 1972, an important turning point had been reached in the story of
CSCE. Much had changed since the Bucharest Declaration of 1966. Each side had
made concessions, but reflecting the progress of détente, the West was willing to go
forward on an essentially Soviet project, while the East, at least at this stage, was
willing to compromise considerably to gain the conference they deemed so important. The "Autumn of Détente" was ready to begin.

THE PROCESS OF NEGOTIATION:
PERSPECTIVES, POSITIONS, AND ISSUES

By the time ambassadorial-level representatives of the thirty-four participants
(Monaco joined later) assembled in Helsinki on November 22, 1972, the "dialogue
of communiqués" between blocs and the other discussions previously mentioned
had succeeded in establishing four or five major topics for consideration by CSCE.
What was unclear, however, was whether enough "give" existed in the positions
of the participants to allow meaningful results. One diplomat at the beginning of
the talks characterized them as "a dialogue of the semi-deaf," while another more
colorfully compared the participants to "a pack of 34 dogs warily circling and
sniffing at each other."[14]
Those assembled at Helsinki for this novel experiment—the proper collective
term may have been a "jamboree of nations"[15]—represented great diversity. Some-
how they had to find the means of gaining enough agreement to formulate a
detailed agenda, to establish rules of procedure, and to determine the structure and
timing of successive stages of the conference. While these steps are common to any
international conference with complex subject matter and many participants, they
are clearly more difficult when objectives vary widely and when the participating
nations are suspicious of each other. *Since the agenda for any conference largely
determines the outcome, it is easy to understand why caution is exercised in developing
it.* The process of building "a consensus of the participating Communist, Western,
and neutral nations,"[16] to quote Finnish President Kekkonen at the initial session,
proved to be almost interminable.

Participants and Goals

The United States can be seen as at best a reluctant participant in CSCE, and some
intimately involved U.S. officials would have preferred to take up the many perplexing issues in a less formal and more private way.[17] Given Soviet insistence on
CSCE as a basis for the entire era of détente, the fact that Western preconditions
had essentially been met, a desire for a unified NATO position on détente, and the
certainty that MBFR could not proceed without CSCE, the United States agreed to
go ahead. But the American approach was essentially passive if not negative,

characterized by a low profile (European critics sometimes saw it as almost invisible) and by an emphasis on damage limitation rather than positive gains.[18] (See Table 6.1.)

As a result of this essentially reactive approach to CSCE, U.S. participation can only be understood in the larger context of the intentions and concerns of the other conferees. In this respect CSCE differs from many post-World War II foreign policy episodes, in which the U.S. policy was much more active, and other states frequently found themselves in more passive roles. It can be argued, however, that as American power becomes less preponderant and as American global activism becomes less acceptable at home, the U.S. posture may be routinely more passive than in the past.

Like the United States, the NATO countries sensed a number of possible pitfalls in the conference. One cause of concern had to do not with Soviet intentions, but rather with NATO relationships. There was some worry in Europe that CSCE might serve to leave the Soviets in a preeminent position there, particularly if, as many believed, the United States was no longer firmly committed to the Atlantic alliance or to maintaining a physical presence in NATO. There was also a fear that the fate of Europe was increasingly being decided through "superpower bilateralism" between the United States and the U.S.S.R., and that the NATO partners were being left with little voice on issues affecting their vital interests.

Although there had been several incidents reinforcing this feeling in previous years, fresh in the minds of NATO members was the Soviet-American joint declaration signed by Nixon and Brezhnev at the Moscow Summit in May, 1972, which

Table 6.1

Participants in the Conference on Security and Cooperation in Europe

NATO* MEMBERS	NEUTRALS	WTO** MEMBERS
Belgium[†]	Austria	Bulgaria
Canada	Cyprus	Czechoslovakia
Denmark[†]	Finland	German Democratic Republic
France[†]	Holy See (the Vatican)	Hungary
Federal Republic	Ireland[†]	Poland
of Germany[†]	Liechtenstein	Romania
Greece	Malta	Union of Soviet Socialist
Iceland	Monaco	Republics
Italy[†]	San Marino	
Luxembourg[†]	Spain	
The Netherlands[†]	Sweden	
Norway	Switzerland	
Portugal	Yugoslavia	
Turkey		
United Kingdom[†]		
United States		

*North Atlantic Treaty Organization.
**Warsaw Treaty Organization.
[†]Also European Community members.

was seen by many as an example of "America's indifferent and even sometimes adversary approach to allies." Procedurally, this declaration of principles to guide relations between the two countries had been worked out over a period of several months and without NATO knowledge, at the same time the NATO Council had been attempting, with active U.S. participation, to develop a joint statement of principles to guide alliance relations with Moscow. Substantively, many NATO governments saw the declaration as "too soft," most notably in its adoption of the Soviet "peaceful coexistence" terminology and failure to go beyond a call for "improvement of relations and contacts" to advocate freer movement between East and West. The United States had earlier agreed with the allies that the former term might imply support of the "Brezhnev Doctrine" and should be avoided, and had urged them to include the latter in the joint NATO statement. One allied leader's conclusion: "You abandoned in Moscow what you were urging us here to support." A last straw for many was Gromyko's assertion in June that the accord represented the "outer limits" of what he would accept at CSCE on these topics and on the right of "self-determination" (which had also been urged on NATO by the United States and then dropped from the U.S.-U.S.S.R. declaration.)[19]

Ultimately, the uneasy state of the alliance led to the ill-fated "Year of Europe" speech by Kissinger in April of the following year.[20] Those in the U.S. government concerned with NATO policy and CSCE (not usually the same individuals dealing with Soviet-American relations) were increasingly aware of such problems, and one of the guidelines given the CSCE negotiators was to avoid exacerbating NATO relationships.[21] These alliance concerns, interestingly, seemed much more in the minds of U.S. officials than any domestic political reactions to CSCE, pro or con, which may be another way in which CSCE is an atypical episode.

Within NATO there were many shared expectations about CSCE, but also differences of emphasis. All the NATO members desired to go beyond mere ratification of the status quo (which many saw as having taken place de facto already) to a positive lowering of barriers between East and West, and to complementing state-to-state cooperation with expanded contacts on an individual level. Another desired outcome was the lessening of Soviet control over Eastern Europe through more direct contacts, advocacy of principles of national self-determination, and modification or elimination of the Brezhnev Doctrine. There was also agreement to leave technical military issues to MBFR (although the U.S. position was more adamant in this regard than many of the others), while allowing more general military topics to be considered. After some early internal disagreement, the West generally came to believe that detailed specific agreements were necessary to achieve positive results, and preferred to set the level of officials attending the final stage of the conference only after intermediate stages had determined whether a high-level finale was justified. A last major concern was to achieve a united position within the alliance through extensive consultations.

There were of course shadings of difference. One commentator suggested in June of 1972 that with respect to the prospect of CSCE, "The French and Scandinavians were enthusiastic, the Americans, British, and Dutch skeptical, the Germans confused, the Greeks, Turks, and Portuguese deeply suspicious."[22]

In general, the smaller powers—whether NATO, neutral, or WTO—saw CSCE as a potential way to gain an independent voice they did not often have; this raised their enthusiasm for the conference above that of the United States and some of the larger NATO powers.

Within the alliance, the French had been the foremost proponents of CSCE, and were in close accord with the Soviets about beginning it expeditiously.[23] They did, however, come to favor extensive preparations, along with the bulk of NATO. Like the Rumanians, they were strongly antagonistic to bloc-to-bloc negotiations, and never agreed to participate in MBFR, conducted on that basis.[24] The Germans generally favored CSCE (although suspicious of Soviet intentions), but their position was complicated by their parallel bilateral negotiations with East Germany and Czechoslovakia. The British shared American skepticism about CSCE, and had some reservations about MBFR. The southern flank countries (Greece, Turkey, Italy, Portugal) were also dubious, fearing that CSCE might dilute NATO's vitality. Norway and Denmark were, by contrast, among the strongest supporters of both conferences,[25] and Belgium, the Netherlands, and Luxembourg were only slightly less upbeat.

In spite of these differences and a rocky beginning, the NATO nations by most counts did remarkably well in maintaining coordinated positions throughout the conference. This was facilitated by what may be one of CSCE's most important outgrowths: the European Community's desire for and ability to develop unified positions through coordination and the use of common spokesmen. The nine member nations came to realize, as one observer noted prior to the conference, that unless they acted jointly, they would remain at a disadvantage vis-à-vis the United States and the Soviet Union, and possibly even the Warsaw Pact in discussions and negotiations concerning the future of Europe and its peoples."[26]

The Warsaw Pact states also had internal differences, although the issues were not usually joined frontally. Soviet objectives seemed clear-cut, as they had throughout the eighteen years the Soviets had pressed for a European security conference: (1) affirmation (some said sanctification) of the status quo in Europe; (2) blockage of West European unification; (3) removal of American presence in Europe (albeit gradually, pending a secure resolution of the German problem, and in a way which did not promote European unification); and (4) expansion of Eastern access to Western science, technology, and culture on a controlled basis (while limiting possible pressure for internal changes or ideological leverage gained from such cooperation). These objectives implied a brief conference, with results couched in generalities.[27] However, such an agenda was called into question by the considerably changed circumstances in which the conference finally took place. The Soviets had to adapt to Western modifications of the conference concept, they had to allow their WTO allies greater freedom to interact with the West in return for help in promoting the conference, and they had to slight the security interests of East Germany in order to reach the prerequisite Berlin agreement with the Western powers.[28]

The conference did not seem to bear out some initial Eastern European expectations that CSCE might provide greater direct contact with Western Europe, and serve as a means of advancing their own national interests with some independence from the Soviets. The WTO states did, in fact, follow Soviet orchestration. As one American participant asserted, "They would stand up, insisting on expressing the opinion of their Government, and read verbatim the speech just made by the Soviet representative all over again."[29]

There were three exceptions to this pattern of East European submissiveness. The Albanians, alone among the states invited, declined even to attend the conference. Although some assumed they would provide a "Chinese voice," they stated that no security could emerge from a conference organized by the superpowers,[30] an opinion perhaps held more moderately by some who did participate.

Rumania continued to act at CSCE, in line with a pattern discerned by one commentator prior to the conference:

> Always vulnerable to the use of force by the USSR, it has boldly exploited the balance among the big powers while carefully staying within the limits of conduct tolerable to the Kremlin. . . . Rumanian leaders see common European discussions, with the prominent participation of small states on both sides, as the logical culmination of their own diplomatic efforts.[31]

They were joined in this drive for an independent foreign policy by the Yugoslavs, who had their own very specific conference objectives relating to security issues, and particularly to the avoidance of national military measures in border regions and in waters which were "sensitive areas."[32] More generally, they were strongly in favor of a security structure in Europe which allowed a proper role for the smaller powers.

The final group of participants were the European neutrals, most of which took an active approach[33] and were strong advocates of each nation having a voice. Substantively, their position generally differed little from those of the NATO states.

Finland provided a special case, although its views differed little from those of the other neutrals. History and geographic location caused the Finns to walk a careful line between full independence and surviving in the shadow of overwhelming Soviet power. Finland's host role in CSCE reflected a desire for a voice in determining Europe's future, without antagonizing either side.[34]

An Emerging Agenda: The "Baskets"

Four main areas of inquiry for CSCE had emerged through the process described earlier: (1) political and security issues; (2) economic, scientific, and technological cooperation; (3) interchange of ideas, information, and people between East and West; and (4) permanent organizational machinery to enhance further cooperation and the reduction of tension.

Specific items proved very difficult to define, but a stratagem suggested by the Swiss ambassador early in the Helsinki stage of the conference allowed discussion to continue when precise wording could not be agreed upon. These four general topic areas became known as "baskets" I, II, III, and IV, respectively, and in common usage replaced more inflammatory references to what each "basket" contained. Specific titles could have been used, most likely by the Soviets, to limit discussion, excluding subjects which did not explicitly "fit" specific definitions.[35]

A review of how the participants viewed the several "baskets" helps clarify the difficulties. For the Warsaw Pact states, the security and political issues in basket I, especially affirmation of the European status quo, represented the heart of CSCE and the rationale for the conference. They desired "renunciation of the use of force and the threat of force in relations between European states," as well as recognition of "the existing European borders . . . as final and unchangeable."[36]

It was in this area that NATO fears about CSCE were concentrated; NATO members were concerned that unless there were specific safeguards written into the Final Act they might be agreeing not to defend themselves, whatever the provocation by the Soviets. NATO therefore had frequently proposed that any agreement should also contain principles which would govern relations between states, irrespective of their social and political systems. This last phrase was clearly directed at renunciation of the Brezhnev Doctrine and was therefore hardly acceptable to the Soviets as initially proposed. Also implicit was the idea that if such principles were violated, nations would be free to use force for self-protection if needed and therefore there could be no question of abandoning NATO. Basket I also included certain general military aspects of security, while as agreed earlier, more specific military topics were to be taken up by the MBFR conference in Vienna. The final agenda for basket I took the form of two items: principles governing relations among participating states, and "confidence-building measures" in the military sphere. These CBMs, in the conference jargon, consisted primarily of prior notifications of military movements.

Basket II was controversial. Improved economic, scientific, and technical cooperation between East and West, which in practice meant greater access by the East to Western advances and most favored nation trade status, was an important Soviet and, to a lesser degree, Eastern European goal. The West had no objection to this basket (to which environmental matters were later added at NATO initiative), although in the United States there were some reservations as a result of Soviet grain purchases the preceding summer, and congressional desires to tie trade benefits to improving the condition of Soviet Jews. Basket II in the larger scheme of things provided some leverage to the West—it represented something which could be withheld pending basket I and basket III concessions by the Soviets. The final basket II agenda as developed at Helsinki was divided into five categories: trade, industrial cooperation, science and technology, environment, and other (for example, transportation and communications).

If basket I was at the core of Eastern European desires for CSCE and a cause of major concern for the West, the reverse was true for basket III. Ultimately titled, ambiguously, "Cooperation in Humanitarian and Other Fields," as defined by the West it contained several potentially delicate issues such as reducing obstacles to freedom of movement and contact among peoples, which the Soviets opposed on the grounds that such measures could result in "ideological subversion." Basket III also posed certain issues concerning relations between the Soviets and other Warsaw Pact states. More traditional and more easily controllable areas such as expansion of cultural exchanges caused few problems, but with Czechoslovakia freshly in mind, discussion intended to produce "freer movement of people, ideas, and information" was not the foremost priority for the Soviets. Western and neutral governments made their most determined efforts on these issues, and it was generally held that without progress here, no overall agreement, and therefore no summit conference could occur. Basket III represented a Western attempt to have CSCE deal with "intra-bloc" as well as "inter-bloc" relationships. If basket II provided the carrot for the Soviets, basket III was the stick. By the end of the preliminary talks an agenda emerged which mixed the issues: human contacts, information, and cooperation and exchange in the fields of culture and education. Although clearly still on the West's list of "musts," the "freer flow of ideas" was not specifically included in the final pre-conference agenda.

Basket IV, dealing with permanent machinery, was pushed primarily by the East, although ironically it had first been suggested in a NATO communiqué (Rome,

May 27, 1970). Western caution about creating machinery whose purpose was ill defined was occasioned by Soviet hints that such an organ might eventually replace NATO and the WTO. This, it was feared, might lead to Soviet domination of Europe, since the U.S.S.R.'s existing individual treaties with each of the WTO states would survive an end of the two large alliances while no similar individual treaties would bind the United States and its NATO partners together. This concern was strengthened by a further Soviet theme, that sooner or later the time would come when it was more appropriate for Europeans to consider their own problems without the presence of observers—that is, including the Soviet Union but excluding the United States and Canada. It was finally agreed to make such machinery contingent on other accomplishments of the conference, with the coordinating committee charged with consideration of "such measures as may be required to give effect to the decisions of the Conference and to further the process of improving security and developing cooperation in Europe."[37]

These four clusters, or baskets, achieved only after seven months of intermittent but intense negotiations, were presented in July, 1973, to the first formal stage of CSCE.

Timing and Procedures

In addition to questions of the substance of the agenda, issues for the preliminary talks included timing and procedure—both of which were nontrivial since they reflected quite different expectations of the numerous participants.

At the initial session, for example, and over an essentially technical point, the Rumanians served notice that they expected to participate (and be treated) independently,[38] and in this they had strong support from such neutrals as Austria, Finland, and Yugoslavia, as well as from the French. The first important procedural decision was that each nation would participate independently, and that there would be no dealings on a bloc-to-bloc basis. Perhaps even more importantly, this same group of countries succeeded in forcing agreement that all decisions of the conference would be taken by a consensus rather than on formal votes.[39] Quickly interpreted as requiring unanimity, this had the result of lengthening both the preliminary and formal stages of CSCE, but increased the freedom of action of each individual state.

Another procedural issue also had implications for the length of the Conference. In keeping with their desire for a short conference and for general rather than detailed statements, the Soviets at first resisted the idea of subdividing the work of the formal stages of the conference into committees. The West, and particularly the United States, however, continued to insist on careful preparation and on emphasis on substance over "the mere atmosphere of détente" since it would be "difficult to evaluate measures proposed in the name of so vague an objective."[40] Toward the end of the preliminary talks, the Soviets agreed to this condition, and to formation of committees.

Nevertheless, the U.S.S.R. pressed for a prompt conclusion throughout the course of CSCE, as well as for a summit conference at the end, the latter in order to gain maximum exposure and legitimation for the political aspects of security they hoped the conference would ratify. The West would use these Soviet desires as a means to gain substantive concessions. By the time the preliminary talks began, it was possible to discern the format of the formal "stages," as they came to be called, of CSCE: Stage I would be a short meeting of foreign ministers of participating states, to accept the agenda and procedures developed by the coordinating committee in the preliminary talks and to appoint necessary working committees; Stage II would be the actual working out of agreements for each "basket"; and Stage III would be a final meeting to ratify results (although it was unclear well into Stage II whether the West would accept a Stage III summit conference, as they finally did). This scenario was indeed followed: the Stage I Foreign Ministers meeting took place in Helsinki, July 3 through 7, 1973; Stage II began in Geneva on September 18, 1973, and stretched on until July 25, 1975; and the concluding summit occurred, once again in Helsinki, on July 30 to August 1, 1975.

THE MANAGEMENT OF AMERICAN PARTICIPATION IN CSCE

For the sake of convenience, this account has referred to the "American position" or to the position of other governments as if they were the products of single individuals. In real life, of course, modern governments are made up of a multitude of individuals, a surprising number of whom may play major roles, and each of whom has somewhat different perspectives and approaches to issues which concern them. What these individuals do, individually and collectively, is important for what becomes government policy and action. What happens *within* governments must not be ignored if we are to understand what happens *between* governments. To comprehend, therefore, why CSCE (or any other policy process) traveled the course it did, we must look "below" the nation level.

In examining U.S. participation in CSCE, it is useful to start with the prior expectations about what might be accomplished. Then Assistant Secretary of State for European Affairs, Martin J. Hillenbrand, showed in congressional testimony that expectations were distinctly limited:

> We have no illusions that the conference will solve the problems of a divided Europe. Nor do we think that even modest improvements will come easily at a conference of over 30 sovereign states, each of which has somewhat different goals and different perceptions of what the conference should try to accomplish.

He continued by stating that even modest improvements would be heavily dependent upon careful preparations.[41]

Initially, Secretary Rogers and State Department Counselor Richard Pederson had shown considerable interest in CSCE, but more because of its potential effect on relations with the Soviets than because of any direct accomplishments it might bring. Support for CSCE seemed essential for good Soviet-American relations in an election year, since the Russians wanted it so much. After the Moscow summit of May, 1972, which cleared the way for the conference, but also made it less necessary to placate the U.S.S.R., American attention waned. *This points up the fact that many specific foreign policy issues, particularly if their outcomes are ambiguous, as those of CSCE seemed sure to be, are viewed in the context of their possible effects on the progress of more general issues and relationships.* Henry Kissinger, then still at the National Security Council (NSC), was characterized by one official as being "dead set against CSCE," not surprising in view of his belief that private discussions among only those directly involved in a given issue were most likely to further U.S. interests.

Having nevertheless agreed to attend the conference because the costs of not participating seemed higher than those of taking part, the United States made its approach one of minimizing negative outcomes, of avoiding conflicts with the Soviets on issues not of basic importance to the United States, of "detachment," and of letting others take the lead when possible. At the same time, it was viewed as important not to undercut the West European NATO allies.[42] This approach, coupled with CSCE's technical nature, which acted to make it a heavily "experts negotiation," helped to set the mode of U.S. participation. A higher-priority undertaking, or one more general in nature, would likely have resulted in higher-level involvement, and less independence for the delegation.

The U.S. participation in CSCE was organized in Washington by the Department of State, with little attempt at direction by the NSC staff. One participant said that given the desire to keep a low profile and the perceived lack of involvement of fundamentally important U.S. interests, it was deemed preferable to "let State play with it," while two of Kissinger's senior associates at the NSC, Helmut Sonnenfeld and William Hyland, confined themselves to keeping a "weather eye" on how State was proceeding.[43] This served to emphasize caution, given the strength of the NSC staff and the relative weakness of the Department of State at this time (Kissinger became Secretary of State only in September, 1973, about the time Stage II of CSCE began in Geneva, and this change had little effect on how CSCE was conducted). Similarly, there was relatively little of the bureaucratic infighting which is so prevalent when vital issues are at stake.*

Within State, primary responsibility for CSCE rested with the Office of NATO and Atlantic Political-Military Affairs in the Bureau of European Affairs (symbolized by the letters RPM), and secondary responsibility, with the Assistant Secretary for European Affairs (Martin Hillenbrand until mid-1972, then Walter J. Stoessel, Jr., and Arthur A. Hartman, successively). This was natural, in view of RPM's responsibility for NATO matters, in which context CSCE had first arisen. Some in the Department believed that the Bureau of Politico-Military Affairs (PM) was a more logical focal point, but given RPM's experience with the issue and a potential agenda considerably broader than security issues, RPM retained central responsibility. Nevertheless, some sense of competition between the two remained.

The first formal step in bringing the government together to develop a CSCE approach was formation of an inter-agency task force in late 1971, chaired formally by Assistant Secretary Hillenbrand. This group met en masse no more than two or three times. Given the large number of agencies and departments with some interest, the real work quickly came to be done in working groups dealing with potential agenda items, each of which met three to four times on average, in late 1971 and early 1972.** This "working group" procedure continued throughout

---

*Such divisiveness, arising from different agency interests and perspectives, is quite common. This is one reason that the "bureaucratic politics" model of the foreign policy process discussed earlier has received currency in recent years.

**On "basket I" issues, major participants included PM, the Arms Control and Disarmament Agency (ACDA), the Office of the Assistant Secretary of Defense for International Security Affairs (DOD/ISA), the Joint Chiefs of Staff, and to some extent, the NSC. Basket II involved the Bureau of Economic and Business Affairs, in State (EB), EUR/RPE (Office of OECD,

the conference, although once negotiations began there were very few meetings, most coordination being accomplished through obtaining clearances from those involved in a particular issue on position or instruction documents. The process was assured a common focus by the fact that each working group was chaired by a representative of RPM: the Office Director, his deputy, or the head of the political section. Eventually this exercise, intended to provide a U.S. "entering position," culminated in the production of several large books outlining positions on the various issues. After agency and NSC staff review, these books became the basis for U.S. participation in very intensive NATO Council studies preceding the conference. The latter were undertaken primarily by USNATO (the U.S. Mission to the North Atlantic Treaty Organization, Brussels). The final result was the NATO communiqué, issued in May, 1972, at the Bonn meeting, which outlined the common NATO position on CSCE. After the decision was made to proceed with CSCE, the next step was to assemble a U.S. delegation, and once it came into existence, the center of gravity shifted to Helsinki.

The Helsinki Preliminary Talks

Ambassadors accredited to Finland were the official heads of delegations at the Helsinki preparatory talks, although the major nations (for example, the United States, France, Great Britain, West Germany) also sent individuals, usually as deputy heads of their delegations, who had experience working specifically on CSCE issues. In the U.S. case, George S. Vest, previously the Deputy Chief of Mission at USNATO in Brussels, was selected. Although his official duties were to act as advisor to the U.S. Ambassador to Finland, Val Peterson, all interviewed agree that Vest was the de facto head of the U.S. delegation.

The U.S. negotiating team was selected by Vest with some care, in an attempt to establish a small group (never more than six to eight members) which, by virtue of the perspectives of the individuals and agencies represented, would allay the many fears about what the outcome might be and would, as a consequence, give the team considerable latitude in "running" the negotiations.[44] Unlike many complex negotiations, where representatives of various agencies sometimes act almost independently, the preliminary talks were a team operation.

The team approach was facilitated by the fact that the negotiations were run initially in plenary sessions, in order for delegations to make opening statements, and for the rules of procedure to be worked out. The United States, in line with its view that careful preparation was required, advocated that the serious work be accomplished in committees. This was resisted by many for the first two rounds of the preliminary talks (November to late February): by the Soviets (who ultimately agreed once it was clear that if CSCE were to take place at all, it would have to

---

European Community and Atlantic Political-Economic Affairs, State), Commerce, and Treasury on eocnomic matters; and on environmental ones, RPE, State's Bureau of International Scientific and Technological Affairs (now Oceans and International Environmental and Scientific Affairs, OES), the Council on Environmental Quality, Environmental Protection Administration, HUD, HEW, and DOT. Basket III was largely State-centered, as was basket IV, with a number of parts of the Department involved, including the office of the Legal Adviser. Upon occasion, State's Bureau of Intelligence and Research, the Policy Planning Staff, and the CIA were also involved.

include more detail than they originally desired); by smaller nations with small delegations, who feared they would not be able to cover several simultaneous meetings; and by some ambassadors who felt they would lose control of the delegations they nominally headed. Through completion of the "Swiss synopsis," laying out all proposals into the famous "baskets," it was finally possible to establish committees and subcommittees. Agreement about their use was obtained by having them meet sequentially rather than concurrently, to allow even small delegations to be involved in each.[45]

A conventional picture of current foreign relations would lead to the assumption that the CSCE negotiating team would be on a short leash, with its activities bounded strictly by instructions worked out in Washington. The reality was quite different. Vest apparently was adept at the art of consensus building, both in Washington and in Helsinki. By virtue of his experience, he was already well acquainted with both the issues and many of the participants, who had been former NATO colleagues. Throughout the whole Helsinki phase, one knowledgeable officer said that the delegation received no more than three or four explicit instructions of any consequence. These, along with broader, more general instructions, were drafted in RPM. The delegation did, however, keep Washington (RPM generally) informed through periodic cables, usually on Fridays, summarizing the week's developments. Vest deliberately chose not to send daily cables, in order to preserve some independence of action and a certain "Olympian distance" from Washington.[46]

Before the talks began, and during the several recesses, however, Vest would return to Washington, take the "temperature" of senior officials in State and at the NSC, and in consultation with RPM and other members of the "Task Force" as appropriate, participate in drafting his own instructions. In addition to the confidence placed in Vest, his own desire to "keep Washington out of his hair," and the nature of the negotiations, a final reason for the lack of explicit instructions was a belief in RPM that it would be futile to go into great detail, that this would lead to endless clearances, and that a certain blindness or vagueness helped to fend off special pleading and interference by individuals or agencies viewing CSCE from a narrower perspective.[47]

None of this was automatic. *It is always important to remember the personality factor in the policy process. Another delegation chief of staff, perhaps with less Washington influence, less self-confidence, or less skill in attaining consensus of all involved might well have desired, and needed, more instruction.* Similarly, if more domestic interest in or controversy about CSCE had existed, Vest and the delegation almost certainly would have been on a shorter leash.

By the time the third round of the preliminary talks opened in Helsinki at the end of February, 1973, three committees had been established to work in the three major areas (baskets I, II, III), and one member of the U.S. delegation had been designated to be in charge of U.S. involvement with each, under the direction of Vest. In another illustration of how participation was managed through interchange between Washington and Helsinki, the officer who had drafted many of the instructions in RPM, and who had had a primary responsibility for the work of the Washington Task Force and working groups, joined the delegation and assumed responsibility for "basket III" negotiations.

Although with the creation of the "baskets" and designation of the committees the broad outlines of the final CSCE act—still almost two and one-half years away—had emerged, much remained to be done. At Helsinki the preliminary stage took considerable time, since for most delegations "it would not suffice merely to set down the headings of the agenda items, but there should be as uniform understanding as possible on interpretation of the terms used."[48] This view, expressed by the deputy head of the West German delegation (that is, Vest's opposite number) is illustrative of the West European approach. It is interesting to note that the United States did not actively resist a quick and superficial result (although continuing to argue against this in public), and the implication must be that the earlier calls for careful preparation were intended as much to fend off the conference as to put it on firm ground. One knowledgeable observer saw, as a result, the European Community "taking the ball and running with it, while the United States sat on the bench," and believed it was during the preliminary talks that "European Community political consultation came of age."[49]

Basket III proved to be the most difficult to deal with, with the Soviets regarding as subversive the idea that freedom of movement and contact should be allowed to take place under other than controlled circumstances. By late May, however, this reservation was at least temporarily dropped, making it possible to agree to proceed with Stage I of the Conference, the Foreign Ministers Meeting in Helsinki in July 1972. In the end, the Soviets gave way on a number of points, not only because of West European insistences, but also because of the absence of U.S. pressure to check the stronger enthusiasms of others. In addition to inclusion of basket III, there was also much more attention to the idea of confidence-building measures and to the nature of the principles in basket I than the Soviets had originally desired. They also accepted a much less explicit charter for basket II than they had initially desired.[50] Conversely, the "carrot" of greater economic access to the West proved less tempting than originally thought, since it became clear that the Soviets envisaged making advances on this score primarily though bilateral contacts.[51]

The Helsinki Foreign Ministers Meeting (CSCE Stage I)

The meeting of the thirty-five foreign ministers from July 3 to 7, 1973, first adopted the "Final Recommendations," which had been so laboriously hammered out at Helsinki,[52] and then proceeded to cast doubt on much that had apparently been agreed therein. In speeches and "declarations" of the participants, and in responses to them, old differences, presumably reconciled, reemerged in earlier forms. There were clear signs the Geneva stage was likely to be a protracted one, if all the diverse views presented were to be accommodated.

On basket I issues, divergence between the Western position of security resting on renunciation of force (shared by some neutrals) and the Eastern emphasis on inviolability of borders and territorial integrity continued. The range of topics and approaches desired were reflected in the list of "Ten Commandments," or principles guiding relations between states which the Geneva talks were expected to amplify (and which took seventeen months to accomplish.)[53] Confidence-building measures and the relationship of CSCE remained highly ambiguous. Generally speaking, those not included in MBFR wanted that negotiation closely linked to CSCE, while the French at the other extreme wanted total divorce. The superpowers preferred separation, if not purely bilateral agreements, on this score.

In contrast, basket II was much less controversial. The heat over MFN (most favored nation) status and trade obstacles in the final stages of the preparatory talks had been defused by the "magic formula of . . . 'reciprocity of advantages and obligations . . . with due regard for the diversity of economic and social systems'" in the Final Recommendations. There was hope that this would avoid disputes over "most-favored treatment" and "non-discrimination," principles which are almost impossible to apply between planned and market economies because of their lack of correspondence.[54]

Basket III, however, was another story. The final title, "Cooperation in Humanitarian and Other Fields," was an eleventh-hour compromise, papering over a fundamental difference between the East, which desired to concentrate on more controlled, organization-level and government-sponsored exchanges, and the West and neutrals, which emphasized improvement of individual human contacts. The West clearly indicated that specific concessions were expected here. British Foreign Minister Douglas Home said little could be expected from CSCE unless "there are plenty of eggs in basket III," while West German Foreign Minister Scheel served notice that an end to CSCE without a summit conference "would not be a catastrophe for Europe, nor would it be the end of the process of detente."[55]

Basket IV (follow-up) received relatively little attention in the statements of the foreign ministers. In the Final Recommendations, this area was entrusted to "a coordinating committee, composed of representatives appointed by the Ministers for Foreign Affairs," which was also to be charged with other coordinative functions throughout the conference, and with making recommendations about "the organization of its third stage."

U.S. presence at the Foreign Ministers session continued to be understated. Secretary Rogers (accompanied by George Vest) chose tactically to emphasize the importance of the contributions of other NATO nations, and to acknowledge that the superpowers alone could not decide the fate of Europe. It seems fair to say that the United States, as it had earlier in Helsinki and would continue to do in Geneva, served a role as expediter and facilitator as much as engaged participant. While the point remained unstated, CSCE was a low-stakes game compared to SALT and the Soviet-China triangle.

The Geneva Negotiations (CSCE Stage II)

On August 29, the coordinating committee for CSCE, made up of representatives of each participating state, met in Geneva to prepare for Stage II, and the full conference convened on September 18. Committees and subcommittees were formed to deal with the "baskets" and their subdivisions, with every state represented on each.

For the Geneva phase, the U.S. organizational arrangements went through a modest evolution. George Vest was named head of the U.S. delegation (resident ambassadors were no longer even nominally involved) and a number of other nations made similar adjustments. Because the various committees were meeting simultaneously, rather than sequentially as in Helsinki, it was necessary to augment the delegation with specialists, who would "sit in the U.S. chair" for most of the committee meetings. The size of the U.S. delegation grew to average twelve to fourteen (from a previous average of six to eight). The entire delegation would meet each morning to compare notes, and to track the work of each committee in relation to the others.

One need which emerged at the end of the preliminary talks and carried through to Geneva was for a "chef du cabinet" to help keep track of the many simultaneous committee negotiations and to assist the head of delegation develop overall policy. Since initially there was no deputy head of delegation, and since the specialists had their own responsibilities, this position of Secretary of Delegation (later Executive Secretary of Delegation) was an important one. Reflecting the tendency to pick individuals with previous experience with the complex issues involved, the choice for this position was a mid-rank foreign Service Officer who had been chef du cabinet for the Secretary General of NATO. Since he remained in it from the end of the preliminary talks throughout the entire Geneva phase and up to the Helsinki summit, he was able to provide much needed continuity in a delegation whose other members were, almost without exception, replaced at one point or another.

An example of this changing of the guard, which illustrates how organizational decisions can underscore policy decisions, was the replacement of the Head of Delegation. Upon assuming his second "hat" as Secretary of State in September 1973, Kissinger soon decided that he wanted Vest as his special assistant for press relations. Given the Secretary's immediate priorities and an upsurge in press and congressional skepticism about his role, this was understandable, but a change in delegation heads so soon after the beginning of the definitive Geneva stage did little to refute the notion that CSCE was taken lightly at senior levels in Washington.

Vest's interim successor was D. Eugene Boster, formerly the Deputy Chief of Mission in Warsaw, with prior Moscow but not NATO or other "multilateral" experience, who was named formally as a special assistant to the Assistant Secretary of State for European Affairs (since Vest had been a special assistant to the Secretary, this helped convey the same message as the replacement itself). One side advantage of Boster's appointment was that he held ambassadorial rank and therefore it would not be necessary to approach the Senate Foreign Relations Committee for another ambassadorial-level special envoy position, a matter of some touchiness in State's relations with the committee at the time. Within a few months Boster took up his previously scheduled ambassadorship and was replaced by Albert W. ("Bud") Sherer, Jr., Ambassador to Czechoslovakia. Sherer continued to serve concurrently in both positions throughout the Geneva phase of CSCE. This second change, plus the failure to relieve the new delegation head of his other responsibilities, also served to project a lack of concern for CSCE, and probably would have been avoided had the conference been of higher priority to senior officials. In fact, Sherer was in Geneva virtually full time except during recesses of the conference, so any lack of attention was more symbolic than real.

Boster and then Sherer continued Vest's general pattern of operation with a few changes reflecting their individual styles. Sherer accepted the recommendation originally made by Boster that a Deputy Head of Delegation be appointed, no doubt reflecting both his own style (which was to rely much more heavily on his staff than Vest had done), and his continuing responsibilities in Prague (and therefore a need for someone who could act for him in absences from Geneva). Most close observers felt that there was little difference in outcome as a result of these changes, although there was some suggestion (not held valid by Vest himself) that

Vest had an advantage because he was at home in a multilateral environment and had served at NATO while both Boster and Sherer had had almost exclusively bilateral experience.[56]

Throughout the Geneva phase, the U.S. approach continued to be a "team" rather than an "agency" delegation, as one example illustrates. One of the two subcommittees for basket I issues was charged with developing the military "confidence-building measures" (CBMs) mentioned previously. During the earlier period, when the CSCE task force was meeting in Washington, the primary Department of Defense representative on such issues had been a Foreign Service Officer serving an exchange tour in the Office of the Assistant Secretary for International Security Affairs (OSD/ISA), who found it easy to work closely with the State Department. Later, he was assigned to the delegation, with responsibilities for the "CBM" subcommittee. He would sit in the U.S. chair at the table, backed up by a representative from the Arms Control and Disarmament Agency (who represented the U.S. when he did not), and by an officer from the Joint Chiefs of Staff, who was responsible for keeping notes. The three sent joint reports and often joint recommendations, both to State and to Defense. This served a useful coordinative role, and the fact that the Defense Department was getting direct reports was a psychological advantage in maintaining smooth interagency relations.[57] More generally, close contact among representatives of diverse interests in the policy process often helps to minimize bureaucratic battling. Familiarity can breed shared outlooks as well as the oft-noted contempt.

Dialogue between the delegation and Washington, and the intensity and level of Washington concern waxed and waned according to what was occurring at the conference, and developments in the broader East-West context. The Geneva phase of CSCE began with what one participant characterized as a "bull session," and serious drafting did not begin for some months. As a consequence, there were at first no general instructions to the delegation. The need to discuss issues off the cuff, and the infeasibility of running such a diffuse negotiation from afar were among the reasons why the delegation was composed of experts from the responsible offices. When actual drafting began, the delegation began to seek more instructions, especially on issues the delegates themselves identified as potential problems. In some cases, instructions were rather detailed (for example on CBMs), while in others, the delegation, as another member said, felt it was operating in a vacuum. What instructions there were were drafted largely in RPM, sometimes with guidance from higher levels, and occasionally with contributions by other agencies. The policy-planning staff in the Department of State (S/P) made contributions to the general effort, but its role amounted to one officer following what was happening, injecting ideas, and occasionally helping in some drafting. On one occasion S/P produced a general paper (February, 1974) for the Secretary, but fundamentally it had a "watching brief" until the last six months or so of Geneva. At that time, concern with follow-up (basket IV issues) brought S/P somewhat more to the fore.[58]

At more senior levels of the government, there was very little attention to CSCE until the very end of the Geneva phase, and even then it was hardly intense. In part this was because for the first year the distractions of Watergate left much substantive policy—domestic and foreign—unattended by the White House, and in part it was because of the low priority given the conference. Kissinger had an evident distaste for CSCE and dealt with the issue only when it could not be avoided. Even attempts by the delegation and Washington "backstoppers" toward the end of 1975 to formulate a public affairs policy foundered as a result of his lack of interest.[59]

More generally, this aspect of U.S. participation (or lack thereof) in CSCE is indicative of the fact that top-level officials cannot and do not give close attention to every issue. Since there was not much domestic or congressional interest in CSCE and, with few expectations, not much chance of major gains or losses, senior policy makers, who in any case prefer to deal directly with the Soviets on fundamental security issues, had few incentives to spend time on CSCE. *This not infrequent "leadership vacuum" means that much national policy, with the exception of major issues, will be developed at lower levels, with personal consideration by top officials coming only at the end, if at all.* This is of course one reason that a view of policy making which treats national governments as single, united actors is likely to be misleading.

As the stakes in CSCE varied, senior attention levels did also. In the spring of 1974, interest heightened as a result of the Soviet push for an early conclusion to the conference, if possible before the Nixon-Brezhnev summit scheduled for July. Because they were importuned by Gromyko to encourage speed (and on the other side by Allied governments not to permit undue haste), Kissinger and his surrogate for CSCE, Helmut Sonnenfelt (by now moved from the NSC to become Counselor of the Department of State), paid closer attention to CSCE, and transmitted a number of rather explicit instructions to the delegation. Once the accelerated schedule was deflected interest lessened, but picked up again in the late winter and spring of 1975 as the conference worked its deliberate way toward conclusion.

One additional aspect of the link between Washington and Geneva is that the nature of what instructions there were changed, once actual negotiations and drafting of the Final Act began. The task force in Washington virtually ceased to exist; its job of preparation was over. In place of substantive instructions, matters of "general conduct" came to the fore, and the delegation needed to be privy to the tactical preferences of the Secretary. The delegates requested and received an increasing amount of backstopping. Kissinger's decisions were conveyed to RPM in the European bureau through Sonnenfelt, and were generally cleared just within the State Department (while substantive instructions throughout the conference were cleared as appropriate with other interested parts of government).[60]

The issues at Geneva continued in a familiar mode; compromise in difficult cases was even harder to obtain, because all parties realized this was for all practical purposes the last chance. National concerns sometimes preempted those of the major alliances, and at a broader level, differences of philosophies and goals often seemed less surmountable than ever.

Perhaps the first major breakthrough occurred on April 5, 1974, with respect to "inviolability of frontiers," the third of the ten "Principles Guiding Relations between Participating States" in basket I.[61] Unrestricted interpretation of this principle, which had been a bedrock Soviet position, would have prevented even peaceful change upon agreement of two states. This reflected the Soviet Union's obvious desire to keep the two Germanys permanently divided. Naturally the West Germans insisted upon inclusion of the right of peaceful change of frontiers, and they were joined by the other members of the European Community, who wished to hold open the possibility of future political unity. The United States believed that the most important principle was renunciation of the use of force, including across borders, but that this could not rule out "peaceful changes in frontiers if such changes are based on popular will and mutual agreement between states."[62]

Under the compromise finally agreed to by the Russians (who were in their 1974 diplomatic offensive to gain an early conclusion to the conference), principle III upheld inviolability of frontiers from assault; the acceptability of peaceful change was to be incorporated elsewhere in the text. Even so, the final compromise did not take place for eight more months, until December. Work on the other principles proceeded at a plodding pace, almost as if the orchestration required a set amount of time to complete each. They were not fully negotiated until the very end of the Geneva phase.[63]

Military aspects of security also proved difficult. Some Western states, notably the British, insisted that at least some military confidence-building measures be placed on the CSCE agenda, even though more technical details would be left to the MBFR negotiations. These "CBMs" fell into three categories: (1) prior notification of major military maneuvers, (2) exchange of observers for such military maneuvers, and (3) prior notification of troop movements. The issues were difficult conceptually: what counted as troops for notification purposes (for example, border guards?) and what territory was to be included under agreement (if the entire territory of participants was included, all of the U.S.S.R. would be; but if only border strips were involved, then the entire territory of some smaller nations would be covered, but only a fraction of the U.S.S.R.).

In general, the Soviet approach was to be as inclusive as possible, applying any aspect covering Soviet territory to U.S. and Canadian territory as well, even though they are physically far from Europe. They also opposed notification of military movements, and in general any mandatory limitations to their freedom of action. This made the Western and neutral states (and more than one of the Warsaw Pact nations as well) distinctly uneasy, in view of prior interventions. This was also one of the few areas in which divisions occurred within the U.S. government, with the Department of Defense more skeptical than the State Department, since the military feared such agreements might hinder American military operations.

Ultimately, the Final Act did contain confidence-building provisions (see Figure 6-1). Given their mildness, they did not tread unduly upon Soviet sensitivities. An evaluation of their worth must await further evidence about how the participating nations actually behaved (in the fall of 1975, NATO did notify others of maneuvers and sent an invitation to the Soviets to send observers, which they ignored; and in January, 1976, the Soviets did send notification of some of their own maneuvers—but did not invite observers).

One other aspect of the CBM question was whether CBMs should apply to the Mediterranean area. Dom Mintoff, the volatile Maltese Prime Minister insisted throughout CSCE that they should, and for a period in 1975 threatened to delay or thwart the final summit (under consensus, the blackmail possibilities were high, unless all other participants were willing to change the rules, which many were reluctant to do).[64] However, the Mediterranean littoral, or coastal, states finally accepted limited pledges of equal status and treatment as perhaps the most they could obtain.

Basket II issues, although in some ways the most technically complex of any, generated relatively less heat than I or III, but the negotiations here were by no means as smooth as suggested in some reports. This was true even though it came to be generally agreed that significant progress on economic and commercial issues was more likely to occur bilaterally, or in more specialized multilateral meetings. Broad guidelines and general principles were essentially all that could be hoped for or achieved, and firm commitments to action were rare. Much the same was true in the other topics in basket II.

Issues of human contacts and information in basket III were closest to the core of Western and neutral interests, and a major stumbling point. The Soviets, in particular among the Eastern states, were sensitive to anything that might lead to "pollution of the mind" (to quote one American delegate), and made concessions in basket III only when it became apparent that the conference would not be concluded (and the much-desired summit would not take place) without them.

It was in this area, as well, that NATO differences were most felt. The West Europeans believed that, having decided to participate in CSCE, they should make every effort to achieve positive results, and that basket III issues provided the best opportunities for this. The United States, as has been mentioned before, had lower expectations about what could be achieved, and in any event thought additional Soviet concessions would better be sought in other areas, such as SALT and perhaps MBFR.

The potential for disagreement arising from these differing calculations about CSCE was compounded by a somewhat erratic U.S. approach. Secretary Rogers had shared the Western European enthusiasm for freer exchange of peoples, and had emphasized the importance of this area in his speech at the Helsinki Foreign Ministers meeting in July, 1973. Secretary Kissinger, in contrast, was much less consumed by the issue:

> A point was reached in 1973 where the Europeans accused [him] of being ready to sell out their interest, on what he seemed to consider an idle piece of paper, in return for Soviet concessions in Washington-Moscow deals on strategic weapons and Indochina.[65]

Alliance tensions were increased by non-CSCE issues as well. The promised "year of Europe" ended with what one observer called "the biggest rift in the 24-year history of the alliance," as a result of lack of consultation about and radically different reactions to the "Yom Kippur War" between Israel and the Arab states in October, 1973, and the subsequent U.S. global military alert the night of October 24-25, during which a "virtual communications breakdown existed between Washington and its chief European allies."[66]

At the time of the Nixon-Brezhnev summit in July, 1974, there appeared to be another NATO falling out. Some West Europeans accused the United States of yielding to the Soviets on the issue of winding up CSCE, and thereby undercutting Western leverage on basket III. Eventually, the United States moved closer to the other Western states on these issues, and decided to press for an "acceptable" basket III. Some speculate that an important reason for this shift in position was that Kissinger realized that a Ford participation in a summit—desired for domestic political purposes, since presidential popularity almost always rises as a result of such preeminently "presidential" activities—would have to be justified by real or apparent Western gains, and that a stronger basket III presented the only possible candidate. Illustrating another of the complexities surrounding CSCE, U.S. pressure on this issue was exerted most tellingly outside the conference environment.

Kissinger, in his meetings with Soviet Foreign Minister Gromyko in Vienna in February 1975, made it clear the Soviets must accommodate or there would be no summit and CSCE would die.

Until the very end, movement on the substance of basket III was glacial. Only in early May did the basis of agreement emerge on human rights issues, in the form of "substantially a Soviet acceptance of a joint Western proposal that was made as a final agreed position."[67] One observer's evaluation of the outcome of basket III, while somewhat cynical, is nevertheless germane: "The East accepted the idea that human contacts, flows of information, and the right to travel were subject to international discussion even though the permanent clauses were so punctured as to become about as impenetrable as cheesecloth."[68] Given the ambiguities, those close to the negotiations put a great deal of emphasis on the need for assessing implementation—what actually happened as a result of the negotiated agreement—before deciding whether basket III had any meaning.

The final basket, concerning follow-up measures to the conference, remained in question until the last days in Geneva. Only the Rumanians, Finns, and Yugoslavs, enjoying their ability to participate directly in the process of détente, pushed energetically until the very end for full-scale follow-up procedures, which they hoped would allow that opportunity to continue. But a number of other delegations cared strongly about the outcome, although they had widely differing reasons for supporting or opposing elaborate follow-up. The U.S. role "above the din" was illustrated very well in this instance: standing aloof from differences among the NATO allies and letting others take the lead, but attempting to keep perspective on the problem and to insure that essential American interests were taken account of in the Swedish sponsored compromise on the issue.[69] The issue was no longer whether there should be permanent machinery; from the beginning of the Geneva phase no delegation strongly advocated this. Rather, it was whether periodic follow-up meetings should be provided for, or just one. The compromise which emerged was characterized by one U.S. official as an agreement to hold "a meeting to discuss further meetings," scheduled for June 15, 1977, in Belgrade (see Figure 6.1).[70]

THE HELSINKI SUMMIT (CSCE STAGE III)

Many of the important provisions of the Final Act were completed only at the last minute; firm scheduling of the Helsinki summit was completed only on July 21, and final negotiations of the Geneva phase concluded a day or so later. Once it had been established that the Final Act was going to be fleshed out in detail, it was inevitable that the Geneva stage would be protracted. This was partially due to the sheer complexity of obtaining agreement of thirty-five nations on every word of more than a hundred pages of text, and partially because, until the very end, the Soviets were not prepared to sacrifice much of substance to obtain their preferred timing and the summit. They may have calculated that the United States would encourage Western acquiescence to their choices of wording; only when this did not occur were they willing to compromise to obtain the summit, which would cap their twenty-year push to regularize the outcome of World War II.[71]

FIGURE 6.1. Summary of Provisions: Final Act of the Conference on Security and Cooperation in Europe (Helsinki, August 1, 1975). (*Source:* "Conference on Security and Cooperation in Europe: Final Act," reprinted in *Department of State Bulletin,* 73, no. 1888, September 1, 1975, 323–350.)

"The High Representatives of the participating States have Solemnly adopted the following:"

BASKET I ("Questions Relating to Security in Europe")

A. Declaration on Principles Guiding Relations between Participating States

Participants "Declare their determination to respect and put into practice," regardless of their own system, location, or level of development, the following principles:

1. Sovereign equality, respect for the rights inherent in sovereignty
2. Refraining from the threat or use of force
3. Inviolability of frontiers
4. Territorial integrity of States
5. Peaceful settlement of disputes
6. Nonintervention in internal affairs (of another participating State)
7. Respect for human rights and fundamental freedoms, including the freedom of thought, conscience, religion or belief
8. Equal rights and self-determination of peoples
9. Cooperation among States
10. Fulfillment in good faith of obligations under international law

B. Document on confidence-building measures ("CBMs") and certain aspects of security and disarmament

1. Prior notification of major military maneuvers (3 weeks in advance if to occur within 250 km. of frontier and/or if more than 25,000 troops involved); encouragement to notify of other maneuvers
2. Exchange of observers at military maneuvers, voluntarily and on a bilateral basis
3. Prior notification of major military movements, at State's own discretion, but encouraged "with a view to contributing to confidence building."

Also affirmed need to work for disarmament, and took note of complementary nature of political and military aspects of security; interrelationship between European security and security of each state; and importance of exchange of information in security area.

(Continued)

BASKET II ("Cooperation in the Field of Economics, of Science and Technology and of the Environment")

Recognized cooperation in these areas can best be developed on the "basis of equality and mutual satisfaction of the partners and of reciprocity"

1. Commercial Exchanges: resolved to promote expansion; recognized beneficial effects of "application of most favored nation treatment," improved business contacts and facilities, promotion of exchange of economic and commercial information, improvement of marketing techniques

2. Industrial cooperation and projects of common interests to be pursued

3. Provisions concerning trade and industrial cooperation, including harmonization of standards, arbitration, encouragement of specific bilateral arrangements

4. Science and technology: possibilities for improving cooperation in fields of agriculture, energy, new technologies and rational use of resources, transport technology, medicine and public health, and a variety of hard science areas; and suggested a number of forms and methods of cooperation

5. Environment: agreed to cooperate in studies and in developing more effective measures to bring improvements in fields of air and water pollution, protection of marine environment, land utilization, conservation, environmental conditions, fundamental research and assessment regarding environmental changes, legal and administrative measures; and suggested forms and methods of such cooperation

6. Cooperation in other areas: development of transport, promotion of tourism, solving migrant labor problems, training of personnel

Questions Relating to Security and Cooperation in the Mediterranean

Participants pledged to promote good relations with nonparticipating Mediterranean States, and to conduct their relations with these states in the spirit of the "Declaration on Principles Guiding Relations between Participating States" (basket I); and stated intention to cooperate with these states in a number of specified ways

BASKET III ("Cooperation in Humanitarian and Other Fields")

In order to "contribute to the strengthening of peace and understanding among peoples," a number of steps proposed:

1. Human contacts: aimed to "facilitate freer movement and contacts, individually and collectively, whether privately or officially, among persons, institutions, and organizations, and to contribute to the solution of humanitarian problems arising in that connection; specific references to contacts among and reunification of families, easing restrictions on marriage between citizens of different states, facilitating professional and personal travel, improvement of conditions of tourism, encouragement of meetings of young people, sports exchanges, and general expansion of contacts.

2. Information: aimed for improvement of circulation of, access to and exchange of oral, printed, filmed, and broadcast information; proposed cooperation in a number of specific ways; expressed intent to improve working conditions for journalists.

3. Cooperation and Exchanges in the Field of Culture: proposed a number of fields and forms of cooperation to extend and improve mutual knowledge and relations.

4. Cooperation and Exchanges in the Field of Education: expressed intention to extend educational relations, to improve access and exchanges; and to do this particularly in the fields of science, foreign languages and civilizations, and teaching methods.

BASKET IV ("Follow-Up to the Conference")

Participants declared their resolve to pay regard to and to implement the provisions of the act—unilaterally, bilaterally, and multilaterally; and to continue the multilateral process initiated by CSCE through exchange of views on implementation; to organize meetings to these ends, beginning with one at the level of representatives appointed by Ministers of Foreign Affairs, which would explore the "appropriate modalities for the holding of other meetings which could include further similar meetings and the possibility of a new Conference;" and set the first of these meetings for Belgrade in 1977; and concluded with final logistical arrangements for conclusion of the current conference.

That the summit was not delayed even further (as late as early July some press reports predicted that it was not likely until October) owed to a change in the psychology surrounding the negotiations, particularly on the part of national leaders not at the conference. Soviet leaders concluded that the time had come for compromises in basket III; once this was done, the carrot of the promised summit could not be denied. While there was some fear among Americans that the summit would place too much emphasis on the Conference, and perhaps release a "détente euphoria," this was balanced by a domestic political consideration—President Ford apparently wanted to go to a summit—and by a realization that it would have been very awkward to demand a lower-level meeting. Typical of the cautious approach and understatement was Kissinger's reminder that the United States had not agreed to the summit until all major Western European countries had done so and that "it was our view that nuances that might separate one in one's assessment of this did not warrant breaking allied unity on the subject."[72]

In any event, the thirty-five heads of state or their representatives, and hundreds of lower-ranking officials gathered at the austere Finlandia house in Helsinki on July 30. Their meeting was variously compared to the Congress of Vienna in 1815 and to the last full gathering of the old era of European royalty at the funeral of King Edward VII in 1910.[73]

More than two full days were devoted to speeches, each head of state interpreting the results of the thirty-month negotiation and underscoring his nation's own concerns, along familiar lines. Predictably, Brezhnev emphasized that the results did not give any country the right to tell another how to manage its internal affairs, in apparent reference both to basket III and to U.S. congressional pronouncements of support for measures intended to modify Soviet treatment of their own Jewish population. For the United States, Ford emphasized that the conference was a part of a process which would lead to easing of tensions and not a conclusion; that much would depend upon the dedication of the participants to making the declarations of the Final Act come true; and perhaps most importantly in view both of Soviet goals and of the recent rocky history of the NATO alliance, that the United States had a "vital interest in Europe's future," and intended "to participate fully in the affairs of Europe and in turning the results of this conference into a living reality," and with respect to NATO, would "continue to be a concerned and reliable partner."[74] The latter was intended, and apparently received, as a much-needed reinforcement of allied relationships.[75] Throughout their public utterances, both Ford and Kissinger kept to the low-key approach followed for so long, pointing out what remained to be done, and characterizing CSCE as a "useful step" but hardly as a panacea.

With the conclusion of the statements, the Final Act was signed in a sober ceremony lasting only seventeen minutes. An unusual, protracted, and ultimately ambiguous chapter in European politics had at last come to an end.

EVALUATION AND AFTERMATH

Although our focus has been almost exclusively on CSCE itself, it is almost impossible to evaluate the outcome without some sense of the broader European political and security environment. Moreover, the Final Act was essentially declaratory: U.S. officials repeatedly emphasized to the author that the proof of the worth of CSCE must rest upon how well such statements of intent were followed by performance. This would depend on how the whole course of détente progressed, and on the advantages that the participating states perceived in carrying out the declaration. There are no legal penalties for noncompliance, only political and economic quid pro quos which could be withheld, and the limited weight of public opinion. Some go so far as to say that if CSCE fails to succeed, it is an irrelevance.

European security in its fundamental sense was clearly not much affected. The exclusion of force reduction issues limited progress on military matters (MBFR, which it was hoped conclusion of CSCE would facilitate, remained stalled as of mid-1976), and strategic arms limitation talks, perhaps most important of all, will take place between the superpowers alone. It is still true that "For the present, security in Europe, defined as the absence of war across the line between the blocs, will depend on the will of the two essentially non-European powers to maintain the balance."[76]

At the same time, in the human rights and cooperation areas, CSCE did provide a means for further accommodation, if not the solution to all outstanding issues. As one commentator wrote:

> Part of the headache for Moscow is that nearly everybody there with a griev-ance on human rights grounds these days is citing the Helsinki agreement to support their case. Moreover, the Soviets have found it necessary to discuss more candidly than in years, such sensitive subjects as censorship, the impact of Western radio broadcasts and travel abroad to justify the way the accord is to be implemented.[77]

Almost immediately after the Helsinki summit, Western governments and journalistic commentators pressed the Soviets on the basket III declarations. The issue was highlighted by the Soviet reluctance and eventual refusal to allow Nobel laurate designate Alexander Sakharov to go to Stockholm to accept his prize. In October, 1975, Georgi Arbatov, a foremost Soviet commentator on détente and the United States, complained that provisions on the freer flow of people and ideas appeared "to be the only point of interest to the West in the entire document signed this summer," and suggested that trying to make it appear the U.S.S.R. was violating the agreement, or arguing that the Soviets owed something in return for the security aspects of the Final Act, would lead "to a questioning of the validity of the agree-ments and of détente as a whole."[78] In December, Brezhnev made many of the same arguments, and objected to some "influential circles in the Western countries," and their "campaigns of misinformation, of slander against socialist countries, all sorts of pinpricks," which were not in accordance with "the spirit of the decisions adopted at the European conference."[79]

Nevertheless, there were indications that the Soviets, having initiated CSCE in the first place, were reluctant to repudiate it, if not shy about trying to shape it to their larger purposes. A revised Soviet-East German friendship treaty, signed in October, 1975, for the first time in such documents made no reference to the de-sirability of the reunification of Germany, which would have conflicted with the inviolability of frontiers principle.[80] In January, some travel restrictions on newsmen in the Soviet Union were relaxed, notification of forthcoming military maneuvers near the Turkish frontier was made, and a campaign to promote pan-European conferences on economic matters was begun. However, the Warsaw Pact states seemed interested in excluding U.S. participation in the latter, doing so in part by proposing geographically limited topics such as transport, regional energy problems, and some environmental issues. The Soviets also picked up their old theme of opposition to proposals for European community political unity.[81] By the end of the first year after the Conference, the reviews were distinctly mixed; some asserted there had been positive gains in both security and human rights areas, while others thought very little had been accomplished.[82]

Western criticism of CSCE came forth from a number of sources. Those suspicious of the Soviets and critical of détente loudly protested what they saw as ratification of the status quo, in that the Final Act seemed to rule out any rollback of Soviet hegemony in Eastern Europe; and doubted the worth of announced Soviet concessions with respect to freer movement of individuals and ideas. Some commentators called the agreement "fraudulent,"[83] or "unfulfilled"[84] and during the 1976 political primaries and fall campaign, the Final Act and Soviet behavior presented an easy target for critics of détente.

Those more favorably disposed to détente argued that "basket I" at most accepted what was de facto, the prevailing (and likely to prevail) situation in central Europe, and retained the possibility of peaceful change and realignment (including reunification of Germany). They also noted that the Soviets had made little progress in excluding the United States from Europe, that both baskets I and III provided standards for measuring (and commenting upon) Soviet actions, and that CSCE had broadened the range of issues considered subject to international discussion and negotiation. While gains were admittedly modest, little had been lost, and in the context in which CSCE was first advanced, this was held a reasonably satisfactory outcome.

The next formal part of the CSCE process was to be the 1977 Belgrade meeting. The basic U.S. posture toward it apparently would be to avoid turning the meetings into name-calling and mud-slinging sessions, but nevertheless to be strongly concerned with implementation, and to be attentive to Warsaw Pact performance in this regard in the interim. The election of Jimmy Carter and his subsequent human rights offensive merely added steel to previously stated positions. Further, the United States would continue its somewhat detached approach, not favoring a full-fledged "CSCE II" as an outgrowth of Belgrade. As before, EUR/RPM was the primary government unit concerned with the forthcoming meetings, and something similar to the task force operation preceding CSCE itself began to emerge as the date grew closer, with many of the same individuals involved.[85]

In one respect, however, U.S. participation at Belgrade was likely to differ from that at Helsinki and Geneva: in the degree of congressional interest and involvement. For example, a number of members of Congress concerned with basket III issues, led by Representative Millicent Fenwick, forced passage of a bill, signed by President Ford on July 3, 1976, which created a fifteen-member commission (twelve members of Congress and three representatives of the administration) whose responsibility was to "monitor the acts of the Helsinki signatories . . . with particular regard to the provisions related to cooperation in humanitarian fields." The Ford executive branch, both because it desired to continue a low-key approach and not allow CSCE to become a point of contention with the Soviets, and because of its distaste for what it regarded as congressional interference with its management of Soviet relations, was unenthusiastic about the commission, but nevertheless resigned to including it in the process leading to Belgrade.[86] Early signs, however, suggested that the Carter administration would move much closer to the congressional position and treat the commission more as a partner in the process.

Perhaps the most accurate assessment of CSCE was made by Arthur Hartman, the Assistant Secretary of State for European Affairs, when he said just prior to the Helsinki summit that the conference "must be seen in perspective as but one aspect of our continuing efforts to move from confrontation to negotiation in strengthening East-West relations in Europe."[87]

Although CSCE may have been derided by some as "a masterpiece of weasel-wording," to quote one U.S. negotiator,[88] and an "ersatz peace pact," to quote one commentator,[89] it was seen by others, including another U.S. official, as a "reflection of our times."[90] Where it will lead is unknowable, but it was an extraordinary gathering and exercise, unthinkable a few years earlier. The future will depend on the attitudes of the governments involved, and this may pose a dilemma. It can be argued that heretofore détente has revolved around a series of practical understandings between Eastern and Western European states, and especially the U.S. and the U.S.S.R., but that fundamental issues of philosophy, political status, and legal rights have been avoided. As the two sides have begun to approach the practical limits, further progress may depend upon accommodation on deeper issues, and this will be much more difficult. In this context, it may have been much too sanguine for anyone to think CSCE would result in a fundamentally changed Europe; the conference may have achieved all that very disparate national interests would permit.

A major element of uncertainty about the future is the role the United States will be willing to play. The flush of enthusiasm about détente has clearly dissipated, whether in the executive branch, the Congress, or the country at large. Skepticism about Soviet intentions is on the rise, and there seems a clear disposition to insure full value received before making any further arrangements with the U.S.S.R. The degree to which accommodations should be made will clearly be a much more visible domestic political issue than was the case with CSCE. Somewhat paradoxically, this tougher predisposition at home may not be matched by a willingness to provide strong leadership abroad, although in its first months the Carter administration seemed less inclined to defer to established policies. Old European fears about the strength of the United States have reemerged, and talk of American "eclipse," "withdrawal," "paralysis," and "neo-isolationism" is increasingly heard.[91] Whether such worries are justified or not will depend not only on what the Soviets do, but upon the domestic political climate in the United States. Ultimately, no foreign policy can be successful, once it becomes visible at home, unless it is in reasonable accordance with public opinion. East-West relations have become an issue of heightened public attention, and development of future policy will of necessity need to take domestic perspectives into account to a greater extent than was true for CSCE. As a result, what lies ahead is even more opaque than is usual in foreign policy.

IMPLICATIONS FOR AMERICAN POLICY MAKING

It is now possible to place CSCE in the larger context of American foreign policy making. In some respects, it was not at all typical of what is likely to be the model pattern in the future and was in some ways an example of an earlier and simpler period.

The degree to which the Department of State was allowed to play the primary role was unusual at a time when more and more parts of the executive branch, not to mention the Congress, are increasingly involved in foreign policy, and when major action flows to the White House. In systems language, both inputs (demands and supports) for CSCE, and the outputs (policy declarations) were largely external to the domestic political system. Except for hearings held by the Subcommittee on Europe of the House Foreign Affairs Committee on the eve of CSCE in 1972, a few brief trips by some committee members to the field for briefing, and some suspicious resolutions introduced largely for nuisance value just prior to the Helsinki summit in 1973, there was almost no direct congressional involvement. From this stand-point, CSCE was conducted the way most in the executive branch believe *all* foreign policy should be. At least until Vietnam, many in Congress were also uneasy about challenging the executive on Foreign Policy in marked contrast, for example, to the energy field. This was not true of all détente-related issues (for example SALT, troop reductions, grain sales to the Soviets, Soviet treatment of minorities), and as argued above, is unlikely to be true in the future.

Second, CSCE at no time became subject to major policy debate, particularly among those actively engaged in the process, in part because of the low-profile approach decided upon by the administration. Up to a point, political leadership has usually been able in the past, as in CSCE, largely to determine when foreign policy issues become prominent and when they do not. Lack of leadership emphasis was one reason for lack of public involvement in this case (with the exception of the summit, which did receive attention, as the President and Secretary of State knew it would in choosing to attend). Finally, and largely because it was not a first-order issue, CSCE received less continuing top-level attention than many issues, and thus reveals more clearly the important part the working-level bureaucracy at home and delegations abroad can play in such cases.

In other respects it does give indications of some future patterns of policy making. Many observers believe that multilateral conference diplomacy on a variety of specialized and general topics will be increasingly prevalent in years to come. If CSCE is an appropriate model of this, some of our conceptions about how policy is made may need adjustment. Because of the many participants, multilateral diplomacy is likely to be conducted more openly than the more traditional bilateral variety. Outcomes are likely, as one official noted, to be "softer," and to reflect attempts to find compromises acceptable to all participants, as compared with the more confrontational bilateral encounters. Smaller states may be able to play a larger role than has usually been true since World War II if CSCE represents a model of international interaction going beyond the bloc-to-bloc approach typical of the past three decades. As issues become more economic in nature, all this is particularly likely to be true, since economic influence is likely to be more widely dispersed than political power.

CSCE does fit most of the features of the simple model of the foreign policy process presented at the beginning of this case. Its collective nature, involving many participants (even if not Congress) should be amply demonstrated, as should its place in a continuous web of related détente and alliance issues, such as the German problem, SALT, MBFR, and great-power bilateral relationships. It was a prime example of complexity, both substantively and in terms of the process and actors involved. The many influences which permeated the open system of CSCE did add considerably to the uncertainty of outcomes and their meaning.

The picture is less clear from the American point of view with respect to what caused CSCE to take place. The United States was not dissatisfied with most aspects of the European security picture taken up by CSCE, at least in the sense of wanting a change, because it was felt real improvement was impossible. Had it not been for the interests of its allies and the perception that CSCE was a Russian quid pro quo for agreements in other areas, the United States would probably have chosen to have no conference at all. It has been argued that foreign policy is often the result of reaction to problems, rather than the result of a conscious effort to advance abstract goals. CSCE certainly did show U.S. policy in a reactive mode, but unlike many instances, this was a consciously chosen posture. A choice was made to allow others to lead in developing and advocating Western proposals, and this policy was generally followed. Similarly, the interplay of personal and organizational factors was present, most noticeably in the way the U.S. delegation functioned under its three heads. Broader policy choices and the mode of the conference set the parameters of possibility, but within such limits, there was ample room for individualized styles of operation.

Finally, the outcomes of CSCE clearly fit the "disjointed and incremental" pattern, and were distinctly ambiguous. Most of the final language was evolutionary, rather than the result of conscious and clearly charted changes of course. One official interviewed felt there were only two instances during CSCE when U.S. policy was changed abruptly: a decision in late 1974 strongly to support the West Germans on inclusion of the possibility of peaceful change of borders, which was then negotiated with the Soviets at senior levels, thus eliminating one of the major difficulties in concluding the conference; and a somewhat similar decision, described earlier, to press for a stronger basket III, at the insistence of the Western Europeans. Otherwise, gradual evolution was the norm.

That there is no one set process or pattern by which foreign policy is made is a major lesson of the U.S. involvement in the Conference on Security and Cooperation in Europe. Under conditions of complexity with multiple governmental actors, a variety of approaches are possible at each stage of decision making, and outcomes are by no means predetermined. When the locus of action moves from a U.S. government decision to international policy, additional sources of uncertainty about final results are added. The lack of control of the international political environment is an important difference in foreign policy compared with most domestic policy, and in the last analysis, the most important distinction between the two policy arenas.

7

Policy Making and Politics in America

David A. Caputo

These five case studies have provided a variety of perspectives on the American policy-making process, and the reader has probably drawn a variety of conclusions concerning that process. This short concluding section places the cases in a broader theoretical framework and emphasizes the implications of the cases for the study of American politics.

The systems model, introduced in Chapter 1 as a useful device for analyzing the cases, can now be utilized for comparing them and deriving general conclusions from them about American policy making. The components of the systems model provide the focal points for summary and comparison of the cases. As these components are reviewed, the reader may wish to refer to the diagram of the systems model back in Figure 1.1.

A COMPARISON OF THE CASES

Demands

Consider, first, the demands portion of the systems model. Remember that demands represent the various requests by groups or individuals for specific policy action. The demands articulated in these five case studies illustrate the differences in scope, origin, and degree of conflict which may characterize policy demands.

Demands may have either broad or specific objectives, as shown by a comparison of the demand for the Equal Rights Amendment and the demand for campaign finance reform. ERA proponents advocated the ERA not as an end in and of itself, but as an opening wedge in the achievement of a broader policy demand—the elimination of sexual discrimination from all aspects of American society. The campaign finance reform legislation, despite the public rhetoric which dominated the discussion and the legislative decision making, was a demand for quite specific legislation limiting campaign contributions and expenditures and increasing the extent of public financing of campaigns. Though a broader purpose was envisioned, namely, equalizing financial resources and increasing access to political office, this objective was much more diffuse and difficult to specify.

Policy demands are generally associated with interest groups outside the government. But though interest groups such as NOW, in the ERA effort, and Common Cause, in the campaign finance reform effort, were actively involved in both proposing and attempting to gain support for specific policy demands, groups within the government also played an active role in generating policy demands. Professor Davis points this out in his references to Vice President Rockefeller's energy proposals and the proposals of the various energy agencies set up at the federal level. An even more dramatic example is President Nixon's special revenue sharing proposals, which were eventually enacted through the housing and community development legislation. Thus the systems model should include policy demands generated by groups or individuals within the various governmental structures as well as demands generated by groups outside the government.

Issues of broad public interest frequently give rise to conflicting demands from different political sectors. This was evident in the Ford administration's apparently contradictory policies on energy supply and consumption, which reflected an attempt to meet the demands of various interested parties, including the oil companies, farmers, and the military. The case of energy policy is also important because it illustrates the problems the United States has when it must respond to interests beyond its control—in this case the oil-exporting countries and the other industrialized nations of the world. The housing and community development case offers another illustration of conflicting demands—some, such as those from developers and participants in poverty programs, for protection or modification of existing programs, and others, such as those from the administration itself, for substantially different programs. The Housing and Community Development Act, by shifting the federal programs from a specific program-by-program approach to increased block funding, signified a major shift in the demands of city officials, federal bureaucrats, and congressional decision makers. By contrast, the Conference on Security and Cooperation in Europe, which attracted little public interest in America, resulted in the formulation of rather narrow policy demands by the State Department, with little policy debate.

The existence of conflicting demands guarantees that at some point in time proponents and opponents of a specific policy will attempt to increase their support by soliciting public support, the support of key interest groups, or the support and cooperation of prominent political leaders. Once this is done, the policy process takes on a new dimension. With the increase in participants and resources involved comes an increase, too, in political interaction and debate.

Supports

The cases in this volume offer interesting insights into the specifics of the supports component, as well as the demands component, of the systems model. The importance of this component was stressed in Chapter 1. All five case studies demonstrate the willingness of concerned groups and individuals to pursue their policy objectives through the legitimate policy-making process. For example, the advocates of ERA and campaign finance reform had to deal with numerous problems and setbacks throughout the policy process. But rather than withdrawing from the system when they met difficulty, they simply tried another tactic or tackled another aspect of the problem. In other words, both proponents and opponents of change accepted the basic rules of the political system and attempted to utilize them for maximum gain. In this respect, the case studies, since they focus on the active participants in recent policy-making decisions, may convey a limited picture of American reality.

It is entirely possible that large numbers of the general public are either apathetic (choose not to participate because they lack interest) or alienated (choose not to participate because they feel that the costs of such participation are too high or that the results are foregone conclusions) and that the public support for governmental action is actually far less than it appears to be.[1] The case studies, with their necessary focus on overt decisions, do not indicate the actual level of underlying support for the political system. Certainly the reports in recent years of low voter turnouts and the reasons cited by nonvoters suggest that apathy and alienation may be on the increase in the United States.[2] Difficult as it is to weigh these variables, it is important not to overlook them in our concentration on specific policy decisions. The reader might well consider the implications for the policy process, and the American political system as a whole, if apathy and alienation should reach high levels.

The Decision-Making Process

While the input variables of demands and support are interesting and important to an understanding of American politics, they are less important than the decision-making process itself—the so-called block box of the systems model, in which policy actually gets developed and adopted. These case studies are particularly helpful in describing this component.

Three main conclusions can be drawn from these cases about the decision-making process itself. Each of these describes a characteristic of decision making in contemporary America, and taken together they aptly illustrate the complexity of American policy making. The first conclusion regards the large number of participants involved in decision making. As Table 7.1 indicates, a wide variety of

Table 7.1

Institutional Participants in the Policy-Making Cases

CASE STUDY	INSTITUTIONAL PARTICIPANTS
Equal Rights Amendment	Congress, 50 state legislatures, courts
Energy Policy	President, State Department, Defense Department, various energy offices, Congress, foreign countries
Campaign Finance Reform	Congress, Courts, President
Community Development Act	Congress, President, Department of Housing and Urban Development
Conference on Security and Cooperation in Europe	State Department, President, Department of Defense, Congress

formal governmental institutions were involved in each of the areas under study. Each of the five cases involved a complicated array of groups, and these groups represented diverse sets of interests. Thus congressional and presidential interests were far apart on the issues of both campaign finance and energy policy. The main lesson is that not only are there large numbers of governmental groups involved in public policy making, but these groups often represent different and even conflicting interests.

Perhaps the best example of this is the traditional opposition between the President and the Congress. Since their electoral bases are different, it is only reasonable to expect the President and the various members of Congress to advocate different policy positions. This is not to say that the presidential position is the "correct" one or the one in the "public interest," but that members of Congress and the President may in fact differ on what exactly is in the national interest. Thus it should not be assumed that the interests and desires of the various institutional groups active in the policy-making process are the same. The fact that different governmental groups have different political bases of support is important in determining the diversity of political views in the American system. Certainly the debate over energy policy aptly demonstrates this point. A member of the House of Representatives representing an agricultural district dependent on mechanization will be unlikely to support stringent rationing of gasoline or propane supplies since such policy may have an adverse impact on his district. The President, however, may see such rationing as absolutely essential to a coordinated national energy policy.

It must also be remembered that each of these institutions has its own set of rules and procedures which help to structure its action. Thus congressional decision making follows certain procedural processes which may appear antiquated or irrelevant, but which are generally necessary for careful and complete consideration of an issue. Similarly, presidential proposals are developed with the aid of executive staff specialists and the appropriate executive agencies. They cannot be enacted without congressional approval, but the form in which they are presented can influence their chances for passage. Thus the decision-making process, if it is to be fully understood, must include a thorough understanding of the individual processes and procedures by which the different institutions reach agreement on different policy issues. These procedural norms and practices often play a decisive role in determining which aspects of demands become policies and which do not.[3]

The second major point about the decision-making process itself is that it is often quite cumbersome, slow, and complicated. This is the case for several reasons. In the first place, as each of the case studies indicates, it is a time-consuming and often tedious task to get any group of decision makers to change the way things are. This is not always due to the decision makers' desire to protect the status quo; it may be due simply to the innate difficulty human beings often have in accepting change of any sort.

Thus decision-making institutions may be in danger of lagging behind technological developments, as claimed by Alvin Toffler in his widely read treatise *Future Shock*.[4] Toffler submits that technological change may have simply overwhelmed the average individual and that unless change is better understood, the individual's and society's adaptive capacities will be greatly hampered. This sudden surge of technological change has also hampered government's ability to resolve pressing problems and issues. An excellent example of this technological change is the development of the electronic media in the past twenty years, with its impact on political reporting and the interpretation of political events by the American citizenry.

The decision-making process is made all the more difficult and time-consuming by the large number of participants involved. Whether individuals or institutions, the participants in each of the five case studies were numerous and diverse. The ERA case illustrated the wide variety of groups which must be mobilized for the passage of an amendment to the Constitution. The chapter on the European Security Treaty showed the complexity of the decision-making process when several nation-states with competing interests are maneuvering for influence and control. If the cases demonstrate any general point, it is the multiplicity of individual and institutional actors involved in decision making.

In addition to the innate resistance to change and the large number of participants in policy making, there is another important factor which accounts for the slowness of the decision-making process. This is that, regardless of the issues, there are bound to be those who win and those who lose, and that the losers will try to exhaust every procedural tactic available to them in the hopes of postponing the final decision. Certainly the campaign finance reform illustrates this point, as the House of Representatives, through the Government Operations Subcommittee on Elections, attempted to thwart major campaign finance changes after 1972. It was only after repeated and persistent efforts on the part of the Senate and a variety of public interest groups that the House decided to take action. The point is that delay is often deliberate and calculated to achieve certain well-defined goals, including, often, the preservation of the status quo. Thus the person interested in bringing about change will probably have to confront substantial opposition to a rapid settlement of the questions involved. Such delaying tactics, as the energy and community development chapters indicate, clearly favor some groups at the expense of others.

The third and final conclusion that can be made about the decision-making process is that the decisions resulting from it are apt to be less than definitive. If politics is the art of the possible, and policy is made through compromise and consensus building, it is understandable why the final policy decisions are not always clear-cut and decisive. In fact, as each case study indicates, it may not be necessary to win at every point during the policy-making process, if the participants can remain in the fray to influence developments at a later stage.

Given these basic characteristics of the policy-making process or black box itself, what can be said about the decisions or outputs which emerge from that process?

Outputs

Probably the most important descriptive aspect of policy outputs is their typically incremental nature. Incremental is a term, in this instance, used to define the output itself and not just the decision-making process which produces it.[5] Incremental decisions build on prior precedent and usually involve only marginal changes. Certainly the 1974 campaign finance reform can be seen, as Chapter 4 indicates, as an incremental decision. The 1974 legislation follows patterns found in prior legislation and also details some new procedures. Similarly, the Conference on

Security and Cooperation in Europe can be viewed as a largely incremental set of decisions. Perhaps the best illustration of incremental outputs is the set of energy decisions reached by the Ford administration. Each was quite tentative and did not involve major new departures from past practices. The important thing to remember about incremental policy change is not that each specific change may be marginal, but that over a period of time, incremental change can in fact lead to major change. Thus a decision-making process which appears quite slow and conservative over a period of time can produce dramatic change in public policies.

Another important aspect of any policy reached via the policy-making process in the United States is the likelihood that it will be characterized by a high degree of consensus. This is not meant to imply that there will not be opposition to it, but that policy outcomes, because of the complexities of the decision-making process, need to have general consensus from a large and diverse set of political participants before they can become overt policies. Certainly the Housing and Community Development Act of 1974 aptly illustrates this point. As Professor Cole points out, the substantially new legislation and programs it created were the result of extensive legislative compromise and interaction. If a major legislative group or individuals with access to the President had opposed the legislation, it would have been highly unlikely that the legislation would have been enacted. This case exemplifies the general conclusion that policy outputs require the tacit and often the active support of those with power in the policy-making process.

A final observation about policy outcomes is that they are often more important when implemented than when enacted. This implies that even the most promising policy decision, with the most far-reaching provisions, must await implementation before its ultimate success or failure can be ascertained. Certainly the debate over ERA is a good example of this. While proponents and opponents differ over the impact of the ERA, final judgment will have to await its implementation. Only then can one say with certainty that it has or has not reduced or eliminated sexual discrimination in this country. The Housing and Community Development Act legislation is an excellent example of a program whose actual implementation appears to have fallen short of expectations for it. Certainly congressional debate over various aspects of the program during early 1977 indicated dissatisfaction with several of its major provisions. Thus, while debate and concern over a policy's impact are justifiable parts of the decision-making process, the final evaluation of a program's effectiveness must wait till after the policy has in fact been implemented.

Feedback

The reader will recall that the policy-making diagram represented in Figure 1.1 also contained two additional items: feedback loops, which permitted policy outputs to influence subsequent demands and supports, and the environmental setting. Certainly the case studies provide excellent examples of the importance of each. The energy and campaign finance reform chapters illustrate how specific policies generate a variety of new demands and influence supports. As Professor Davis points out, President Ford responded to specific requests by farmers and other groups to change energy policy when they expressed their demands for such changes or when it became obvious that the Republican administration was in danger of losing their electoral support. In the campaign finance reform case, it was obvious that each set of congressional decisions resulted in a specific response from those persons and groups interested in and affected by campaign finance reform. Perhaps the best example of this is represented by John Gardner's rather blunt request that the House Administration Committee, under the leadership of Wayne L. Hays, take action on the Senate-passed legislation during 1973.[6]

One of the difficulties in analyzing case studies such as those presented in this volume is the lack of a broader time perspective which would permit analysis of the policy output's impact on subsequent support levels. This point is difficult, but important. The cases here emphasize short-range supports—support for a particular policy, officeholder, or administration. But another and far more important question is that of the long-range impact of outputs on support levels. Presumably, if individuals or groups are constantly disappointed or frustrated by the policy outputs of the decision-making process, their basic commitment to the political system will diminish and ultimately the system's legitimacy and authority will be eroded to the point that finally its very stability is threatened. It should be clear that this question cannot be explored through the cases in this volume because of their limited time frames. Nevertheless, the cases themselves can be seen as examples of how dissatisfied groups, over a long period of time, may attempt to alter the basic decision-making process in order to strengthen their influence on, or increase their share of, policy outputs.

The Environment

Finally, the environment both affects and is affected by what transpires in the policy-making process. For example, technological developments in the field of energy will have considerable impact on subsequent energy policy decisions by the United States government. If more efficient energy sources were developed, or if the automobile's internal combustion gasoline engine were replaced by a more fuel-efficient powering device, energy demand would be substantially met without increasing other new sources. Similarly, the growing public recognition of human rights will have an impact on legislation affecting the role of women in American society. While this may not take the form of ratification of the ERA, it should result in greater awareness and legislative gains for women and minority groups. Environmental constraints and influences are difficult to isolate and measure, but they certainly do set the broad parameters of policy making in American society. Underlying cultural values will be important considerations in any future attempts to affect decision making.

THE EVALUATION OF POLICY IMPACT

As the comments on the feedback process suggest, relatively little is known about several important aspects of the policy-making model. Social scientists in general and political scientists in particular have concentrated on the institutions and processes which are most readily analyzed and which appear most critical to policy making. Far too few attempts have been made to evaluate the impact the implementation of a particular program might have on society or on the other components of the policy-making process. Professor Cole's essay is an excellent example of an attempt to consider the impact of a program in a systematic and careful fashion. Program evaluation and analysis of a program's impact and implementation require considerable and careful research efforts, which many social scientists have ignored. The result has been a concentration on the input and decision-making process components of the model.

This has usually meant that when new programs or policies are being actively considered, sophisticated analyses are made of the groups for and against the proposal, but no such analyses are made of the program's potential impact on the particular problem. Thus political scientists have ignored to a very large degree the policy output and feedback components of the policy-making model. This has led to a lack of information on the critical questions of policy implementation and impact.

It should be kept in mind, however, that the complexity of the policy-making process poses immense difficulties for the analyst. In order for an accurate measurement to be made of the impact of a specific program or policy, a research methodology must first be developed which permits screening out of irrelevant and unimportant variables. Furthermore, causality must be established. The analyst must be able to prove, not just that A and B are associated, but that A causes B. Unless causality can be clearly established, the policy maker may be quite reluctant to accept the analyst's interpretation. There has been quite an interesting and lively debate in recent years among policy analysts over the research methodology to be used to ascertain causality.[7] The difficulty of establishing causality in a system as complex as the American system of policy making must be seriously considered by any individual interested in analyzing the impact of a particular policy.

AMERICAN POLICY MAKING

What, then, are the implications of the cases presented here for American policy making? What general conclusions are possible? While any speculation must be tentative and cautious, consider the following possibilities.

Certainly one possibility is that the American decision-making process is simply too slow-moving to respond effectively to the accelerating changes in American society and the world, and that ultimately the entire process will have to be radically changed. However, in rebuttal to this suggestion, one could maintain that the American political process and institutions have changed significantly over the two-hundred-year history of the country and that there is no reason to think that they will not continue to adapt to changing conditions. History will be the arbiter on this point, but it is interesting to speculate whether the institutions and processes can adapt to a faster rate of change and greater social complexity.

A second concern is whether the policy-making process as described in this volume is responsive enough—or, paradoxically, too responsive—to public demands. On the one hand, increased governmental reliance on technical expertise to deal with increasingly complex problems threatens to widen the communications gap between the general public and its elected leaders. On the other hand, increased responsiveness to public demands could result in a variety of decisions and policies beneficial to special interests but inimical to the country as a whole. The debate over energy policy illustrates this point well. Alternatives are being sought by technical experts, but quite often policies setting energy distribution and consumption are being made with specific political overtones. Thus it does the government little good to declare energy independence if that is in fact impossible or to decide that gasoline or oil is to be rationed if allocation practices are constantly influenced by political considerations. Thus the future roles of the citizen, the expert, and the elected political leader require careful consideration. In fact, the relationship between the general public, political leaders, and technical experts may be the most important issue facing American society in the next twenty-five years.

Finally, consideration needs to be given to the growing reality of global interdependence and its impact on American policy making. No longer is this country able to reach decisions without considering both their impact on other nations and the limitations that other nations may impose on our range of options. Certainly the energy case aptly illustrates this point. But energy is only one of the areas of political interdependence. The fact of interdependence must be taken into account in the whole range of American policies. If policies are developed which do not adequately consider this fact, one could well argue that such policies will, at best, simply not work, and at worst, be detrimental to American interests.

In sum, then, the American policy-making process is complicated and even confusing, but always interesting. If one intends to influence this process, one must understand its basic characteristics. Describing these characteristics, from both the practical and the theoretical viewpoint, has been the aim of this volume.

Notes

CHAPTER 2

1. In the case of the first alternative, a majority of both houses of a state legislature must vote in favor of the proposed amendment.
2. Lower courts also can interpret the meaning of the Constitution, and if the Supreme Court lets a lower court's decision stand, a precedent is set for the interpretation of future cases.
3. Martin Grunberg, *Women in American Politics* (Oshkosh, Wisc.: Academia Press, 1968), p. 4.
4. Eleanor Flexner, *Century of Struggle* (Cambridge, Mass.: Harvard University Press, 1959), p. 8.
5. Eight states in the United States, however, still apply common law doctrine in areas of the law concerning domestic relations. See Barbara A. Brown, Thomas I. Emerson, Gail Falk, and Ann E. Freedman, "The Equal Rights Amendment: A Constitutional Basis for Equal Rights of Women," *Yale Law Journal,* Vol. 80, No. 5 (April, 1971), p. 937.
6. *Minor v. Happersett,* 88 U.S. (21 Wall.) 162 (1875).
7. Grunberg, p. 4.
8. *Ibid.,* p. 64.
9. Ruth Bader Ginsberg, "The Need for an Equal Rights Amendment," *American Bar Association Journal,* Vol. 59 (September, 1973), p. 1013.
10. Lois W. Banner, *Women in Modern America: A Brief History* (New York: Harcourt Brace Jovanovich, 1974), p. 171.
11. The following year, 1945, the House passed the Equal Rights Amendment for the first time. The Senate, however, failed to act on it.
12. Kirsten Amundsen, *The Silenced Majority* (Englewood Cliffs, N.J.: Prentice-Hall, 1971), p. 32.

13. Many women and men disliked the assertive tactics used by the women's groups, but were sympathetic to the cause.

14. U.S. Dept. of Health, Education, and Welfare, Public Health Service, *Monthly Vital Statistics Report*, Vol. 24, No. 2, (Rockville, Md., 1975), p. 512.

15. U.S. Dept. of Health, Education, and Welfare, Public Health Service, *Vital Statistics of the United States, 1973*, Vol. II, Section 5 (Rockville, Md., 1975), p. 6.

16. Esther Peterson, "Working Women," in *The Woman in America*, ed. Robert Jay Lifton (Boston: Houghton Mifflin, 1965), p. 145.

17. Louis Harris and Associates, *1972 Virginia Slims American Women's Opinion Poll, A Survey of the Attitudes of Women on Their Roles in Politics and the Economy* (New York: Phillip Morris, 1972), p. 4.

18. Women's Bureau, United States Department of Labor, *Fact Sheet on the Earnings Gap* (Washington D.C.: U.S. Government Printing Office, 1972), p. 2.

19. Cynthia Fuchs Epstein, *Women's Place* (Berkeley: University of California Press, 1971), p. 7.

20. U.S. Civil Service Commission, Manpower Statistics Division, *Study of Employment of Women in the Federal Government, 1971* (Washington D.C.: U.S. Government Printing Office, 1971), p. 15.

21. U.S. National Center for Education Statistics, *Digest of Education Statistics, 1973 Digest*, p. 107.

22. Citizens' Advisory Council on the Status of Women, *Women in 1974* (Washington D.C.: U.S. Government Printing Office, 1975), p. 13.

23. Center for the American Woman and Politics, Eagleton Institute of Politics, Rutgers University, *Report 1974–1975*, pp. 6 and 7.

24. Margaret Mead and Frances Bagley Kaplan, eds., *American Women: The Report of the President's Commission on the Status of Women and Other Publications of the Commission* (New York, 1965), pp. 147–157. The opposite trend can be seen in such cases as *Rey v. Rey*, 279 So. 2d 360 (Fla, App., 1973).

25. Women, however, often receive preferential treatment in divorce, alimony, and child custody proceedings, and for this reason many oppose the ERA as a method of correcting other injustices.

26. Susan C. Ross, *The Rights of Women* (U.S.A.: Sunrise Books, 1973), p. 166.

27. *Ibid.*, p. 170.

28. In 1970 the Supreme Court upheld a lower court decision instructing the previously all-male University of Virginia at Charlottesville to admit women. The all-male barrier at the prestigious Stuyvesant High School in New York City also was knocked down. But other attempts have not been so successful. Texas A & M, an all-male state university, was sued twice in the early 1960s, but it remained segregated even though both cases went to the United States Supreme Court. (Later the college voluntarily desegregated). In early 1971 a lower federal court refused to admit men to Winthrop College, an all-female state college in South Carolina. The Supreme Court approved the decision without discussing the issues.

29. The fifteen states are Alaska, Colorado, Connecticut, Hawaii, Illinois, Maryland, Massachusetts, Montana, New Mexico, Pennsylvania, Texas, Utah, Virginia, Washington, and Wyoming.

30. Barbara A. Brown and Ann Freedman, "Equal Rights Amendment: Growing Impact on the States," *Women Law Reporter*, November 15, 1974, pp. 63-67.

31. *Ibid.*, p. 64.

32. To obtain this information, Ruth Bader Ginsburg and Brenda Feigen Fasteau, law professors at Columbia University, worked from a computer printout provided by the U.S. Department of Justice. The list of key words that triggered the computer call-up ran from "widowerhood," "girl," "boy," "masculine," and "sister," through "prostitution" and "rape," but left out such pronouns as "he," "she," and "her."

33. Barbara A. Brown, Thomas I. Emerson, Gail Falk, and Ann E. Freedman, "The Equal Rights Amendment: A Constitutional Basis for Equal Rights of Women," *Yale Law Journal*, Vol. 80, No. 5 (April, 1971), p. 875.

34. *Reed v. Reed*, 404 U.S. 71 (1971).

35. *Stanley v. Illinois*, 405 U.S. 645 (1972).

36. *Frontiero v. Richardson*, 44 U.S. 677 (1973).

37. The scheme was invalidated insofar as it required a female member to prove the dependency of her spouse.

38. *Kahn v. Shevin*, 94 S. ct. 1734 (1974).

39. The Fourteenth Amendment was ratified in 1868.

40. *Minor v. Happersett*, 88 U.S. (21 Wall.) 162 (1875).

41. *Bradwell v. Illinois*, 83 U.S. 130 (1873).

42. *Muller v. Oregon*, 208 U.S. 412 (1908).

43. *Lochner v. New York*, 198 U.S. 45 (1905).

44. At that time, however, such legislation was strongly supported by many women's groups and proponents of the progressive movement.

45. *Goesaert v. Cleary*, 335 U.S. 464 (1948).

46. *Hoyt v. Florida*, 368 U.S. 57 (1961).

47. 116 *Congressional Record* 7948, 7953 (Daily ed., August 10, 1970); 116 *Congressional Record* 17631-36, 17639-71 (Daily ed., October 9, 1970).

48. Disagreement existed, however, among the proponents about the concrete impact of the amendment on existing laws, especially those concerning the Selective Service Act. Representative Griffiths said the ERA would require women to serve in the armed forces, though as true for men, only in positions for which they were suited. Senator Bayh maintained that the amendment would allow Congress to exempt women from military service on the grounds of "compelling reasons" of public policy.

49. Jo Freeman, *The Politics of Women's Liberation* (New York: David McKay, 1975) p. 217.

50. *Ibid.*, p. 218.

51. Lisa Cronin Wohl, "Phyllis Schlafly: Sweetheart of the Silent Majority," *Ms.*, March 1974, p. 56.

52. Brown, Emerson, Falk, and Freedman, p. 889.

53. *Ibid.*, p. 920.

54. Wohl, p. 55.

55. Brown, Emerson, Falk, and Freedman, p. 945.

56. Civil law concerns relations between individuals or organizations, such as divorce actions, or suits for violation of a contract or for damages arising from

an automobile accident. Criminal cases concern crimes committed against the public order. Most crimes are defined by local, state, and federal statutes, which set forth a range of penalties as well.

57. The reasoning used to strike down state legislation under Title VII differs considerably from the Equal Rights Amendment's standards of allowing differentiation only on the basis of unique physical characteristics of one sex or the other. The practical effect, however, is much like intended effect of the Equal Rights Amendment.

58. Brown, Emerson, Falk, and Freedman, pp. 992 and 993.

59. Under the ERA it could be argued in defense of such maternity leave laws and state regulations that they deal with unique physical characteristics of women. It is possible for the state to regulate conditions on this basis, but the kind of legislation imposed would be subject to "strict scrutiny" by the courts.

60. *Griswold v. Connecticut,* 381 U.S. 479, 486 (1965).

61. Wohl, p. 57.

62. The exception to this is Senator Birch Bayh, who maintained that for "compelling reasons" of public policy, the amendment would allow Congress to exempt women from military service.

63. In 1950 and 1952 the question whether a provision for exceptions should be written into the amendment, particularly with regard to military service, was debated. The Senate, under the leadership of Carl Hayden, concluded it should be, and amended the ERA in those two years to provide that "The provisions of this article shall not be construed to impair any rights, benefits, or exemptions conferred by law upon persons of the female sex."

64. Citizens' Advisory Council on the Status of Women, *Women in 1973* (Washington D.C.: U.S. Government Printing Office, 1974), p. 18.

65. Hearings on S. 1614 before the Subcommittee on Organization and Mobilization of the House Committee on Armed Services, 80th Congress 2d Sess. No. 238 at 5564–64 (1948).

66. Brown, Emerson, Falk, and Freedman, pp. 906 and 907.

67. "Equal Rights For Women—Is '75 the Year?," *U.S. News and World Report,* February 17, 1975, p. 49.

68. League of Women Voters of the United States, "The ERA Meets the Press," *The National Voter,* Vol. XXVI, No. 2 (Summer, 1976), p. 24.

69. "Equal Rights For Women—Doomed?," *U.S. News and World Report,* April 28, 1975, p. 45.

70. *Coleman v. Miller,* 307 U.S. 433 (1939).

CHAPTER 3

1. General Services Administration, National Archives, *Presidential Documents,* Vol. 10, p. 1033.

2. *New York Times,* August 20, 1974.

3. Federal Energy Administration, *Project Independence Report,* November, 1974, p. 76.

4. See Mancur Olson, *The Logic of Collective Action,* (New York: Schocken, 1968), pp. 60–65.

5. *Presidential Documents,* Vol. 10, p. 1164.
6. *Ibid.,* p. 1184
7. See Robert W. Tucker, "Oil: The Issue of American Intervention," *Commentary,* January, 1975, pp. 21–23.
8. *Presidential Documents,* Vol. 10, p. 1183.
9. *Ibid.,* pp. 1182–83.
10. Federal Energy Agency *Project Independence Report,* p. 26.
11. *Presidential Documents,* Vol. 11, pp. 48–51.
12. *New York Times,* August 22, 1975; *Congressional Quarterly Weekly Report* 33:39 (September 27, 1975), p. 2045.
13. *New York Times,* February 13, 1975.
14. Murray Edelman, *The Symbolic Uses of Politics,* (Urbana: University of Illinois Press, 1964), pp. 152–171.
15. *Congressional Quarterly Weekly Report,* June, 1975, p. 1255.
16. National Academy of Sciences, Committee on Nuclear and Alternative Sources, Synthesis Panel, Decision-Making Resource Group, "The Decision-making Process for Coal for Electric Generation," 1976.
17. Edward C. Banfield, "Ends and Means in Planning," *International Social Science Journal* XI (1959):3.

CHAPTER 4

1. For an enlightening discussion of this point, see David W. Adamany, *Campaign Finance in America* (Belmont, Ca. Wadsworth, 1972), pp. 1–15.
2. While it is impossible to list all the useful references on the subject of campaign finance, a partial list would include the following: David W. Adamany, *Campaign Finance in America* (Belmont, Ca.: Wadsworth, 1972); Herbert E. Alexander, *Regulation of Political Finance* (Berkeley, Ca. and Princeton, N.J.: Institute of Governmental Studies and Citizens' Research Foundation, 1966); Herbert E. Alexander, *Financing the 1968 Election* (Lexington, Mass.: Heath Lexington Books, 1971); Herbert E. Alexander, *Financing the 1972 Election* (Lexington: Mass.: Heath Lexington Books, 1975); Herbert E. Alexander, "Political Finance: Reform and Reality," *The Annals of the American Academy of Political and Social Science,* Vol. 425 (May, 1976); John F. Bibby and Herbert E. Alexander, *The Politics of National Convention Finances and Arrangements* (Princeton, N.J.: Citizens' Research Foundation, 1968); Common Cause, *1972 Federal Campaign Finances: Interest Groups and Political Parties* (Washington, D.C.: Common Cause, 1974); Congressional Quarterly, *Dollar Politics, Volumes I and II* (Washington, D.C.: Congressional Quarterly, 1971 and 1974); William G. Domhoff, *Fat Cats and the Democrats* (Englewood Cliffs, N.J.: Prentice-Hall, 1971); Delmer D. Dunn, *Financing Presidential Campaigns* (Washington, D.C.: The Brookings Institution, 1972); Alexander Heard, *The Costs of Democracy* (Chapel Hill: University of North Carolina Press, 1960); Robert L. Peabody, Jeffrey M. Berry, William G. Frasure, and Jerry Goldman, *To Enact A Law: Congress and Campaign Financing* (New York: Praeger, 1972); Howard Penniman, *Campaign Finances: Two Views of the Political and Constitutional Implications* (Washington, D.C.:

American Enterprise Institute, 1973); President's Commission on Campaign Costs, *Financing Presidential Elections* (Washington, D.C.: Government Printing Office, 1962); Twentieth Century Fund Commission on Campaign Costs for an Electronic Era, *Voter's Time* (New York: Twentieth Century Fund, 1969).

3. Congressional Quarterly, *Dollar Politics, Volume II* (Washington, D.C.: Congressional Quarterly, 1974), p. 69.

4. For a discussion of the 1972 figures, see *Dollar Politics, Volume II,* pp. 64–72. For the 1976 campaign see "Tight Budget for Presidential Candidates," *Congressional Quarterly Weekly Report,* Vol. XXXIV, No. 31, pp. 2036–2037.

5. For a discussion of George Wallace's success with the Richard A. Viguerie Company's direct mail approach, see *Dollar Politics, Volume II,* p. 52.

6. The Political Broadcast Act of 1970, vetoed by President Nixon on October 12, 1970, helped to pave the way for the 1971 legislation. For a discussion of the legislative debate and history of this act see Robert L. Peabody, Jeffrey M. Berry, William G. Frasure, and Jerry Goldman, *To Enact A Law: Congress and Campaign Financing* (New York: Praeger, 1972).

7. This point and the discussion of Watergate activities are based on the Report of the Senate Select Committee on Presidential Campaign Activities (Washington, D.C.: Government Printing Office, 1974). For a journalistic account of Watergate see Carl Bernstein and Robert Woodward, *All the President's Men* (New York: Simon & Schuster, 1974).

8. Excerpt from transcripts of White House tapes released August 5, 1974.

9. For details on these activities see the appropriate sections of the Report of the Senate Select Committee on Presidential Campaign Activities.

10. For a discussion of Gardner's philosophy see, John W. Gardner, *No Easy Victories* (New York: Harper & Row, 1968).

11. See Theodore Roosevelt's State of the Union Address, 1905.

12. *Ibid.*

13. See "Federal Election Laws: A History of Loopholes," in *Dollar Politics Volume 1* (Washington, D.C.: Congressional Quarterly, 1971), pp. 15–18, for a description of this legislation.

14. *Ibid.*

15. Wayne L. Hays, Statement before the Subcommittee on Elections of the Committee on House Administration of the House of Representatives, June 22, 1971 (Washington, D.C.: Government Printing Office, 1971), pp. 6–7.

16. Edmund S. Muskie, Statement before the Subcommittee on Communications of the Committee on Commerce of the United States Senate, March 3, 1971, p. 365.

17. Mike Gravel, Statement before the Subcommittee on Communications of the Committee on Commerce of the United States Senate, March 2, 1971, p. 167.

18. *Dollar Politics, Volume 1,* pp. 16–18.

19. *Ibid.,* p. 18.

20. *Ibid.,* pp. 16–17.

21. *Ibid.,* p. 9.

22. Statement of Dr. Herbert Alexander to the Subcommittee on Communications of the Committee on Commerce of the United States Senate, April 1, 1971 (Washington, D.C.: Government Printing Office, 1971), p. 637.

23. *Ibid.*
24. Public Law 92-225, Section 202.
25. Public Law 92-225, Section 205.
26. *Ibid.*
27. Public Law 92-225, Section 104.
28. *Ibid.*
29. Public Law 92-225, Section 103.
30. For a summary of the National Association of Broadcaster's position, see the Statement by Vincent T. Wasilewski to the Subcommittee on Communications of the Committee on Commerce of the United States Senate, March 5, 1971 (Washington, D.C.: Government Printing Office, 1971), pp. 481–483.
31. See Public Law 92-225, Sections 301–311 for the specific legislative provisions.
32. Public Law 92-225, Section 301.
33. Section 310 of the Senate version of this legislation would have created a bipartisan Federal Elections Commission. The House-Senate Conference Committee dropped this Senate provision in the legislation. The members agreed to report back to their respective Houses.
34. Statement of Richard G. Kleindienst to the Subcommittee on Elections of the Committee on House Administration of the U.S. House of Representatives, June 22, 1971 (Washington, D.C.: Government Printing Office, 1971), p. 117.
35. *Dollar Politics, Volume 2,* p. 61.
36. United States Senate Select Committee on Presidential Campaign Activities, *Final Report* (Washington, D.C.: Government Printing Office, 1974), p. 445.
37. *Dollar Politics, Volume 2,* p. 62.
38. *Ibid.*
39. *Final Report,* p. 445.
40. *Ibid.,* pp. 445–577.
41. *Ibid.,* pp. 563–577.
42. John W. Gardner, Statement to the Subcommittee on Elections of the Committee on House Administration of the U.S. House of Representatives (Washington, D.C.: Government Printing Office, 1973), pp. 385, 391.
43. See *Dollar Politics, Volume 2,* pp. 29–33 for a discussion of the legislative history of the 1974 legislation.
44. Gardner, Statement, pp. 384–385.
45. For a discussion of the lawsuit, the Appeals Court decision, and the Supreme Court decision, see *"Buckley v. Valeo," Supreme Court Reporter,* Vol. 96, No. 8 (February 15, 1976), pp. 612–796.
46. For a discussion of the Appeals Court decision see "Campaign Reform: Success on First Legal Test," *Congressional Quarterly Weekly Report,* Vol. XXXIII, No. 34 (August 23, 1975), pp. 1857–1858.
47. *"Buckley v. Valeo,"* pp. 635–636, 640.
48. *Ibid.,* p. 651.
49. *Ibid.,* pp. 622–653.
50. *Ibid.,* pp. 644–650.
51. *Ibid.,* pp. 692–693.
52. *Ibid.,* p. 671.
53. Albert J. Rosenthal, "The Constitution and Campaign Finance Regulation After *Buckley v. Valeo," The Annals of the American Academy of Political and Social Science,* Vol. 425 (May, 1976), p. 133.

54. For a discussion of this controversy, see "Election Commission: Regulator or Refuge?" *Congressional Quarterly Weekly Report,* Vol. XXXII, No. 52 (December 28, 1974), pp. 3342–3443.

55. See "Election Commission: Independence at Stake," *Congressional Quarterly Weekly Report,* Vol. XXXIII, No. 39 (September 27, 1975), pp. 2073–2074.

56. *Ibid.*

57. *Congressional Record,* Vol. 120, No. 151 (October 7, 1974), p. 10042.

58. "Election Commission: Independence at Stake," pp. 2073–2074.

59. *Ibid.,* p. 2074.

60. *Ibid.*

61. For a discussion of this interaction see, "Partisan Wrangle Delays Campaign Bill," *Congressional Quarterly Weekly Report,* Vol. XXXIV, No. 12 (March 20, 1976), pp. 603–604, and "Congress Clears New Campaign Finance Law," *Congressional Quarterly Weekly Report,* Vol. XXXIV, No. 19 (May 8, 1976), pp. 1104–1106.

62. "Congress Clears New Campaign Finance Law," p. 1106.

63. *Ibid.*

64. P1 94-283, Section 105.

65. P1 94-283, Section 107.

66. P1 94-283, Section 109.

67. P1 94-283, Sections 107, 109.

68. P1 94-283, Section 105.

69. *Ibid.*

70. *Ibid.*

71. Alexander Heard, "Establishing Public Confidence in the Electoral Process," *The Annals of the American Academy of Political and Social Science,* Vol. 425 (May, 1976), p. 144.

CHAPTER 5

1. The full text of the President's remarks may be found in the *Weekly Compilation of Presidential Documents* (Washington, D.C.: U.S. Government Printing Office, 1974), August 22, 1974, pp. 1059–1061.

2. As quoted in *National Journal Reports,* September 14, 1974, p. 1369.

3. These figures are derived from *The Statistical Abstract of the United States, 1974,* U.S. Department of Commerce (Washington, D.C.: U.S. Government Printing Office, 1974), p. 249. The urban renewal program is discussed in greater detail below.

4. As quoted from President Nixon's 1971 State of the Union Address, the full text of which may be found in the *Weekly Compilation of Presidential Documents* (Washington, D.C.: U.S. Government Printing Office, 1971), pp. 50–58.

5. For a classic statement of the incremental nature of decision making in American politics see Charles E. Lindblom, *The Intelligence of Democracy* (New York: Free Press, 1965).

6. A more thorough discussion of the Housing Act of 1934 and of the FHA may be found in David C. Ranney, *Planning and Politics in the Metropolis*

(Columbus, Ohio: Charles E. Merrill, 1969), p. 72; and Glen H. Beyer, *Housing and Society* (New York: Macmillan, 1965), pp. 448–483.

7. A more detailed discussion of this program may be found in Ranney, pp. 72–73; and Warren E. Farb, Jane D. Katz, and Francis R. Parente, *Housing—Low and Moderate Income* (Washington, D.C.: Library of Congress, 1975), p. 1.

8. See Ranney, pp. 73–75; and Herbert J. Gans, *The Urban Villagers* (New York: Free Press, 1962).

9. For a more complete discussion of the 1954 Housing Act, see Ranney, pp. 75–76; Richard L. Cole, *Citizen Participation and the Urban Policy Process* (Lexington, Mass.: D. C. Heath and Co., 1974), pp. 12–13; and Melvin B. Mogulof, *Citizen Participation: A Review and Commentary on Federal Policies and Practices* (Washington, D.C.: The Urban Institute, 1970), p. 64.

10. See Ranney, pp. 76–77 for a discussion of the 1956 Housing Act.

11. See Ranney, pp. 76–77 for a discussion of the 1959 Housing Act.

12. Financial data are taken from *The Statistical Abstract of the United States, 1974*, p. 249. For a more complete discussion of the text see, Cole, pp. 14–15; and Ranney, pp. 79–80.

13. U.S. Congress, House Committee on Banking and Currency, *Investigation and Hearings of Abuses in Federal Low and Moderate Income Housing Programs*, 91st Cong., 2d Sess., December, 1970.

14. For a more complete discussion of the 1968 Housing Act see Robert Schafer and Charles G. Field, "Section 235 of the National Housing Act: Homeownership for Low-income Families?" in *Housing Urban America*, eds. Jon Pynoos, Robert Schafer, and Chester Hartman (Chicago: Aldine, 1973), pp. 460–471. It is interesting to note, as well, that faced with increased legal challenges, President Ford, on October 17, 1975, announced the release of 235 funds, but only for families whose income fall in the $9,000 to $11,000 category.

15. Report of the National Commission on Urban Problems to the Congress and to the President of the United States (commonly called the "Douglas Commission Report"), *Building the American City* (Washington, D.C.: U.S. Government Printing Office, 1968), p. 180.

16. These data are derived from *The Statistical Abstract of the United States, 1974*, p. 249.

17. As quoted in *National Journal Reports*, December 16, 1972, p. 1909.

18. For a full discussion of the New Federalism philosophy and background see *National Journal Reports*, December 16, 1972, pp. 1907–1904.

19. As quoted in the President's *State of the Union Address*, January 22, 1971.

20. *Ibid.*

21. The complete text of this March 5 message to the Congress may be found in the *Weekly Compilation of Presidential Documents*, March 8, 1971, pp. 430–436.

22. *Ibid.*

23. A Standard Metropolitan Statistical Area (SMSA) is defined by the Bureau of the Census as, "Any area containing a central city or cities with an aggregate population of 50,000 or more and those surrounding counties which have a metropolitan characteristic and are socially and economically integrated with the central city."

24. *Weekly Compilation of Presidential Documents*, (Washington, D.C.: Government Printing Office, March 8, 1971) pp. 430–435.

25. U.S. Congress, Senate Subcommittee on Housing and Urban Affairs of the Committee on Banking, Housing, and Urban Affairs, *Proposed Housing and Community Development Legislation for 1973*, 93rd Cong., 1st Sess., July 1973 [Hereafted cited as 1973 Senate Report], p. 28.

26. *Ibid.,* pp. 452–453.

27. U.S. Congress, House Subcommittee on Housing of the Committee on Banking and Currency, *Housing and Community Development Legislation—1973*, 93rd Cong., 1st Sess., October 1973 [Hereafter cited as 1973 House Report], p. 518.

28. *Ibid.,* pp. 800–802.

29. For a full report of House and Senate action of this bill see *National Journal Reports*, April 13, 1974, pp. 554–562; *National Journal Reports*, September 14, 1974, pp. 1369–1379; and *Congressional Quarterly Weekly Reports*, August 24, 1974, pp. 2319–2322.

30. For a comprehensive review of the provisions of the Housing and Community Development Act of 1974 see *National Journal Reports*, September 14, 1974, pp. 1369–1379; and *Congressional Quarterly Weekly Reports*, August 24, 1974, pp. 2319–2322.

31. The full text of the President's remarks may be found in the *Weekly Compilation of Presidential Documents*, August 22, 1974, pp. 1059–1061.

32. For a detailed explanation of the elements used in this formula see U.S. Department of Housing and Urban Development, *Community Development Block Grant Program, Directory of Allocations for Fiscal Year 1975* (Washington, D.C.: U.S. Government Printing Office, 1975), p. ii [Hereafter cited as 1975 HUD Directory of Allocations].

33. *National Journal Reports*, September 14, 1974, p. 1370.

34. U.S. Department of Housing and Urban Development, *Community Development Block Grant Program, A Provisional Report* (Washington, D.C.: U.S. Government Printing Office, May, 1975) [Hereafter cited as 1975 HUD Report].

35. Of course it also is true that the consolidated categorical grant programs, on the whole, stressed physical development as opposed to social service programs.

36. It should be pointed out that a number of these are the smaller cities which were not fully participating in all consolidated categorical grant programs.

37. Unpublished report prepared by David A. Caputo of Purdue University and Richard L. Cole of The George Washington University, 1976.

38. U.S. National Advisory Commission on Civil Disorders, *Report of the National Advisory Commission on Civil Disorders* [Kerner Report].

39. See E. E. Schattschneider, *The Semi-Sovereign People* (New York: Holt, Rinehart, & Winston, 1960) for an elaboration of this point.

CHAPTER 6

1. Graham T. Allison, "Conceptual Models and the Cuban Missile Crisis," *American Political Science Review*, 63 (September, 1969), pp. 689–718; elaborated in Allison, *Essence of Decision: Explaining the Cuban Missile Crisis* (Boston: Little, Brown & Co., 1971).

2.   Graham T. Allison and Morton H. Halperin, "Bureaucratic Politics: A Paradigm and Some Policy Implications," *World Politics*, 24 (Spring, 1972, Supplement), pp. 40–79.
3.   Morton H. Halperin, *Bureaucratic Politics and Foreign Policy* (Washington, D.C.: The Brookings Institution, 1974).
4.   John D. Steinbruner, *The Cybernetic Theory of Decision: New Dimensions of Political Analysis* (Princeton, N.J.: Princeton University Press, 1974).
5.   David Howard Davis, *How the Bureaucracy Makes Foreign Policy: An Exchange Analysis* (Lexington, Mass.: D.C. Heath-Lexington, 1972).
6.   Charles E. Lindblom, *Intelligence of Democracy* (New York: Free Press, 1965), *The Policy Making Process* (Englewood Cliffs, N.J.: Prentice-Hall, 1968); Charles E. Lindblom and David Braybrooke, *A Strategy of Decision* (New York: Free Press, 1963); James G. March and Herbert A. Simon, *Organizations* (New York: John Wiley & Sons, 1958); Karl W. Deutsch, *The Nerves of Government: Models of Political Communication and Control* (New York: Free Press, 1963); Harold L. Wilensky, *Organizational Intelligence: Knowledge and Policy in Government and Industry* (New York: Basic Books, 1967); and Anthony Downs, *Inside Bureaucracy* (Boston: Little, Brown & Co., 1967).
7.   Samuel P. Huntington, *The Common Defense: Strategic Programs in National Defense* (New York: Columbia University Press, 1961); Richard E. Neustadt, *Presidential Power: The Politics of Leadership* (New York: John Wiley & Sons, 1960); Thomas Schelling, *Arms and Influence* (New Haven: Yale University Press, 1966); Roger Hilsman, *To Move A Nation: The Politics of Foreign Policy in the Administration of John F. Kennedy* (New York: Doubleday, 1967); Richard C. Snyder, H. W. Bruck, and Burton Sepin, *Foreign Policy Decision Making: An Approach to the Study of International Politics* (New York: Free Press, 1962).
8.   This model is a refinement of one presented in my *Foreign Policy and the Bureaucratic Process* (Princeton, N.J.: Princeton University Press, 1974), pp. 28–38. Conceptually, it is largely compatible with the Allison-Halperin approach presented in the works cited previously.
9.   See James D. Thompson, *Organizations in Action: Social Science Bases of Administrative Theory* (New York: John Wiley & Sons, 1967), pp. 6–10.
10. For some recent case studies of congressional participation in the foreign policy process see Alton Frye, *A Responsible Congress: The Politics of National Security* (New York: McGraw-Hill, 1975), published for the Council on Foreign Relations.
11. Information on the period leading up to CSCE has been drawn from the following, which should be consulted for additional detail: Wolfgang Klaiber et al., *Era of Negotiations: European Security and Force Reductions*, Atlantic Council of the United States (Lexington, Mass.: D.C. Heath-Lexington, 1973), which is the most balanced and complete coverage of the origins and issues of CSCE; Francis T. Miko, "Conference on Security and Cooperation in Europe: The Soviet Approach," Congressional Research Study 75–91 F (Washington, D.C.: Library of Congress, April 3, 1975); Mojmir Povolny, "The Soviet Union and the European Security Conference," *Orbis*, 18 (Spring, 1974), pp. 201–230; John C. Campbell, "European Security: Prospects and Possibilities for Eastern Europe," East Europe, 19 (November, 1970), pp. 2–8;

and Robert Legvold, "The Problem of European Security," *Problems of Communism,* 23 (January–February, 1974), pp. 13–33.

12. See Josef Korbel, *Detente in Europe: Real or Imaginary?* (Princeton, N.J.: Princeton University Press, 1972); and Lawrence L. Whetten, *Germany's Ostpolitik: Relations between the Federal Republic and the Warsaw Pact Countries,* published for the Royal Institute of International Affairs (London: Oxford University Press, 1971), for full treatments of West German initiatives and their subsequent history. Conclusion of the nonaggression treaties with the U.S.S.R. and Poland in 1971 was to provide a major impetus in clearing the way to CSCE.

13. This was an indirect reference to the "Brezhnev Doctrine," enunciated by the Soviets after Czechoslovakia, which justified such interventions when they were necessary to preserve "Socialism," and therefore set clear limits on national independence. The NATO position was contained in the Final Communique of the NATO Ministerial Meeting, Brussels, December 4, 1970. Unless otherwise stated, citations in this study from WTO and NATO communiqués are from versions printed in the very useful appendices to Klaiber et al., *Era of Negotiations.* These communiqués and statements can also be found in the appropriate issues of *The Atlantic Community Quarterly* or *Survival* and *The NATO Review.*

14. Quoted in John M. Goshko, "European Talks Raise Conflicts," *Washington Post,* November 25, 1972.

15. "On To The Next Round," *The Economist,* 243 (June 3, 1972), p. 12.

16. Quoted in James Feron, "European Security Talks On in Finland," *New York Times,* November 23, 1972.

17. Personal interviews. This and all other personal interviews cited as sources were conducted by the author with U.S. officials who had direct involvement with CSCE.

18. Personal interview.

19. Paragraph based on Flora Lewis, "Soviet-American Accord Embitters NATO Officials," *New York Times,* July 26, 1972.

20. Henry A. Kissinger, "1973: The Year of Europe," speech to Associated Press Editors, New York, April 23, 1973, reprinted in *Current Foreign Policy,* Department of State Publication 8710, June, 1973.

21. Personal interview.

22. Roger Berthoud, "East and West Approaches to the European Security Conference: Eliminating the Brezhnev Doctrine," *London Times,* June 6, 1972.

23. Scott Sullivan, "Next: Tough European Conferences," *Baltimore Sun,* June 4, 1972.

24. Maurice Schumann, press conference, Budapest, reprinted in *Le Monde,* September 11, 1971.

25. Klaiber et al., pp. 40–45.

26. Michael Palmer, "The Prospects for a European Security Conference," *Atlantic Community Quarterly,* 9 (Fall, 1971), p. 296; this argument was also made by some of those interviewed.

27. Listing from Miko, pp. 16–17.

28. Klaiber et. al., p. 85.

29. *Ibid.,* p. 51.

30. James Feron, "The European Security Talks On in Finland," *New York Times,* November 23, 1972.

31. Campbell, pp. 6–7.

32. C. L. Sulzberger, "Tiptoeing to Security in Europe," *New York Times,* August 4, 1972.

33. For example, see "Talks on Europe to Get Swiss Plan: Proposals to be Offered to Settle All Disputes," *New York Times,* November 19, 1972.

34. James Feron, "Finland Still Wary of Moscow, Covets World Role at European Security Parley, *New York Times,* September 9, 1972.

35. Personal interview.

36. Warsaw Pact Nations' Communiqué, Moscow, December 4, 1969; Communiqué of Warsaw Pact Foreign Ministers Meeting, Prague, October 31, 1969.

37. "Final Recommendations of the Helsinki Consultations," Helsinki, July 7, 1973, reprinted in *Department of State Bulletin,* 69, No. 1779 (July 30, 1973), pp. 181–188. The quotation is from paragraph 53, p. 185.

38. John M. Goshko, "Rumanian Step Sets Tone at Helsinki Talks," *Washington Post,* November 24, 1972.

39. Götz von Groll, "The Foreign Ministers in Helsinki," *Aussenpolitik* (English ed.), 24 (3rd Quarter, 1973), pp. 271–272.

40. Richard Nixon, "United States Foreign Policy for the 1970s: The Emerging Structure of Peace," Report to the Congress, February 9, 1972, p. 48.

41. "Conference on European Security," U.S. House of Representatives, Subcommittee on Europe, Committee on Foreign Affairs, April 25, 1972 (Washington, D.C.: Government Printing Office, 1972), p. 8.

42. Personal interviews.

43. Personal interviews.

44. Personal interview.

45. Götz von Groll, "The Helsinki Consultations," *Aussenpolitik* (English ed.), 24 (2nd Quarter, 1973), pp. 123–124.

46. Personal interviews.

47. Personal interviews.

48. von Groll, p. 125.

49. Personal interviews.

50. Personal interview.

51. von Groll, p. 126.

52. See note 37 for location of text.

53. See von Groll, "Foreign Ministers," p. 260. The list of principles under basket I in Figure 6-1 is virtually the same as those proposed in the preliminary talks. The Communiqué for the Helsinki Foreign Ministers Meeting is reprinted in *Department of State Bulletin,* 69, No. 1779 (July 30, 1973), 178.

54. von Groll, pp. 264–266.

55. *Ibid.,* p. 269.

56. Personal interviews.

57. Personal interview.

58. Personal interview.

59. Personal interview.

60. Personal interviews. Note applies to this and previous paragraph.

61. von Groll, "The Geneva CSCE Negotiations," *Aussenpolitik* (English ed.), 25 (2nd Quarter, 1974), 158. See also Figure 6-1.

62. William P. Rogers, statement to Helsinki Foreign Ministers Meeting, July 5, 1973, reprinted in *Department of State Bulletin*, 69, No. 1779 (July 30, 1973), 178.

63. David Binder, "European Summit Likely in Summer: U.S. Sees Enough Progress at Geneva to Begin Plans," *New York Times*, January 21, 1975; personal interviews.

64. A somewhat similar ploy had been attempted, with the threat of delaying a final communiqué, at the CSCE Stage I Foreign Ministers Meeting in Helsinki. See note 53 for location of source of final wording.

65. Flora Lewis, "European Parley: End Is In Sight," *New York Times*, July 1, 1975.

66. George Sherman, "NATO Rift Begins to Heal: Misunderstanding Blamed," *Washington Star*, December 10, 1973.

67. Henry A. Kissinger, press conference, Washington, D.C., July 25, 1975, reprinted in Department of State Bulletin, 73, No. 1885 (August 11, 1975), p. 200.

68. Lewis, "European Parley."

69. I am indebted to Robert Legvold for his comments about the international political climate during this period.

70. Personal interview.

71. Personal interview.

72. See note 67.

73. Robert Keatley, "When East Meets West in Helsinki," *Wall Street Journal*, July 9, 1975.

74. Gerald R. Ford, address to the Conference on Security and Cooperation in Europe, August 1, 1975, reprinted in *Department of State Bulletin*, 73, No. 1888 (September 1, 1975), pp. 304–308. Quotations from pp. 306–307.

75. Personal interview.

76. Campbell, p. 7.

77. Peter Osnos, "Helsinki's Final Act: A Dilemma for Moscow," *Washington Post*, October 16, 1975.

78. Georgi A. Arbatov, "Reciprocity After Helsinki," *New York Times*, October 8, 1975.

79. Leonid I. Brezhnev, speech, Warsaw, December 8, 1975, excerpted in *New York Times*, December 10, 1975.

80. David K. Shipler, "New Soviet-East German Pact Omits German Unity as Goal," *New York Times*, October 8, 1975.

81. David Fouquet, "Kremlin Carrying Out Some Helsinki Pledges," *Washington Post*, January 14, 1976.

82. For a summary of developments in the first year after the conference, see David K. Shipler, "Helsinki Accord and the Soviet Union: Effects on Human Rights Seem Mixed," *New York Times*, August 1, 1976; and Murrey Marder, The Helsinki Accord: Its First Anniversary, *Washington Post*, August 2, 1976.

83. George F. Will, "A Farewell to 'Detente,'" *Washington Post*, March 7, 1976.

84. Leonard H. Marks, "The Unfulfilled Promise of Helsinki, *Washington Post*, August 1, 1976.

85. Personal interviews.

86. For details of this Congressional initiative, see Marks, "The Unfulfilled Promise of Helsinki," and Henry S. Bradsher, "Helsinki Pact a Year Later: Basket of Ideas or Troubles," *Washington Star,* July 19, 1976.

87. Quoted in Robert Keatley, "When East Meets West in Helsinki."

88. Quoted in Alfred Friendly, Jr., "Cold War to Cold Peace," *Newsweek,* 86 (July 28, 1975), p. 31.

89. *Ibid.*

90. Personal interview.

91. Flora Lewis, "Europeans Are Worried About U.S. Will to Lead," *New York Times,* March 14, 1976.

CHAPTER 7

1. While the literature on these general topics is voluminous, a useful starting point is Peter Bachrach and Morton S. Baratz, *Power and Poverty* (New York: Oxford University Press, 1970), pp. 3–63.

2. The nonvoter was widely discussed during the 1976 campaign. See, for example, "Carter Squeezes Out a Popular Majority," *Congressional Quarterly Weekly Report,* Vol. 34, No. 51 (December 18, 1976), pp. 3332–3333.

3. Again the literature here is extensive. An excellent descriptive account of the congressional appropriations process can be found in Richard F. Fenno, Jr., *The Power of the Purse* (Boston: Little, Brown & Co., 1966).

4. Alvin Toffer, *Future Shock* (New York: Random House, 1970).

5. For two discussions of incrementalism, see Herbert A. Simon, *Models of Man* (New York: John Wiley & Sons, 1958), pp. 241–260; and Charles E. Lindblom, "The Science of Muddling Through," *Public Administration Review,* Vol. 29, No. 2 (Spring, 1959), pp. 79–88.

6. See p. 88 for the text of Gardner's statement.

7. For a useful starting point for investigating the literature in this area, see the *Policy Studies Journal* Vol. 2, No. 1 (Autumn, 1973), pp. 4–71; and *Policy Studies Journal,* Vol. 3, No. 3 (Spring, 1975), pp. 222–292.